A comprehensive and well-researched ~~book~~ of ideas I intend to use in my family!
    –Debra Bell, author of *The Ultimate Guide to Homeschooling*

❖ ❖ ❖

Christine Field has done it again! *Life Skills for Kids* reflects the simple, practical lessons she (and her husband) have gleaned from organizing and raising a homeschooling household with four children. . . . Christine has thoughtfully laid out a topical list of skills along with practical suggestions on what to do and say in order to effectively equip our children. Parents should read and reflect on these chapters together—they (and their children) will be richly rewarded.
    –Rob Shearer, publisher, Greenleaf Press

❖ ❖ ❖

Not only is this book excellent for parents, . . . it is also an excellent resource for all those who want to teach life skills to their students. It is a very comprehensive curriculum guide for equipping children for the real world. If you are one who lives life with purpose, you will find this an excellent source for instruction.
    –Emilie Barnes, director of More Hours In My Day

❖ ❖ ❖

Teaching children important life skills is one of the greatest things a parent can do for a child. *Life Skills for Kids* is a wonderful resource for every parent's library.
    —Kathy Peel, president of Family Manager, Inc. and author of *Be Your Best: The Family Manager's Guide to Personal Success*

❖ ❖ ❖

Is your child really prepared for life? You may think so until you read *Life Skills for Kids*. Christine Field takes you step by step through a carefully thought-out series of Maxims of Maturity (MOMs), helping to guide parents in teaching skills to their children in fourteen crucial areas. This book is well researched, practical, and best of all—doable.

–Rhonda Barfield, author of *Eat Healthy for $50 a Week*

❖ ❖ ❖

In an era of rapid and radical cultural change, many Christian parents have developed blurred vision when it comes to family life. *Life Skills for Kids* is a corrective lens that will help them see clearly that God designed children to grow best at home with their parents. Christine's practical insights not only restore vision for *why*, but bring into clear focus *how* to restore home life to the center of your child's life. Read and see!

–Clay Clarkson, Executive Director of Whole Heart Ministries and author of *Educating the Whole Hearted Child*

❖ ❖ ❖

Every family should read this book! Christine has provided dozens of practical steps to help us equip our children for life. This is a book that I will be referring to for the rest of my parenting years.

–Jonni McCoy, author of *Miserly Moms* and *Frugal Families*

❖ ❖ ❖

Life Skills for Kids is easy to understand, with uncomplicated principles that promote success as soon as they are practiced! For any mom who has dreams and goals for her child, Christine provides the directions necessary to reach those goals.

–Ellen Banks Elwell, author of *The Christian Mom's Idea Book*

EQUIPPING YOUR CHILD
FOR THE REAL WORLD

Life Skills for Kids

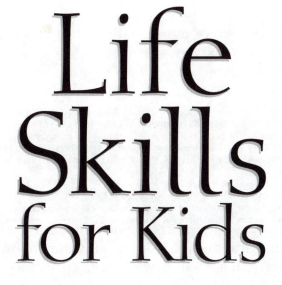

Christine M. Field

SHAW

WATERBROOK
PRESS

Life Skills for Kids
A SHAW BOOK
PUBLISHED BY WATERBROOK PRESS
2375 Telstar Drive, Suite 160
Colorado Springs, CO 80920
A division of Random House, Inc.

All Scripture quotations, unless otherwise indicated, are taken from the HOLY BIBLE, NEW INTERNATIONAL VERSION®. NIV®. Copyright © 1973, 1978, 1984 International Bible Society. Used by permission of Zondervan Publishing House. All rights reserved. The "NIV" and "New International Version" trademarks are registered in the United States Patent and Trademark Office by International Bible Society. Use of either trademark requires permission of International Bible Society.

Scripture quotations marked NRSV are from the New Revised Standard Version of the Bible, copyrighted 1989 by the Division of Christian Education of the National Council of the Churches of Christ in the United States of America, and are used by permission. All rights reserved.

ISBN 0-87788-472-2

Copyright © 2000 by Christine M. Field

All rights reserved. No part of this book may be reproduced or transmitted in any form or by any means, electronic or mechanical, including photocopying and recording, or by any information storage and retrieval system, without written permission from the publisher. Shaw Books and its circle of books logo are trademarks of WaterBrook Press, a division of Random House.

Edited by Miriam Mindeman and Mary Horner Collins
Cover design by Tobias Design
Typesetting by Carol Barnstable/Carol Graphics

Library of Congress Cataloging-in-Publication Data
Field, Christine M., 1956-
  Life skills for kids: equipping your child for the real world / by Christine M. Field.
  Includes bibliographical references and index.
  ISBN 0-87788-472-2 (pbk)
  1. Children–Life skills guides. 2. Child rearing. I Title.
  HQ781 . F48 2000
  649*.1—dc21   99-055081

---

05 04 03 02
10 9 8 7 6 5

This book is lovingly dedicated to
my best friend, my husband, Mark.
Thanks for all the wonderful years
of this great adventure of family life!

❖ ❖ ❖

A special thank you to my artists-in-residence,
Clare and Caitlin, who drew some
of the illustrations for this book.
A big hug to Gracie and Daniel,
who inspire me to press on.

Contents

Preface

I wrote this book because I needed it for my own family. We have chosen to order the super-sized plate of parenting. That is, we have them, we train them, we homeschool them, we mentor them. A few years into this process, we observed that our academic program was going great, but issues of character development, life vision, and practical life skills needed serious attention. How, I asked, were we to accomplish that?

Even with four great kids and a lifestyle I dearly love, I had begun to feel that the super-sized plate was a little excessive. I had too much work to do. Teaching the children was a full-time job in itself, and added to that was the task of running a home, our involvement in church, and our support of our children's other interests. I found myself resenting the extra work while still feeling growing concerns about the big gaps in my children's education. My eight year old could read almost any book in the library, but she didn't know how to dry dishes. And I saw so many other areas in which she would need instruction before becoming an adult. My children needed practical life education in order to know how to take care of themselves and their loved ones in the real world.

How overwhelming! The last thing I needed was another project or program to do with the kids. How could we fit another commitment into our already overcommitted lives?

Then it became clear to me that the solution was so obvious—get the children involved in everyday life alongside the adults in the family. If they spend time with adults, they will learn to be adults. If we intentionally expose them to the everyday life skills we take for granted, they will become equipped for adulthood.

What if you don't homeschool? You're probably even busier than our family with work and other commitments. But you are still your child's first teacher, and you possess a wealth of information and practical skills. Why not share these with your children and give them a legacy of life skill confidence?

It's not too hard. It's just living life and letting your children come alongside you. It's intentionally letting them in on the seeming minutia of everyday life. When this is done with a loving heart and a light-hearted spirit, you will be having fun with your children while teaching them valuable life lessons.

Your children only have one childhood. Share your life with them. Love them passionately. Learn together, and you will all look to the future with confidence. My prayer is that you may find joy in the journey.

Introduction

What Will Our Children Need to Know?

The irresponsible teenager has become the caricature of modern adolescence. He can't find his school books to do his homework; he regularly runs out of clean underwear; he has to borrow money from Dad to go to the mall; and his "cooking" consists of knowing how to operate a microwave oven. The young lady of similar age often does not fare much better. It seems the days are gone that girls learned homemaking skills, much less money management and life organization. At the end of their teen years, young men and women are *chronologically* ready to be launched into the real world where Mom is not around to cook, launder, and clean and where Dad is not available to whip out his wallet to lend twenty dollars. But are they equipped to handle it?

I wasn't. In fact, part of my frustration in parenting is that I wasn't raised to be a wife and mother. My generation was groomed for careers and accomplishments in the world, so when some of us landed at home with kids, we were clueless about parenting and domestic skills. Children, however, are resilient and allow us to practice on them. And as we learn, we find ourselves reevaluating what is important for our children's lives. Can we give them what we seem to have missed?

We desire so much for our children. We want the best education and the most enriching life. Of course, it would be lovely as well if they had stable, loving marriages and produced well-behaved grandchildren. Too often the process of enriching children's lives translates into lots of sports or art activities and classes galore. These are important, but are they really preparing your son or daughter for the everyday challenges of adulthood? Will your children be equipped to care for themselves and others, along with doing whatever else God has in store for them?

Adult Life Skills

In a world whirling with choices and opportunities, sometimes the best educational opportunities lie within our own homes in our own families. Let's say your child, boy or girl, is in early childhood, and you want to profitably use the next ten years of that child's life in your home to teach him or her how to manage as an adult.

What are the needs of an adult? These fall into the three broad areas of *public, personal,* and *family life.* Each of these divides into distinct categories that form the basic topics of this book: people skills, in and around the home skills, life navigation skills, time organization, space organization, money management, healthy lifestyle skills, healthy mind skills, spiritual habits, decision-making skills, creative skills, and celebration skills.

Author Robert Barnes agrees that we need to teach our children to function in those three basic arenas of life—public, family, and personal. He also notes, "If there is no plan, no philosophy of life, there can be nothing but conflict between the three primary areas of life."[1] We see that scenario today in people who are overcommitted to work, overworked at church, and underconnected at home. There is no balance because they have failed to keep the Creator at the center of their lives and have given undue attention to one arena or another.

Barnes says that keeping these three areas in balance defines *success,* and he concludes, "It's the parents' job to raise an employable child. It's the parents' role to raise a marriageable child. And most important, it's the parents' job to raise children who are able to be used by God to fulfill God's purpose for each child when that child reaches adulthood."[2]

Lest we think this is too great a burden, Pastor S. M. Davis reminds us that many Christian leaders proved their leadership ability between the ages of twelve and twenty. For exam-

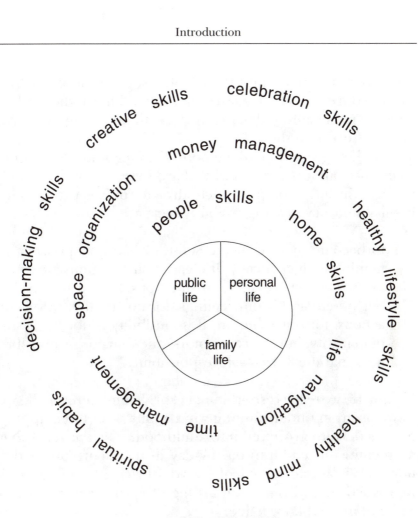

Adult Life Skills

ple, while yet a young adult, David conquered Goliath, and Charles Spurgeon pastored a church at sixteen. Also, Jesus was introduced at the Temple at age twelve. He goes on to cite seven character qualities that our twelve year olds can have in place: (1) a godly attitude, which will defuse the teenage time bomb, (2) a sense of responsibility, (3) discernment about the right kind of friends, (4) a hunger for the truth, (5) a spirit of spontaneous obedience, (6) a respectful attitude, and (7) a life fully committed to Jesus Christ.[3]

A thirteen year old today is generally more worldly than

wise. We must not mistake that shallow sophistication for true wisdom or responsibility. True maturity will mean they will be effective personally and in the world, without letting the world be too effective in them.

In their ground-breaking book *Teaching Your Children Responsibility,* authors Linda and Richard Eyre emphasize as well the necessity of preparing our children for public, private, and family life. They say responsibility means

> to become mature in the sense of being responsible *to* family, *to* self, *to* society. It means being responsible *for* all aspects of our lives and our situations: for our talents, for our potential, for our feelings, for our thoughts, for our actions, for our freedom. Responsibility is not the result of maturity, but the cause of it—and a major responsibility of parents is to teach responsibility.[4]

So, how do we teach responsibility? For that matter, how do we move on from understanding what adults need to equipping our children to grow well into adulthood? The answer is that we mentor our children day-by-day in the laboratory of our homes. We take advantage of everyday teachable moments, as well as activities we purposely arrange, to provide our children with the needed knowledge.

That's where this book comes in. Starting when your children are very young, you can use it as a handy guide to life skills training in your home. Older children can study this guide themselves, or use it as a checklist of desired skills and knowledge to be mastered. Parents can use this book to refresh their memories on their own rusty life skills or to learn new strategies for managing these aspects of maturity. In doing my research for the book, I learned a great deal that has equipped me to teach certain things to my children, particularly in the area of money management. I honed my skills so they could learn many things earlier and more expeditiously than I did.

Our culture may tempt us to assume we have done our job as parents if we provide our children with a superb education and stimulating enrichment opportunities, but for their sake we must take the time and effort to provide them with basic life skills. Author Patricia Sprinkle reminds us: "Training happens at home. It requires dedication and consumes time. It can't be hurried. It is woven day by day on the loom of family life."[5] That "loom of family life" is full of exciting opportunity.

What Do We Want?

When I pray for my children, I ask a lot. I go for the big stuff. I pray that they will love the Lord for a lifetime and that they will exhibit that love in their lives. I pray that it will be God's will that they may experience the joy of marriage, children, and family life. I pray that God will give them a vision for their lives that will lead them down proper paths of training, equipping, and career development. But I have never prayed for them to learn to balance a checkbook or clean a bathroom. Those things seem so mundane and trivial. Yet aren't these small skills essential, along with hundreds of similar ones? Getting along in adulthood consists of the ability to handle both small and large, routine and unusual life skills.

What will happen if children are not equipped? In my own case, because I never learned homemaking skills from my mother, I approached motherhood at a real deficit. But a lack of life skills can also affect children long before they reach adulthood. *Parents Magazine* discussed this issue with Carol Held, a veteran kindergarten teacher, reporting that

> she sees a marked change from her early years in the classroom in the 1970s. Her kindergartners today at Emerson School (ironically a school for gifted children) have more trouble learning their way around the school—where items belong, how to clean up after themselves—than earlier cohorts. . . . "It's not a joke to see how kids can't function on their own anymore," Held says. "Children don't see messes anymore because their parents pick them up. Kids can't even push their chairs in under the table."[6]

15

Many of us see this every day in our environment. I spoke to a teenager who couldn't read an analog watch, and I have taught four year olds at church who did not know how to care for themselves in the bathroom. I have met babysitters who cannot correctly count change, and the level of service I have received from some younger workers is appalling. In our own children's lives, we parents can do much more than shake our heads in dismay at this state of affairs. Bob Barnes notes,

> It's a parent's job to establish a plan that will train a child in the skills he or she will need to be a responsible adult, rather than a forty-year-old adolescent. To send a child off without the necessary training is to put him in a position of being most likely *not* to succeed![7]

Taking on this job requires us to look at our vision of parenting, and it may require us to make serious changes. This was certainly true in our home.

Parents Are Not Cruise Directors

I must confess that I had not given much thought to training children prior to having them. We believed that love would cover it all. We didn't need discipline or structure or regulation in our home. Love would solve all of life's problems. Our first child, consequently, spent her early years in a very child-centered environment. Our goal was to make sure she was happy and having fun. It was only after the second child, and then two more, came along that we truly began to realize that we are not the cruise directors for our children's voyage through a fantasy world of blissful irresponsibility. When I realized that my main job was to equip my children, not merely entertain them, my vision for parenting changed radically. Yes, we would instill in them the joy of living, but they would certainly not be strangers to hard work or to accountability for their actions.

A main purpose of childhood is to prepare children for adulthood. It is not to push them or to force them to use abilities that have yet to develop, but to slowly, sequentially prepare them to be productive adults and to know the satisfaction of productivity. They already know how to be children. They need guidance in learning to be adults.

Only after turning to the true source of wisdom, the Word of God, did we realize that our obligation to train our children went still further. It wasn't enough that we had happy, well-adjusted kids who were gaining discipline and practical living skills. We needed to help them learn wisdom. Indeed, gaining wisdom and knowledge of God is a lifelong pursuit. The earlier we encourage our children to seek wisdom, rather than mere earthly knowledge, the more obedient we are as parents. Such preparation blesses us and our children.

The writer of Proverbs states, "Happy are those who find wisdom, and those who get understanding, for her income is better than silver, and her revenue better than gold. She is more precious than jewels, and nothing you desire can compare with her" (3:13-15, NRSV). By training our children to be wise, responsible adults, we are giving them the most precious inheritance. More than that, we are giving in them a gift to their future spouse, children, employers, coworkers, friends, and their community at large.

Home: The Learning Laboratory of Life

What is it about the home that makes it such an effective learning laboratory? Many factors of family life work together to stimulate growth and development. Of course, no family is perfect, and therefore we cannot claim perfection for the learning laboratory, but families include by definition a great many of the ingredients for effective and realistic training in life skills. Added to that, families are the best setting for learning forgiveness and tolerance and love when the imperfections in the family and its individuals come to light.

Acceptance and encouragement set children free to learn.

In a healthy family, members extend both encouragement to learn and tolerance for the inevitable mistakes in the process. Sometimes children (and adults!) are reluctant to learn new things. They are afraid of failure or they may not know how or where to begin. In the home, we can make sure our children have positive experiences when the stakes are low, and we can praise them for their good efforts, encouraging them to greater independence and capability.

When learning life skills, there is no failure. If the chore isn't done properly, it will improve with practice. If manners need polishing, practice! If sewing skills are uneven, practice! If children can take chances and make mistakes while they are at home and the consequences are meted out with large measures of love and responsiveness, they will be more receptive to the correction they receive in the world. Instead of shouting, "I can't," they will develop the habit of asking, "What can I learn?"

Relationships build learning and learning builds relationships.

Most children are highly motivated by the time and attention paid them by an adult who loves them. This means your home is a perfect place to be teaching life skills while focusing on relationships and sharing your life with your child. You can share your passions while kindling and fostering that passionate parent/child bond.

But what if you can't stand to be around your kids? Some parents dread summer vacations and holidays because the children will be underfoot all day. If you have reached that stage in your lives, think back for a moment. Can you remember the intense love you felt for your child as an infant? You held and nurtured her and your heart sang. When you were apart, your arms ached. Those tender baby years teach us that togetherness, living together, and sharing life make you close.

Perhaps your older child rarely inspires such warmth in

you now. It may be difficult to accept, but sometimes the child whose behavior is the most annoying to you is the one who needs your attention and time the most! Author Deborah Carroll notes, "As you spend time with him, do even mundane things with him, you'll find yourself falling in love with him over and over again."[8] Time spent together can be the healer of wounded hearts and the vehicle of life instruction. Whether you are cooking together, doing a home repair, or engaging in a familiar holiday ritual, the shared time and experience can bring more depth and understanding to your relationship with your child.

The real world of the home transfers to the real world of work.

Many writers in the field of career education have identified essential employability skills. In our increasingly technical society, computer and math skills are often near the top of the list. On a more basic level, however, many employers are having trouble merely finding workers who can read or write. Communication skills, interpersonal skills, work responsibility skills (like coming to work regularly and on time), and problem solving and reasoning skills are all highly valued in the workplace.

Job Savvy: How to Be a Success at Work lists the following ten self-management skills that employers want to see in their employees:

1. Concern for productivity
2. Pride of craftsmanship and quality of work
3. Responsibility and ability to follow through on assigned tasks
4. Dependability
5. Work habits
6. Attitudes toward company and employer
7. Ability to write and speak effectively
8. Ability to read and apply printed matter

9. Ability to follow instructions
10. Ambition/motivation/desire to get ahead[9]

So many of these skills are learned at home in daily interactions and in being called to be accountable for one's actions within the context of family relationships.

The attitudes and attributes that make a good employee are the same attitudes and attributes that make a good kid. A child who can learn to do chores cheerfully stands a better chance of becoming an employee who performs work with a good attitude. A child who has been taught to value honesty will be an employee to be trusted. A child who has been trained in good work and study habits at home will transfer those skills to the workplace. In addition, while children may study some problem solving theory in middle school, they learn the real art of this at home in performing family service, working out sibling disputes, planning personal finances, and negotiating a host of other everyday activities.

What about the skills one needs to bring to marriage? Openness, honesty, the ability to communicate and solve problems, the ability to withstand stress—these are just a few. All of these relationship skills are practiced and honed at home, in relationships with parents and with siblings. The transferability of our influence at home is clear. We have a tremendous opportunity to make an impact on our children's future, both in their work and in their relationships. But we must be willing to do the job.

Parents are the most reliable experts on their own children.

As a society, we have given over so much to institutions and experts. We rely on them to teach academics, sex, drugs, death education, consumer education, conflict resolution, and more. Those needs that are not filled in school are fair game for willing entrepreneurs who will teach our kids sewing, cooking, woodworking, babysitting, manners, or study skills—for a fee. The actual cost is dollars, lost family time, and loss of control over our children.

In light of increasing youth violence, many writers have commented on family time and its value. A recent *Wall Street Journal* article reports:

> A discussion group of Maine adults was organized by pollster Peter D. Hart to explore declining values. Just what, specifically, are they concerned about? One huge problem, they say, is that family routines have broken down. "It used to be, you came home from school, and an hour and a half later you all sat down and ate dinner. Then you watched one show on TV and did your homework," says Nancy Thompson, a middle-aged telephone operator. "You had a Sunday afternoon dinner. There's none of that today. It's all haphazard." The consequences are serious: lack of involvement by parents in the lives of their children. . . . In a nationwide survey of 2,011 adults last week by Mr. Hart and Robert Teeter for the *Wall Street Journal* and *NBC News,* a whopping 83 percent of the respondents said that lack of involvement in their children's lives is a "very serious problem" facing society.[10]

Why aren't we more involved? I believe there are two reasons. First, we are simply too busy. Second, and even more significant, we have come to be over-reliant on experts to teach our children. We have forgotten that when it comes to parenting and instilling life skills in our own children, we are the true experts. Bob Barnes observes,

> Despite America's reputation for resourcefulness, this country hit a point where it no longer knew what to do with its children. . . . Within barely a decade the American parent had become less a parent and more of a taxi driver, making sure that the children got to the proper subcontractor.[11]

Instead of purposefully involving our children in work and activity at home, we drive them from place to place to let someone else teach them something which may or may not be of value. Then when we do come home, we are too tired and stressed out to take advantage of the teachable moments that occur in family living every day. And we find ourselves having to work to be somehow knitted back into a family because our wide ranging pursuits have carried us so far from one another.

While parents are busy playing taxi driver (and actually gloating over how many activities they are able to squeeze in), they are abdicating so many wonderful opportunities. By keeping their children with them more, they could be the ones to truly impart their values, life view, morals, and standards. The Delany sisters, centenarians noted for their common-sense wisdom, remind us, "If you live right, chances are your children will, too. But teach them everything. What you don't teach them, someone else will—and you may not like those lessons!"[12]

Taking back the responsibility for your children may not be easy. People may wonder why you aren't running everywhere for enrichment in their little lives. But you will be gaining enrichment which can only be found by spending lots of time together, doing big and little, important and seemingly insignificant things. Rick Boyer, homeschooling father of ten says,

> Life skills are the building blocks of the business of living, the skills we need to serve God in the life to which He has called us. They come to us as we explore our interests, fulfill our responsibilities, receive instruction, spend time with other people, and meditate on Scripture. God has developed a life curriculum for each of us, only a fraction of which will be learned in a classroom. The experiences we need to form both skills and character will be built by a loving Designer into the fabric of our lives to help prepare us for the rest of our lives.[13]

With God designing the life curriculum for your family, think of the possibilities!

Making a Life Skills Checklist

This exercise is for parents. Imagine your child as an adult. Don't focus on careers or jobs for purposes of this exercise, but on independence and character qualities. Start one notebook for each child, and describe this person as a young adult. Be as specific as you can about the areas on this list:

- ◆ people skills
- ◆ home skills
- ◆ life navigation skills
- ◆ time organization
- ◆ space organization
- ◆ money management
- ◆ healthy lifestyle skills
- ◆ healthy mind skills
- ◆ spiritual habits
- ◆ decision making skills
- ◆ creative skills
- ◆ celebration skills

Jot down your thoughts, dreams, and priorities in these areas. As you read through this book, you will flesh out these areas and perhaps add others of your own. (The appendix contains information on additional helpful resources for your planning and teaching.) Keep this Life Skills Notebook for your child to track her own progress. You may also add sections of your memories of mentoring as well as treasured photos. Our family's notebooks have included photos of bread baking sessions, summer lemonade stands, and favorite pets who have helped teach responsibility.

As your child gets older, let him keep the notebook himself. It will be a treasured possession. As he becomes more skilled at life skills, he can add his own materials, resources he has uncovered, and perhaps information on career areas to explore. The point is to begin today to develop a tool to help you and your child plan ahead for independence. It will be here faster than you think.

How to Use This Book

First, *read it through in its entirety.* This will help you to develop an overview of life skills, refresh your memory about skills you may not even be conscious of anymore, and give you some ideas about what your children need to know. Choose the area in which your child needs the most work. Do not expect your child to master all areas at the same time. Imagine if someone expected you to correct all your faults overnight! You would be resentful and resistant to change. Likewise, children can only be expected to focus on one major area at a time. For our family, sharing the load of household chores came first. We spent many months working on this area before moving onto another.

Then, *proceed through the needed skill areas, focusing on each for at least a month.* The following chart gives a brief summary of each of the building blocks, or what I call *Maxims of Maturity.* As the children mature, repeat the areas each year with increasing complexity. This year for teaching money skills you might simply make the goal of having your child identify coins and use a piggy bank. Next year she can begin to save for larger goals and consistently tithe her money. An even older child could work out an entire budget and do his own banking. The skills will grow as your children grow.

Of course, for different families the choice of skill areas and the order and activities will vary. There is not enough time to teach our children everything they will need to know. *We must focus on the best pursuits for the individuals we have been given to love and care for and prepare for adulthood.* What will make them feel competent in the world? What will help them become the people God has given them the potential to become?

When you have established some goals that fit your family, delve in and enjoy yourselves!

MOMs: Maxims of Maturity

❖ **Maxim One:** Responsibility begins in small things, and it should be timed well. By starting too early or too late to expect things from a child we may groom a child who can't do anything for himself or others.

❖ **Maxim Two:** Children must learn to get along with others and to resolve and manage conflict on their own. This starts at home with parents and siblings.

❖ **Maxim Three:** Everyone lives somewhere. We need to take care of that place and make it a haven to nourish ourselves and others—a place to call home.

❖ **Maxim Four:** It's a big and sometimes uncertain world out there, and our children need to navigate it safely.

❖ **Maxim Five:** We are given only a certain amount of time. We have to use it wisely.

❖ **Maxim Six:** We all work and live in a physical space. We need to manage that space. Our children's future spouse and employer will appreciate this especially.

❖ **Maxim Seven:** Things break and need maintenance. The more we can learn to do on our own, the more self-reliant we will be.

❖ **Maxim Eight:** Much of life involves money. Either we learn to handle it or it will handle us.

❖ **Maxim Nine:** Each of us has only one body. We have to take care of it.

❖ **Maxim Ten:** A brain is a valuable thing. We should aim to make it work at peak performance.

❖ **Maxim Eleven:** If God is not at the center of our life, it will ultimately be unsatisfying.

❖ **Maxim Twelve:** We must make lots of decisions in life. The more decisions we make, the better decision makers we will be.

❖ **Maxim Thirteen:** All of life involves creativity. From artists to accountants, we can all develop and nourish that creativity.

❖ **Maxim Fourteen:** Rejoice and be glad! This day is all we have.

CHAPTER 1

Responsibility in the Small Things

Don't Start Too Early or Too Late

✤ First Maxim of Maturity

Responsibility begins in small things, and it should be timed well. By starting too early or too late to expect things from a child we may groom someone who can't do anything for himself or others.

✤ Transferable Skills

Positive attitude toward work and a good work ethic; eagerness to continue to grow and learn; ability to take responsibility for, and accept consequences of, own actions; adaptability to helpful routines; attention to detail; capacity for staying with a job until completion.

I heard once that God made time in order to prevent everything from happening all at once. His graciousness extends to human growth as well. Imagine the stress of having to mature in one year, or having to complete a high school education by age ten. God had a better plan—to allow human beings to mature, learn, and grow at a saner pace.

A child cannot read the classics of literature without wading through some phonics training. She can't be expected to solve algebraic equations without first counting many beans. Learning life skills is the same. We can start while our children are young to teach them to be self-reliant and productive. Taking advantage of the learning opportunities in the small moments and the small tasks of everyday life not only cements the bond of relationship, but also lays the foundation for learning bigger things. We have the time, if we will seize the small moments. Bonnie McCullough and Susan Monson, in their idea-packed book, *401 Ways to Get Your Kids to Work at Home,* tell us,

> By the time your children reach eighteen years of age, they will have spent 32,234 hours under your guidance and training. Consider that it takes only 2,100 hours of classroom and outside study time to complete a bachelor's degree in college and half that time to learn some skilled trades. Your home has sixteen times more teaching hours than does the university. What do you want to do with this time?[1]

Reading that forced me to look at how I was using my own time. Am I engaging my children in life-enhancing activities, or are we just passing time? I don't want to be an ogre who nags the children to do more, more, more, but I want to be a faithful steward of the precious time that we have together. Having come to motherhood a bit later than most, perhaps I am especially aware of how quickly these years are passing.

Seeking the Road to Independence, Security, and Maturity

Patricia Sprinkle notes, "Children who do too little in childhood may not grow up capable of doing enough as adults."[2] What have we expected of our children? Too often, it has been simply that they feel good about themselves. The goal of enhancing, or at least not damaging, children's self-esteem pervades the books and magazines we read, the discussions we participate in, and every aspect of the educational system. Seminars and school assemblies are devoted to helping children feel good about themselves. However, we have to ask, is this goal a worthy one? Will it lead to beneficial results?

James Tobin, like many parents, questions this trend to

do everything possible to boost a child's self-esteem. Speaking of his thirteen-year-old daughter, he notes,

> Eager to boost Lizzie's self-esteem from babyhood on, we hurrahed each tiny step forward and rushed to reassure her at every setback. We wanted a Superkid in school and sports, but asked little from her around the house or in the community. As a result, we've sometimes wondered, Will she really be ready to tackle adulthood?[3]

Parents who make the choice to sacrifice a child's well-being at the altar of self-esteem may discover not only that they have given up too much, but also that the gain is not worthwhile.

William Damon's research shows that scientists have not been able to find *any* correlation between a child's self-esteem and any important behavior or skill in a child's social, emotional, or intellectual life. Adults who offer general praise, such as "You're terrific," are sometimes doing children a disservice because the praise is not tied to any specific mastery. The message this sends is confusing to children and leads them to not take adults at their word. It also leads, Damon believes, to an over-preoccupation with self. He says, "When we tell children that their first goal should be self-love, we are suggesting to them that they are at the center of the universe. By contributing further to the already child-centered orientation of modern culture, this emphasis can push a child towards a narcissistic insensitivity to the needs of others."[4]

Our Christian faith, likewise, warns us about having an unbalanced view of ourselves. While affirming our inherent worth as creatures of God the Creator, the Bible cautions, "Do not think of yourself more highly than you ought, but rather think of yourself with sober judgment, in accordance with the measure of faith God has given you" (Romans 12:3).

Damon also observes that the humblest people are often the most secure and that those who are most self-aggrandizing are often quite insecure. Jesus is the greatest example of that strength of humility. Philippians 2:7 says that Jesus "made himself nothing, taking the very nature of a servant." He humbled himself as much as he possibly could to do his work among us.

What are the long-term results of the short-sighted self-esteem fix? (I like to call it the "self-esteem monster.") Children who have spent their lives being told how wonderful they are eventually reach an obstacle which comes as a shock to them. Perhaps it is in the form of a tough teacher who expects more than good feelings in a student's work. Perhaps it is an employer who wants the young adult to work hard, regardless of how he feels about himself. The collision of reality and the cocoon of self-esteem woven in childhood can be harsh and devastating.

A recent newspaper article in my area was headlined, "Self-Esteem Taught by School as Important Life Skill." In it Teresa Mask interviewed a college teacher who said that her students often get angry when they are told that they haven't written a coherent paper because all their lives they have been led to believe that everything they have done is wonderful. Then reality sets in. Mask comments, "The harm comes from people who develop low self-esteem when they learn they aren't as great as they think they are."[5]

My own transition to the real world contained some of this element of shock. I finished high school at a small private school where I earned good grades and received much attention and praise for being so bright, gifted, and funny. Then I went to a large college where there were many, many people who were bright, gifted, and funny. It was a shock to learn I was not the only one. I completed undergraduate school and went on to law school, a place full of people who have done very well up until that point, or else they would not have been accepted into law school. The rigor of that training teaches young law students that they aren't so special and that they essentially know nothing. Then, practicing law with the full realization of my own ignorance was the next transition. Being able to whisper to myself, "I am special" when faced with a formidable adversary in the courtroom was of absolutely no value to me. My security and confidence required a stronger basis.

Gaining Real Self-Confidence through Competence

Children will only truly believe in themselves when they have done something competently, something to feel good about. And it is involvement in real things in the real world that leads to such competence. The home provides a natural training ground where even the very young child can feel valued and have a sense of belonging, as he or she contributes while at the same time learning life skills in the family.

As your child's coordination, ability, and understanding increase, so can her level of responsibility in the home. She can also learn the value of constructive feedback in learning to do chores well. According to Damon,

> Children must learn to hear negative as well as positive feedback, to care about it and to act on it. This can only occur in relationships where they have full respect for the person who offers the child feedback. It is best for children to learn this while young, well before the adolescent years. . . .The only effective route is through a continuing succession of specific actions and achievements, such as *taking on genuine family responsibilities around the house* [emphasis added]. The process must be sustained, in small and large ways, over the years. There is no quick fix.[6]

We have the tools we need to produce self-confident, competent children. We must give our children real things to do in a stable predictable routine so they can know they are needed and important, and then we must praise them for doing something real.

Starting Young When Chores Are Fun

You will notice that from about ages two to five, children *love* routine. They crave to know what will happen next in the day. Also characteristic of this age is the growing spirit of independence. Your child wants to "do by myself," which is the marvelous beginning of self-confidence. You can capitalize on these two factors by bringing your very young children alongside you as you go through daily routines. As you wash the dishes, get him a stool and give him the plastic cups to dry. As you fold clothes, let her fold the washcloths and kitchen towels. As your children grow, so will their skills. Maria Montessori had this to say about work and children:

> The adult in our culture is unprepared to recognize and accept the young child's desire for work and therefore, is not only amazed when it appears, but refuses to allow its expression. He instead tries to force the child to play continuously. Adults must learn to recognize the child's instinct for work and cooperate with it.[7]

Many of us have been brainwashed into believing that childhood is a time for unfettered play. The opportunity we are missing is that a fun, light-hearted approach to work *is* play for a child, and it paves the way for the development of a strong work ethic.

My son, Daniel, begged to be involved with me starting when he was about sixteen months of age. If there was a basket of laundry in sight, he would carefully take it out piece by piece. Instead of viewing it as an annoyance or distraction, I learned to give him the washcloths to fold. If I didn't want "help" with the laundry, I learned to whiz through the task behind closed doors so he wouldn't be disappointed.

My son also enjoys order. When he is not creating chaos in our home, he helps me to place unbreakable cookware in the lower cabinets or refile and stack books in the bookshelf. Even in these very early years, children *want* to help. The problem for us as parents is that their help takes too much of our time. We waste the opportunity to teach, because we just would rather do it ourselves. In a survey for this book, one Oklahoma mom wrote,

> I begin giving little jobs to my little ones. I hand my

twenty month old laundry from the washer and she glee-
fully tosses it into the front loading dryer. Around two and
a half years, I start having them get the newspaper from
the front lawn in the morning. Around age three they
wash dishes, usually mugs, bowls, and spoons. Around age
five they add lunch dishes, usually just plates and cups.

Is it more trouble to have your children "help"? Often it is. But
to allow them to do so makes them feel valued and needed in
the family, and this paves the way for better attitudes about
chores when they are older.

Continuing Even When They Have Other Important Things to Do

As children grow, parents often desire to excuse them from
chores because they have other important things to do, such as
schoolwork and extracurricular activities. But what message
does that send? It says that work outside the home is more important than family and may perhaps breed the adult who will
stay at the office longer rather than come home to deal with
the children, a tired spouse, and a sink full of dishes. Don't we
really want to communicate that nothing is more important
than helping and nurturing those closest to us—our family?

Being called to be a parent or homemaker can be perceived as boring when there are so many other things to do in
the world. But, if we devalue this calling, what message are we
giving our children about their own value and about the importance of parenting and child-rearing? When we place value
on these nurturing behaviors, we show the value of the
nurturers and the people they nurture. Our world could
certainly use more caring people, and we have a prime opportunity to help our children become such people when we give
them a part in making a house into a home.

This apprenticeship in real life will help our children in
work and marriage, but it also has benefits even earlier.
McCullough and Monson note, "If young adults know how to

clean a house and keep it that way, how to select and cook good food, or how to budget money, then they are released from the extra time it takes to learn these things when time is needed to concentrate on studies, career, or other areas of living."[8] In my own experience, I would have been better off not having to invest catch up time in learning practical skills at the same time I was launching my career. A person who makes the transition straight from school to a homemaker role is often similarly ill-equipped.

We must seek a balance for our family which validates the children's outside achievements while also calling upon them to be contributing members of the family. Then our children, at maturity, will have a fighting chance of finding balance in personal, public, and family life.

How Do We Teach Responsibility and Chores?

Think about the amount of time you have available in a week with your children. There are 168 hours each week. Let's say you and your child spend about 70 of them sleeping and approximately 3 of them going to church. If your child attends school, subtract another 35 for 60 free hours per week that you spend with your child. For preschool children, figure back in that 35 hours for a total of 95! What can you do with that time?

If used wisely, with effective expectations and methods for teaching, this can be a goldmine in child training time. Elisa Morgan, founder of MOPS (Mothers of Preschoolers) and author Carol Kuykendall note, "As much as kids seem to resist responsibilities, deep down they need to know they are counted on. Yet they often need help in learning how to tackle their chores, and those chores need to be age appropriate."[9] How do we teach chores to children, and what can we expect of children at various ages?

Give little jobs and little tools to little people.

If you want to have your child help with cleaning, provide

appropriate tools for her use, such as child-size sponges. Her own spray bottle with her name on it (containing water) is an irresistible item to get a child interested in cleaning. If you want him to hang up jackets and jammies, make sure you have reachable hooks or clothes bars. Clothing rods in closets can be lowered by hanging a dowel at the child's height with rope tied to the original clothes rod. Low shelving and easy-to-open storage areas also make it easier for the very young child to help put things away.

Train them step by step in excruciating detail.

Michael Jordan was not born a basketball superstar. He learned his skills sequentially and methodically. Dr. Stanley Greenspan notes, "In much the same way, many tasks that your school-age child needs to master are made up of separate steps. . . . By teaching her how to apply a step-by-step method to any task she sets out to master, you're giving her a tool she can use throughout her life."[10]

When teaching a new skill, like dishwashing, to my children, I follow these steps. First, they watch me do the dishes. Then I watch them do it a few times, and make helpful, non-critical suggestions, such as reminding them to turn cups upside-down to drain, or to place silverware in the holder so it will dry out. After they have watched me, and I have watched them a few times, then they are ready to begin doing the task on their own.

Have some fun with the training!

When teaching a child a new responsibility, it can actually be fun to have training sessions. You can pretend that you are doing a television documentary such as, "Taking out the garbage through the ages." It might sound something like this:

DAD: Primitive man threw his trash outside his cave.
MOM: We are much more sophisticated and sanitary.
DAD: This is what we do . . .

Then he demonstrates properly securing the bag, carrying it to the trash can, then placing a fresh bag in the can.

Teaching a lesson on how to clean the bathroom might sound like this:

> DAD: Scrubbing bubbles alone won't clean the bathroom—they need your help!
> MOM: This is how we clean the bathroom. Observe the following . . . Scrub, scrub, scrub!

Offer visual reminders.

Once a task is learned, it is sometimes helpful to make task cards with pictures for younger children to remind them of the details of multistep jobs. For example, my daughter Grace's task card for cleaning her room uses pictures and text and says, "When Mommy or Daddy say it's time to clean my room, I make my bed, pick up all the clothes off the floor, put clean clothes away, put dirty clothes down the laundry chute, put the books on the bookshelf, put the toys in the box, and pick up any trash or papers on the floor." The task card remains posted in her room so that she can refer to it and I can refresh her memory when necessary.

Use summer or school break as a teaching time.

Summer is a good time to learn new responsibilities. Taking out trash or doing yardwork can be taught sequentially on a slow summer day. A school break might be the perfect time to organize your child's room to make it easier for him to maintain. If new routines are established over break periods, they will be in place when school resumes.

Write down some of the things you would like to have your child tackle this year on a goals sheet. Put them into the notebook described earlier at the end of the introductory chapter. In this way, you can track your child each year and watch her ability and confidence grow.

Age Appropriateness: What Can Your Child Do?

OK, you are looking down at your eighteen-month-old toddler and saying, "Sounds great, but I guess it will have to wait." Not so. A child of that age can be asked to fetch items, fold washcloths, pick up toys, and carry plastic dishes to and from the table. We can ask and train, even at this age. And as they mature, our children are capable of much, much more.

The following chart gives some ideas of what is possible at what ages. These are merely guidelines—your child may do more or less. Knowing that learning life skills is a process, don't expect perfection from him. The intent here is to give you ideas to try out in your family.

Age-Appropriate Chores for Children

Ages 2-3

Begin to dress self	Put silverware in dishwasher
Help make bed—at least pull covers up	Help feed animals
Pick up toys	Help wipe up spills
Hang clothing on hooks	Dry unbreakable dishes
Carry laundry to and from laundry area	Sweep
Help fold towels	Bring in newspaper
Empty light trash cans	Mop a small area
Dust	Pour from a small pitcher
Carry plate to sink after meals	Pull weeds
	Fetch diapers
	Help pick up livingroom

Ages 4-5

Dress self	Help in kitchen—stirring, ripping lettuce, drying dishes
Make own bed	Help carry and put away groceries
Clear dishes from table	Wash toys when needed
Set table	Help rake yard
Retrieve the mail	Help wash car and clean interior
Dust	
Water plants	

Ages 4-5 *cont.*

Sweep patio
Wash floors, low walls with sponge
Put away own clothes—put dirty clothes in hamper
Sort clean clothes by family member
Sort dirty clothes by color
Hang towels after bath
Help load dishwasher

Note: Ages five to twelve or so are golden years for teaching children at home. These kids are increasingly capable and yet not too preoccupied with school and extracurricular activities. Make sure you start to give both boys and girls the opportunity to do outside chores and to do maintenance-type tasks with Dad. Don't neglect teaching both your son and your daughter to do chores inside the home, like cooking and cleaning. You will shortchange them for life if you do.

Ages 6-12

Make bed
Take care of pets—clean cages and feed them
Cook simple foods—use simple recipes
Make school lunches
Help with yard work
Help wash car
Wash, hang, and fold laundry
Vacuum, sweep, and mop
Straighten up house
Wash, dry, and put away dishes
Clean bathroom completely
Rake leaves, shovel snow
Weed and water garden
Use washer and dryer
Take out trash
Strip and change beds
Iron
Polish shoes

Ages 13 and up

Any of the above, plus:
Change light bulbs
Replace vacuum cleaner bag
Wash inside and outside windows
Clean out refrigerator
Clean stove and oven
Prepare a meal
Make grocery lists
Shop for groceries
Cook meals
Do all laundry functions
Iron clothes
Do clothes mending, repairs
Mow lawn
Trim yard
Wash and polish car
Maintain a bicycle—fill tires with air, oil squeaks
Help paint and caulk

When all of my children were very young, I would look at lists such as this and laugh. I felt my kids would never reach these levels of ability and my household chore load would remain with me permanently. But time and attention are great teachers, so there is hope for anyone with young children. Patricia Sprinkle encourages us this way:

> Eleven-year-old children can work almost equally with parents in housework, lawn care, meal preparation and cleanup, and laundry. By age fourteen a child should be able to do anything in a home an adult does. The fourteen year old will even be glad to tell you better ways of doing it—whether or not you ask![11]

Compare this with the typical, worldly-wise fourteen year old, obsessed with movies, music, and makeup. How your children will be at age fourteen is largely a result of what your agenda has been and how much you have expected of them up to that time.

Motivation Techniques: Generating Enthusiasm That Keeps Going

You know your children and you know what will motivate them. You can tailor a motivation system to appeal to them more effectively than any commercial vendor. Following is a list of some of the techniques we have found or made up on our own. Be creative and get ideas from your children, and don't forget to move on to something else if your children get bored or you get tired of administering a system. What works this month may not work next, and you may find that just a simple change in the rhythm or pattern can serve as a purposeful way to motivate them.

Use charts.

Charts are a great way to reduce nagging. They are agreed upon, unemotional, and nonnegotiable. They can even allow

Extra Challenges for the Older Child:

Follow your mom or dad around for one day and make a list of every chore she or he performs. Have a meeting with that parent to discuss what you could do to help. You will be helping the parent and broadening your own skills.

Go to the library to research the connection between maintaining a clean home and allergies. Is there a connection? Present your findings to your parents.

the child to exercise some independence in looking at the chart, then choosing which task to do first or when to do the job. There are several kinds of motivational charts you can use.

Assignment charts set up the job requirements and may have a schedule for their completion. By looking at the chart, the child knows what to do and perhaps when it should be done. These charts are as unique as the families who use them. For very young pre-readers, draw or cut out pictures related to the expected chores. The child looks at the picture and knows what to do.

A pocket chart, with job cards that slip in and out, can be constructed with envelopes or library pockets. The jobs to be done are inserted in the top pocket. As the jobs are completed, the card is transferred to the bottom pocket. The cards for each chore can also be hung vertically on brads (fasteners available at your stationery store) and then placed in a pocket at the bottom when completed.

We use a circular chart for kitchen duties at mealtime. An arrow indicator is fastened to the center of a paper plate with a brad and the indicator is moved around the plate to denote various jobs. Depending on the age of your child, you can write out a straightforward daily, weekly, or monthly chart of expectations. Younger children are often motivated by checks or stickers which denote completion of their daily chores.

Pocket Chart

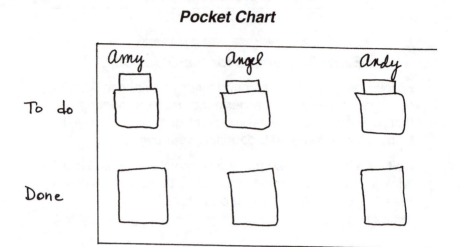

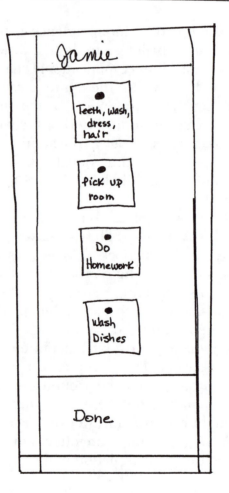

What about irregular jobs that don't fit into the typical day's routine? You can institute the old "job jar" concept. Write the tasks to be done on little slips of paper and put them in a container. Each person draws a task for the day. These are great for busy Saturdays when the whole family can get involved in spring or fall cleanup. A variation on this is to write the jobs on popsicle sticks. Put the sticks in a mug and have each child draw a stick to pick a job.

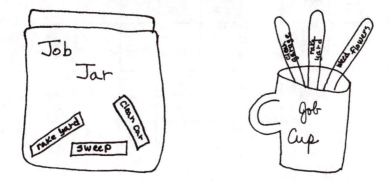

A progress chart keeps track of accomplishments and may provide a reward. These can be used for daily chores, as above, where the parent puts up a star for each time the child brushes teeth, washes hands, brushes hair, makes bed, etc. Progress charts can be in any form and can be used to track a number of activities. For example, we have used a paper tree and leaves to track number of books read. For each book completed, the child got to tape a leaf on the tree. When the tree branch was

41

full, we went out for ice cream. Another progress chart might be in the form of a path or track, such as for a race car. Each day the child takes out the trash, or practices the piano, or does any agreed upon activity, he moves the marker further along the chart. When the marker reaches the finish line, the child receives a special treat.

A recent piece in *Woman's Day* offered an interesting twist on chore charts. This family had each family member trace his or her handprint onto a piece of Fun Foam, and then they

Progress Chart

What Gracie Can Do

	Sun	Mon	Tues	Wed	Thur	Fri	Sat
Brush teeth	☆						
Dressed	☆						
Brush hair							
Make bed	☆						
Pick up clothes, toys							
Bath							
Reading							
Prayers							

Piano Practice Path

decorated the hands, punched holes at the wrist, and hung them on the refrigerator. Self-stick notes were used to post chores on the helping hands.[12]

Use games.

In our home we love to play games and use them as a regular part of our learning program. When the two oldest girls were young, about four and five, we decided to make a game of learning life skills as well. So began The Helpy Helpers Learning Club. Our daughters often referred to themselves as helpy helpers when they had done something helpful for Mom. The rest of the name grew naturally out of what we were going to accomplish.

I began by listing a number of areas in which the children needed instruction. They each had a notebook with a sheet for Mom or Dad to check their progress in each task. For example, on the subject of laundry, these were some of the checkpoints:

1. Sort clothing into lights and dark.
2. Load washing machine.
3. Add detergent and turn on machine.
4. Transfer clothing to dryer when washing is complete.

43

5. Dry all clothing completely.
6. Fold and sort.
7. Put away clothes in appropriate locations.

We needed an incentive for learning, so I got each girl a plain white T-shirt, and with fabric paint we wrote "Helpy Helpers Learning Club" on each shirt, along with the girl's name. I found some iron-on heart patches and star patches on a clearance table and bought several of these. As each girl mastered a skill, a heart or star patch with the name of the skill written in permanent marker was ironed on her shirt.

Our goals for the year were to have each girl be able to manage loads of laundry, prepare a simple meal with no cooking, cook at least one simple dish, learn to wash, dry, and put away dishes, and learn the components of a clean room from the checklists they have learned to complete in their notebooks. As each area of expertise was mastered and a patch earned, the chore would be included in their regular routine of chores. As their proficiency grew, so would their responsibility.

The Seven Dwarfs whistled while they worked. The Helpy Helpers had a song to sing while they did their chores. At "club meetings" and as they worked around the house, my girls sang this to the tune of "Are You Sleeping?":

> I like helping
> I like learning
> How about you?
> How about you?
> I'm a helpy helper
> Be a helpy helper
> You can too.
> You can too.

We had a club meeting once in a while to check the girls' progress and talk things over. I always made it a point to ask them what they were interested in learning or working on. They had some very helpful ideas, such as learning to take care of a pet (and so we got a puppy) and learning the names of different flowers, which we have tried to incorporate in our gardening.

This method can be used for anything you are seeking to teach your child, such as saying their ABCs, picking up toys cheerfully, even potty training! Many children are very motivated by this system and view each patch of accomplishment as a badge of honor. Some would argue that children need to learn responsibility and no one said it should be all fun and games. We believe that life is a joy, that each day holds something to be savored, and that time spent together is to be cherished. The Helpy Helpers Club is one simple thing we tried to help our children learn to be cheerful servants.

When my girls grew out of The Helpy Helpers Club, we had to come up with something new. We also saw the need to work on attitudes as well as work expectations. It was no joy to any of us to have an orderly house, but miserable inhabitants. As we considered motivational techniques, we discussed the area of allowances, but my husband and I disagreed about how allowances should be used. He felt that the children should not be paid for doing chores that they have to do simply because they live in our home. (There is a larger discussion of this issue in chapter 8, which covers the subject of money.) We came up with the idea of "The Field Beans" as a middle ground.

The Field Beans

To earn 10 beans a day, do these things:

1. Teeth, wash, dress, hair neat—without being told
2. Table and kitchen helper—setting, clearing
3. Morning chore/room pickup
4. Do all schoolwork, homework, piano
5. Keep room neat and clean (Includes UNDER beds and furniture)
6. Keep laundry off floor/Put away clean laundry when asked
7. Have a quiet time: prayer and reading
8. Afternoon/evening pickup of house and bedroom
9. Be kind to others at all times
10. Have a pleasant attitude
11. PE training with Dad for extra bean

Each bean = 5 cents. If you earn all 10, you earn 50 cents per day. If you earn 50 cents per day, Monday through Saturday, you earn 3 dollars for the week. (We purposely exclude Sunday.) You lose one bean for each task you omit per day.
Your money: 10 percent goes to church; 10 percent goes to savings; you keep the rest.

We labeled sections of an egg carton with each child's name. The top cup of the carton was filled with ten beans. As each bean was "earned," it was moved to the bottom cup to be tallied and recorded by that day's bean counter.

This was a very motivating system for my growing children. They were at the ages that they wanted to have some money of their own. This gave them money, but it was tied to very specific expectations. With this system, the parents can change the expectations as the need arises, and they can work on attitudes, such as unkindness or harsh talk to one another. When children know they will lose a bean for being rude to a younger sibling, they will often think twice.

Motivating and Establishing Consequences: When Johnny Doesn't Feel Like Taking Out the Trash

These ideas for motivation or charting results are only the beginning. What if your child does not choose to cooperate? The grandest of plans is worth nothing if your child is not on board. Of course, the best way to motivate children is with our unconditional love. Charts, stickers, and motivational devices are cute and interesting, but if we hope to gain our kids' cooperation in life, they must know they are loved completely and totally.

Lay a foundation of unconditional love.

Gary Chapman and Ross Campbell explain this idea well:

> We need to fill our children's emotional tanks with unconditional love, because real love is always unconditional. Unconditional love is a full love that accepts and affirms a child for who he is, not for what he does. . . . Sadly, parents often display a love that is conditional; it depends on something other than their children just being. Conditional love is based on performance and is often associated with training techniques that offer gifts, rewards, and privileges to children who behave or perform in desired ways. Of course, it is necessary to train and/or discipline our children—but only after their emotional tanks have been filled. Those tanks can be filled with only one premium fuel: unconditional love. . . . Only unconditional love can prevent problems such as resentment, feelings of being unloved, guilt, fear, and insecurity. Only as we give our children unconditional love will we be able to deeply understand them and deal with their behaviors, whether good or bad.[13]

When we are certain in our own minds that our love for our children is unwavering, whether or not their room is cleaned, then we can begin the less intimate task of establishing consequences for their work behavior in the home.

Work together to tailor consequences in your family.

According to Robert Barnes, teaching responsibility requires use of the ICE plan. The *I* stands for Instruction, the *C* for Consequence, and the *E* for the Experience portion of the learning process.[14] The critical ingredient in teaching responsibility is to establish consequences for one's actions or lack of actions.

Consequences may require some brainstorming on your part. Elizabeth Crary notes two general types of consequences: "(1) Withdraw a privilege for a short while if the privilege is misused (no television, bike, friends over, etc.) or (2) Retribution. If damage is done, it must be repaid or undone as much as possible."[15] Since the purpose of consequences is not to punish, but to help the child learn, she suggests asking these questions in making a choice: "Is the consequence reasonable? Is the consequence enforceable? Is the consequence clearly related to the offense? Is the consequence consistent with nurturing care? Is there anger, resentment, or retaliation associated with the consequence?"[16]

To get your children on board and brainstorm, start with a family meeting to list work assignments and come up with appropriate consequences. Children can often be your best source of ideas. We had our first meeting when our oldest two were about four and five years old. At that time we were dealing with slapping, leaving bikes out, and yelling. We asked the children what would be an appropriate response on our part to their behavior. They decided that if they left their bikes out, the bikes would be hung up in the garage out of reach for three days. If they yelled unnecessarily, they would have to go to their room for ten minutes. If they slapped a sibling, they would serve a time out. With the rules posted on a chart on the wall, we would merely point to the chart when an infraction occurred and the child would take the punishment. After all, it was their idea.

If you are at a loss for consequences, Patricia Sprinkle suggests, "Ask yourself this important question: What am I doing for my child that, if left undone, would soon teach the child to care for part of his or her own world?"[17] The purpose of this is to give a nexus, or connection, between behavior and results. Here are some examples:

- Not taking dishes from table to sink—scrape all plates off for that meal
- Kitchen not cleaned after one meal—next meal not prepared
- Toys left out—items confiscated for a day or pay a fine
- Garbage not taken out—wash all garbage cans in the house and outside
- Bike left out—can't ride for three days
- Arriving late to dinner—no dinner
- Messy room—stay in room until it is cleaned
- Unnecessary yelling—go to a room where others won't be bothered

The idea of consequences is to create some discomfort for the child. This mild discomfort or inconvenience is often an incentive to remember and obey. You know your children better than anyone else. What could you do to drive home the point of responsible behavior to them?

Offer a chance to grow instead of a rescue operation.

When our children mess up, our tendency is to want to rescue them. This might be in the form of bringing their forgotten lunch to school, or taking out their trash. But this is too short-sighted. Our action may make us our child's hero for the moment, but by it we are teaching that it is acceptable to fail to follow through, to drop the ball on responsibilities. With determination and a willingness to work through conflicts and short-term discomfort, we can spur our children on in their path to maturity.

Of course, we have to make wise choices about how much
freedom and responsibility our children should have. Morris
R. Schechtman, in his book *Working Without a Net*, draws many
analogies between family life and corporate dynamics. He
says, "We don't throw our kids out on the street at an early age
and expect them to grow (emotionally and intellectually) on
their own; we don't give them complete freedom and no limits. We *manage* [emphasis added] our relationships with
kids."[18] Part of this "managing" inevitably involves conflict
and confrontation, which many try to avoid, both at home and
at work. But conflict and confrontation on the part of the parent can be used in a caring approach. If we can navigate these
conflicts wisely at home, we will raise better employees and
spouses who can manage the many conflicts of everyday life.

Schechtman lays out the difference between caring and
uncaring attitudes:

> An uncaring approach avoids conflict and confrontation.
> . . . The more we care, the more we should demand. . . .
> When our kids start learning how to walk, they invariably
> bump into objects and fall down; they scream and cry in
> frustration. Should we as parents prevent this discomfort
> by picking them up and carrying them around? Is it a car-
> ing gesture to delay this natural and productive stage of
> growth? Of course not. The more growth we facilitate, the
> more we care.[19]

Schectman goes on to distinguish the difference between
caretaking and caring:

> Caretaking means that: You do things for people that
> they're perfectly capable of doing for themselves. The
> things you do persuade people that they are unable to
> solve their own problems; that anyone else would be
> better able to solve them. Caring for means that: You
> challenge people to be the best they can be. You tell them
> what they need to hear, not what they want to hear.[20]

The applications of this to parenting are legion. To bail our children out is a form of caretaking. They will never grow to responsibility if we bail them out of every uncomfortable situation. It often takes only one incident of a forgotten jacket on a chilly day or a left-behind lunch on a day of school to cure forgetful behavior.

Another form of bailing our children out is never letting them fail. Let them buy a toy (with their own money) that will fall apart in ten minutes. Let them choose candy that will disappear in a minute instead of a book that can be read and re-read. The next choice may be wiser.

A powerful example of failure to train and manage can be found in the story of Eli in the Bible. His sons, Hophni and Phinehas, became worthless men whom the Lord destroyed. It says in the account of their lives, "Eli's sons were wicked men; they had no regard for the Lord" (1 Samuel 2:12). In reading this story, I cannot help but wonder why Eli didn't take the time to train and rebuke his own children. Was he merely caretaking, not caring?

Handling Grumbling and Complaining: Training Attitudes Toward Work

So much of life involves work. Whether we live in an urban area with the stress and physical challenges of keeping hearth and home together, or whether we live on a farm, work is a way of life. My husband spent much of his childhood working on a farm, and he recounts stories of entire seasons devoted to work from sunup to sundown. It was this early acceptance of the fact of work as a part of life that contributed to his positive, eager attitude towards work as an adult. Training our children to have a healthy, positive attitude towards work may help them and us more than any idea or shortcut we can share. And the benefits of this attitude are not just in the future.

In *Raising Lifelong Learners*, Lucy Calkins and Lydia Bellino say:

When we try to teach children to work hard, frequently we do so only by supervising their chores and stressing the importance of self-discipline. We tell our kids that if they do their work well, if they keep their noses to the grindstone, they'll someday end up with a good job, a good house, a good life. Our message is that hard work pays off in the long run; it isn't fun, but it's worth it. Throughout, we assume and teach that work and play are the opposite of each other. But are they?[21]

Ask your child to look at the attitude they have when they work on something they love, such as a hobby or a project. Such an enjoyable pastime doesn't seem like work. So why not love what we do? If all of life involves work, we can model for our children the enjoyment of working. I have heard that the secret to happiness is not to do what you love, but to love what you do. Do our children see this in their mom and dad?

For my husband and me, there is a thin line between work and play because each of us generally loves the work we have been called to do. If your child hears you or your spouse continually complaining about your work, how will that influence their developing attitude toward work? In contrast to the negative view, Colossians 3:23 gives this admonition, "Whatever you do, work at it with all your heart, as working for the Lord, not for men." So we see that our child's attitude towards work is really more important than the work itself. We can use work in our homes to teach our children positive work attitudes by training them with encouragement and example. When one of our children begins to complain about having to do something, we can remind them, "We serve each other in this family." And we can seek to impress upon them that when we serve one another in the home, we are serving fellow members of Christ's kingdom.

Learning to Do a Job Well

Part of having a good attitude toward work is doing the work right the first time. When I see my children rushing through a job, I remind them that if you don't have time to do it right the first time, you certainly don't have time to do it *over*.

There comes a time in a child's development when haphazard work is unacceptable. A two year old cannot be expected to keep dresser drawers neat and tidy. But you can certainly expect this level of neatness from a ten year old. A ten year old who is held accountable for doing a job well the first time will carry that expectation over into all the places where work will touch her life—school, jobs, volunteer work, service in the church, and future home and family.

Here are some tips for helping your child do it right the first time:

- Slow down! Haste makes jobs that have to be redone.
- Give instructions. Make sure your child understands what is expected.
- Check the work when it's completed.
- Give constructive feedback. Praise your child for the positive aspects of the work before you gently point out the shortcomings.

Achieving Personal Goals: Your Child's Incentive for Learning to Work Well

Working slowly, carefully, and step-by-step has an application to learning any skill, including skills your children choose to learn. McCullough and Monson tell this story about goal setting in the family: "One father asks his children every Friday night, 'What are your goals this weekend?' He says it has taken several months, but they have quit watching so much television and now are working on the things they 'really' want to do. Talents are 'interests' that have been nurtured; goal setting will help talents grow."[22]

You can make it a family project for parents and older children to list five things they want to do, or learn to do. Examples include saving money for an item, learning to ride a two-wheel bike, remodeling a room, reorganizing a closet, etc. Then brainstorm together the steps you can take to reach your goals. Help your child to do the following:

- Define a goal. Answer the question, what is success for this project?
- List the steps needed to accomplish the goal.
- Set a date or deadline for completion.

It is always valuable to build up positive feelings and attitudes towards working hard by doing what it takes to achieve a goal and then being able to look back proudly on your efforts.

Pets: For *Some* Families, a Great Way to Learn Responsibility

Everyone loves the idea of a family pet. That is, until the pet is hungry, dirty, or ill. Then affection can be replaced by annoyance and quarreling. Pets can be used to teach responsibility. They can also be objects of affection for our children and can encourage nurturing behavior. They teach us about the facts of life when they multiply, and they teach us about the fragility of life when they die.

We have learned a lot as a family from the pets we have had. When we only had three children, ages two, six, and seven, we got a golden retriever puppy. Their reputation for being wonderful with children sold me on the idea. The pleading brown eyes of my pet-loving daughter really sold me. So, we got the puppy. Unfortunately, as enthralled as the children were, as the puppy became a little older, the infatuation waned. He ate a lot, he went to the bathroom a lot, and he was getting extremely big. The bigger he got, the less interested the children were in him. He became so large that he would knock over the two year old, and the other two became afraid of him.

We ended up giving away the golden retriever. The two guinea pigs and a rabbit we currently have seem to offer a comfortable level of responsibility for our children. When they start asking for a dog again, I try to arrange an opportunity to dog-sit while a friend goes on vacation. Usually by the end of a week, our children's dog aspirations have vanished.

Before you commit to a pet to help teach responsibility, ask yourself, "Are the children really old enough to care for this pet?" Your second question should be, "Am I, as the parent, willing to take over care of this animal if the children drop the ball?" Unless you can answer both of these questions in the affirmative, don't get a pet. Pets have to be fed on schedule, must always have clean water, and require cleaning and regular maintenance. What are the things you need to do to make a particular animal happy and healthy? What are the costs—both in time and money? Here are some questions to ask regarding any pet:

- How much exercise does this animal require?
- What is the cost to feed the animal?
- How much time will the care of the animal require?
- What are the common illnesses or diseases of the animal?
- What shots are required? How much does this cost?
- Does the animal bite? What first aid care is required for a bite?
- What special ways can you play with this animal, or pamper it?

Pets—from most to least amount of care

- ❖ Dogs
- ❖ Cats
- ❖ Rabbits, hamsters, guinea pigs
- ❖ Turtles
- ❖ Birds
- ❖ Fish

You might try using a contract with your children for pet care. According to Elizabeth Crary,

> Contracts clarify expectations and consequences. . . . Contracts spell out the effort each party provides, the benefits each person receives, and the consequences to each for lack or compliance. A contract is appropriate when *both* parties agree to the goal. The contract outlines how they will work together. Three steps in making a contract are: Clarify the purpose, decide who does what, and establish the benefits and consequences.[23]

Here's how a contract might be used for pet care:

> Dad agrees to buy Johnny a guinea pig. Johnny agrees to feed the pig each day and clean the cage once a week without being told. Dad agrees to not nag Johnny to take care of the pet.
> If Johnny consistently takes care of the pet for one month, Dad will take him to the pet store to buy a special toy for the pet.
> If Johnny consistently fails to take care of the pet, Dad reserves the right to take the guinea pig to a pet shelter for relinquishment.
> Signed:_____

Of course, contracts can be used to outline expectations and consequences for studying, practicing music, chores, and any number of life skills your children are learning. You are the best judge of whether this type of technique works for your family.

In Matthew 25:21, Jesus told of a ruler who praised a faithful servant, "Well done, good and faithful servant! You have been faithful with a few things; I will put you in charge of many things." As a Christian parent, that is a quality I want my children to have. Parents can give children at any age fun opportunities to learn responsibility and faithfulness in their tasks—whether they are small or large ones.

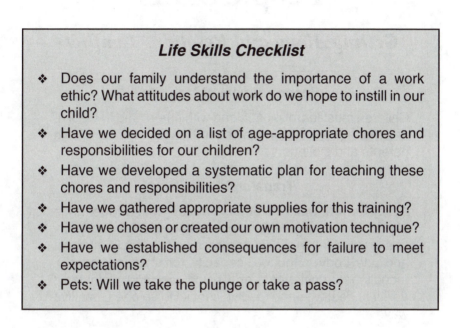

Life Skills Checklist

❖ Does our family understand the importance of a work ethic? What attitudes about work do we hope to instill in our child?

❖ Have we decided on a list of age-appropriate chores and responsibilities for our children?

❖ Have we developed a systematic plan for teaching these chores and responsibilities?

❖ Have we gathered appropriate supplies for this training?

❖ Have we chosen or created our own motivation technique?

❖ Have we established consequences for failure to meet expectations?

❖ Pets: Will we take the plunge or take a pass?

CHAPTER 2

People Skills

Getting Along and Resolving Conflict

Second Maxim of Maturity

Children must learn to get along with others and to resolve and manage conflict on their own. This starts at home with parents and siblings.

Transferable Skills

Ability to work well with others, interact with a wide range of people, recognize the uniqueness of individuals; ability to express feelings, give and receive feedback, interpret and use body language; capacity for showing respect, friendliness, politeness, and using tact and diplomacy; ability to deal with and resolve conflict in an open, positive way.

One of the greatest gifts we can give our children is the knowledge that the universe does not revolve around them. We need to remember that as human beings, we are fundamentally selfish and self-centered from infancy, and we must learn to think beyond ourselves. The risk for any of us if we are indulged too much is that we may learn to expect that kind of treatment everywhere in life, including marriage, relationships, and the workplace.

We tend to indulge our children out of love for them, but love is not indulgence. Love is training your children and sometimes being tough with them, asking them to learn unselfishness, being strong enough to tolerate their not liking you when you try to do the right thing. The Bible clearly shows that if we seek to encourage Christlikeness in our children, we must ask them to look beyond themselves and develop servants' hearts. In Philippians 2 we see both a command, "Each of you should look not only to your own interests, but also to the interests of others" (v. 4), and an example, Christ, who "made himself nothing, taking the very nature of a servant" (v. 7). This ability to look beyond oneself is a critical people skill.

Why focus on people skills? One reason is the skyrocketing divorce rate for new marriages, currently estimated at between 50 percent and 67 percent. And in the workplace? Have you ever seen a work situation without any conflicts between people? Our concern must be to equip our children to be able to deal with people at work, at home, in every aspect of their life. And they will be equipped if they have dealt with and resolved conflict in their formative years.

Getting Along at Home

Service and sacrifice to one another must rule in your home. One of the earliest lessons we much teach children is that we all serve one another in a family. In my early years of mothering, I have been guilty of complaining, "I'm not the maid." No, I am not the maid, but I choose to serve people I love and care for. That kind of healthy modeling and attitude towards service may help your children avoid power struggles in their future relationships. Perhaps with that attitude, they won't argue with their spouse about whose turn it is to change the baby, or who has washed the most dishes. They will do what needs to be done out of love. And so we explain to our children that they have to do things around the house because they belong to a family, and a family works together, and working together as a team and serving one another is a manifestation of love.

Many times my husband, Mark, will find himself in some messy situation, such as spilling something major. Instead of screaming, "How could this happen?" I ask how I can help. When I hear my children voicing a cheerful, "How can I help?" I will know it is a sign of true maturity. I will know that they are indeed grasping the concept that all of life does not revolve around them.

Bob Barnes notes, "This concept of learning to be observant of the needs around you is not easy to teach, especially when we are so interested in communicating our needs to those around us."[1] That ability to step out of our own needs and reach out to help those in need is a part of good citizenship. Help your children be aware of the needs all around them, starting in your home and expanding to the world. Is there a sister whose feelings have been hurt? That relationship must be set right. We never allow our children to go to bed with unresolved issues between the siblings or with Mom and Dad.

On their own initiative, our children have expressed great kindness to one another, such as making cards for a sick sibling or purchasing a little trinket out of their own money just because it would make a sibling happy. They are learning the joy that generous, unconditional giving brings. When they exhibit that type of behavior, they are heartily praised.

One way to encourage thoughtfulness within the home is to play the "Thinking of You Game." Each week, have each family member draw the name of another family member out of a hat. During the week, your mission is to do two or more acts of kindness for that person, without identifying yourself.

At the end of the week, everyone talks about what kind things were done for them, and everyone tries to guess who did them.

My husband occasionally gives the children a paper consisting of a list of blank lines. The paper is captioned "Things I #2 did to show love this week." The assignment is for the children to fill in the blanks with good deeds. They are accountable to Daddy and usually comply cheerfully, often with creative acts of caring.

We have used an idea called the Cup of Kindness when we #3 observe the children exhibiting habitual unkindness. This idea was introduced to me by Kathie Morrissey, who spoke at a homeschooling convention. Each child starts the week with a cup full of nickels. Every time they are rude or unkind, they lose a nickel. At the end of the week, they can keep the remainder.

How can you expand your family's kindness to friends #4 and strangers outside your home? Is there a friend of the family whom they can encourage with a note or a flower from your garden? When my children hear of a sick friend, they often send cards or bring small gifts. Teach them to pay attention to the "sick list" at church. Is there some way they can minister to those in need? Keep your eyes open for opportunities.

For about a year, a homeless woman made her home at our local train station. She would sit on a bench outside the depot each day, engaging passersby in conversation. My family took an interest in her. First, the children would bring her sandwiches. She always enjoyed this, but she enjoyed even more the opportunity to chat with someone. We would occasionally give her money, and when the weather turned cold, we brought her spare blankets from our home. My husband took an interest in her situation as well. On his own initiative, he began bringing home her dirty laundry to wash. We did it together as a family and were happy to provide her with some measure of comfort. Ultimately, my husband worked with the local social service people to have her placed in a nursing home because her medical needs were becoming acute. She is still there, and he and the children sometimes go out to visit her. These were all simple things for our family to do, but they resulted in tremendous discussions. And now, anytime we can lend a hand to someone in need, my children are always eager to help.

How do your children see you treating others? I am often amazed at the rudeness to which service persons are subjected. The person who gives me my cup of coffee at McDonald's is a creation of God, just as I am. I let my children see me treating that person with respect and kindness. What if someone is rude to you? I talk about it with the kids afterwards, pointing out that the person might be having a bad day, and then sometimes we actually pray for that person with the sour disposition. I want my children to know and to see that meeting unpleasantness with more unpleasantness is not what we are called to do as Christians.

Philippians 2:3 says, "Do nothing out of selfish ambition or vain conceit, but in humility consider others better than yourselves." The only way to achieve that spirit of humility is to be grounded in the Lord. If I am Christ-centered in my life, I will have no need of self-aggrandizement, or of making myself look better at the expense of the other person. I won't need it because God has given me all I need to be secure—his unmerited love. If I can help to instill that same confidence in my children, they will be secure enough to be servants as well.

Sibling Sense

If you have multiple children, they may not fully appreciate it, but the mere fact that they have siblings and conflicts with them is a gift. Learning to resolve conflicts at home with siblings may be the most valuable training your child will receive for a healthy marriage. Marriage expert John Gottman says, "A lasting marriage results from a couple's ability to resolve the conflicts that are inevitable in any relationship." He adds, "Many couples tend to equate a low level of conflict with happiness and believe the claim 'we never fight' is a sign of marital health. But I believe we grow in our relationships by reconciling our differences."[2]

Fighting is a part of family life. Learning to do it with self-control and respect for the other party may take years! But daily life with children presents many opportunities to practice fighting. Often a major source of fights is having to share with siblings. Explain to your children that you don't need multiple items in a family when you can share the items you have. What do they have to share? Their parent's time, a bedroom, toys, and sometimes clothing. What can they learn from sharing? Accepting others, patience, taking turns, and leaving things in good condition for the next person. Those all sound like skills they will need for work or marriage.

Another people skill that siblings can learn is teamwork. There can be strength in numbers. Often when children stick together with their siblings, they can reach more common goals. For example, if they are all in agreement about going to the pool, they are more likely to get to go. If one doesn't work on the team, then all will suffer. For example, at the pool we all stay together. If one wanders away, then we all leave. On the way there in the car we discuss this. When we leave the car and enter the pool, we might go through a dialog like this: Dad says, "What are the rules?" The kids say, "Stay together and don't run." Dad says, "And what happens if we don't?" The kids respond, "We have to leave." Dad reminds them, "Remember, you're a team." Their job is to look out for one another and self-supervise. They are a TEAM: Together Everyone Accomplishes More.

Older children should be made aware of their special place and the responsibility they have to younger siblings. The younger siblings look up to older ones as role models. Encourage the older ones to spend some time with the younger ones. Teach them to treat a smaller sibling with special kindness, and they will have a wonderful friend for life. They may even see the younger one start imitating them, which really is a compliment.

A new baby in the house is exciting and annoying to older children. Encourage your children to look at it this way: Parents have most of the work with the baby; older siblings have the opportunity to have most of the pleasure and fun. As the babies grow up, older children may complain that they too often have to take younger ones along with them. As parents, we may forget how annoying this can be, but we should seek a balance—while we may truly need an older child's help, we definitely do not want to have the younger sibling become burdensome.

What about the younger children? They will soon discover that parents are often more lenient with younger children. In other words, they may get to do more sooner because parents have more confidence in their parenting. Clue your younger child in on these benefits, and don't allow him to be a mopey, whiny younger child. Tell him it just makes him seem more like a baby.

What about the children in the middle? It seems they have neither the advantages of the oldest nor the privileges of the youngest. They are truly in the middle, and this can be a negative or a positive. Explain to them that they have the best of both worlds. They have older siblings to look up to and younger siblings to mentor and shepherd in life.

> Ask your children to list five things they can do to show they care for each one of their siblings. Encourage them to act on these ideas, and perhaps to keep a list of "Things I Did to Show Love."

Sibling Disputes: Learning to Disagree

Bob Barnes notes that "any parenting plan needs to include ways for children to practice disagreeing agreeably."[3] This experience teaches children how to negotiate and compromise and is good preparation for marriage. Barnes tells the story of one family that always fought over treats and special goodies.

The parents had to deal with not only incessant nagging for treats, but also the expense of things such as ice cream cones or sodas as they added up over a month's time. This family started setting aside a certain amount each month for such indulgences. The children had to agree on how and when to spend the money, and when the money was spent, it was gone for the month. They all learned a great deal and benefited from the exercise.

To teach our children to resolve their differences, we have tried many things. Our first house had a cramped, bare, kind of scary laundry room. When the children fought, we told them they would have to go to the laundry room to finish the fight. They never actually got into the room because the fight was resolved by the time they reached the door.

When the children were equally at fault for some misdeed, we would require them to hold each other's hand and serve a time-out together. This would usually start out with excruciating complaints and glances of disgust, but would end up with giggling and good friendship.

Children can also learn a lot about conflict resolution by working on a big job together. Give multiple children a large chore, such as cleaning the garage, and leave them to work out the division of labor. They are usually quite capable of coming to a satisfactory resolution, especially when parents are not butting in with suggestions. Another good practice area is deciding what television programs to watch. This is one good reason children should never have their own televisions or computers—if they have to agree together in order to get the privilege of using the machine, they are actually being trained in the art of compromise and conflict resolution.

In families with more than one child, there is often one who emerges as strong-willed at the expense of a more pliable sibling. When the stronger personality takes advantage by always making the decisions or receiving a benefit, the parent may need to intervene. Talk privately with the children. Encourage the strong-willed one to consider the needs and feelings of the other by asking, "How would you feel if you never got to do what you wanted?" Talk with the compliant child about making her needs known. Then make a mental note to keep your finger on the pulse of that relationship to monitor disparities and to step in when necessary.

The Bible is full of sibling stories. Read some of the following stories with your family:

- ◆ Cain and Abel—Genesis 4:2-16
- ◆ Esau and Jacob—Genesis 25:27-34
- ◆ Joseph and his brothers—Genesis 37

Ask your child what caused the fighting in these situations. More importantly, discuss what consequences, sometimes quite grave, resulted from not getting along.

Getting Along with Everyone Else

All of us need to know how to relate to others beyond the home. Of course, as we have seen, many of the skills for this are developed in family life every day. In addition, we can give our children opportunities to learn and practice other attitudes and behaviors that they will need in getting along—from making a first impression to making and keeping a friend.

Practice making a good first impression.

Lead your children through some questions on the impressions people make on each other: Did they ever meet someone who wouldn't look at them? Someone who had nothing to say? How did they feel about that person? Why is it important to make a good impression, preferably without putting on a false facade?

Then take time to evaluate your children's skills in this area. When they meet someone, do they look the person in the eye and shake hands where appropriate? Do they know how to make conversation? If they are weak in this area, one great idea is to let the children greet guests at your home whenever you have visitors. They can take coats and offer soft drinks, all the while making conversation and working on making a good first impression.

You can also encourage your child to be a helper or greeter in Sunday school class. I often teach in my children's Sunday school classes. When a new child comes, I tell my daughters that it is their job to make the new person feel welcome. "Remember how you felt when you first started coming here?" I remind them. They are usually very gracious and help to make the new person feel comfortable. I am told by her teachers that my four year old has done this without any prompting from anyone.

We shouldn't train our children to base their evaluations of people on appearance, but we have to acknowledge that appearance plays a factor in their ability to meet a potential mate and to get or keep a job. In fact, in the workplace, dress and appearance can be as important to success as work skills. Hiring decisions are often based on first impressions. Once on the job, dress and appearance continue to play an important role. Why? "People assume that you will care for your job in the same way you care for yourself," notes LaVerne Ludden.[4] To bring this point home, ask your children which teacher/ doctor/pastor they would rather have: one who is clean, neat, and nicely dressed, or one who is sloppy and unkempt. Lead them into a discussion about how others perceive them, just as they perceive others.

Learn to make friends.

The Bible has a lot to say about friendship. Look up these Bible verses with your child to help him discover the meaning of true friendship: Proverbs 13:20; 17:17; 27:9,17. Also read and discuss with your children these Bible stories of powerful friendships:

- David and Jonathan—1 Samuel 18–20
- Naomi and Ruth—Ruth 1

◆ Jesus, Mary, Martha, and Lazarus—John 11

Does your child appreciate the difference between a friend and an acquaintance? A friend is someone who shares your feelings, is loyal and trustworthy, keeps secrets, shares good and bad times, and stands up for you. An acquaintance is someone who just keeps you company. Many times children will immediately bond and become "best friends" with everyone they meet. Talk to your child about the important responsibilities involved in being a friend. Friendship takes time and talk.

For your younger child, ask him to identify which of these characteristics defines the way a real friend would act. Does a real friend:

◆ Laugh at you when you fall, or help you when you fall?
◆ Share his toys, or refuse to let you touch his toys?
◆ Try to cheer you up when you feel bad, or leave you alone when you feel sad?
◆ Demand to always do things his way, or takes turns?

Making and keeping friends is a complex process. It invites your child to do some self-analysis and to extend herself to others, perhaps beyond her comfort zone. Linda Schwartz offers children these tips on making friends:

Look inward: Examine yourself. What kind of friend are you? What kind of person would you like to have as a friend? Do you know someone who might enjoy your friendship?

Be yourself: You want people to like you as you are. Don't put on an act or pretend to be something you aren't. Instead, be natural, honest, and sincere.

Be considerate: Consider the other person's interests when you are making plans. Consider the other person's feelings when you are talking and listening.

Be diplomatic: Express your opinions carefully. Confront people respectfully. Don't criticize or make unflattering comparisons.

Get involved: Don't let fear of failure keep you from trying a new activity or accepting a new responsibility. Shared effort produces lasting friendships.

Reach out: Invite someone to spend time with you doing something both of you would enjoy. The key to building friendships is to share feelings, ideas, and experiences.[5] [italics added]

For children who are reluctant to meet new friends, this cute idea came from a classroom, which could be easily adapted to a neighborhood or Sunday school class:

One enterprising teacher made up booklets for her kindergartners. On the front of each booklet she lettered the title, "My Friends." Each child was encouraged to ask his friends to do something in the book, such as write their names, draw a picture, outline their hands, or place a thumbprint. The booklet served as a device to encourage children to think about their friends and to interact with other children.[6]

A major part of making friends is paying attention to others, learning the art of listening. Many people don't know how to listen. In our home, we practice taking turns to talk. We want to model good communication for our kids, so one person talks while all the others listen. We also work to teach our children how to reflect back something they have heard. For example, if a friend is telling about falling off a bicycle, a child can comment, "Wow! That must have hurt," letting the speaker know she has been heard and understood.

When entertaining guests at home, turn off the TV, and don't allow your children to read or do anything else when they are supposed to be listening. Teach them to look at the person who is talking. They should act interested and ask questions and not interrupt when someone else is talking. The difference between being interested and being too personal may be a fine line, but people generally will let you know when you've crossed it. Tell your children that people may ask them to be less personal or they may send nonverbal signals, such as turning away or making an excuse to leave.

Try to encourage your child to talk to people other than the ones they usually talk to. This is the best way to meet someone new and to show your interest. Sometimes children hesitate to approach new people out of fear of rejection. Do your children think everyone they meet should like them? Ask them this: "Do you like everyone you meet?" Chances are they do not, so why should they expect everyone to like them? Of course, you can talk to your children all day about how making friends is worth the risks and the effort, but the best training you can give them is to put friendliness into practice in front of them.

Have your child plan a party. It can be a birthday party or an any-day party. Give them a budget to work within, and have them plan refreshments, games, and decorations. Use this as an opportunity to meet and get to know new friends.

Learn to keep friends.

Linda Schwartz offers these hints to children for keeping a friend:

Be trustworthy: When a friend tells you a secret, keep it. Don't repeat it to others. Trust is a vital part of friendship. Loss of trust can destroy a friendship.

Be sensitive: Be aware of a friend's needs. Try to know

when your friend needs to be with you and when your friend wants to be alone. Respect his or her wish for privacy and need for personal space.

Be a good listener: Kids like to talk to someone who listens actively. Show a genuine interest in the things that are important to your friend.

Be dependable: If you make a promise to a friend, keep it. Don't let your friend down. Be there for him or her in bad times as well as good. Let friends know they can count on you.

Be honest: Let a friend know how you feel. If a friend says or does something that hurts you, talk it over with him or her privately. Express your feelings as honestly as you can, and encourage your friend to do the same.[7] [italics added]

Friendship involves respect for other people's privacy. This means avoiding conversations about how much something costs, how much money someone makes, how much someone weighs, and blemishes or physical flaws. Caution your children also to avoid overfamiliarity—doing things such as inviting themselves over to others' houses or to their family events. We have been amazed at the boldness of children who drop in unannounced and expect to be entertained and fed by our family.

My friend Margie Beck, mother of four, has come up with one way to educate visitors about invasive behavior. With neighbors and friends constantly streaming through her door, she became annoyed at the messes they would leave behind, so she created a checklist. Visiting children are required to leave the playroom in good order. If they violate these requirements, they cannot visit her home for one week. She says she is much happier to have children visit now because she is not constantly cleaning up.

What can your child do with friends? Here are some ideas to get them started:

- Start a collection
- Do a hobby
- Practice a sport
- Volunteer somewhere
- Read the same books and discuss them
- Take a walk together

Older children will face complicated conflicts with friends at times. Gone are the days of fighting over what truck to use. What follows is a list of problems that children might encounter with a friend. Increase your children's confidence and understanding by role playing these situations with them. What would they say or do if:

- Your friend says something mean to you.
- Your friend copies your work in class.
- Your friend is jealous because you want to play with other friends too.
- Your friend borrows a dollar and never repays you.
- You find out your friend has disclosed a secret you shared with him.

Because the older child places such importance on friendship, these conflicts may seem earth shattering to her. Take your child's feelings seriously and help her work through the difficulty. You will be equipping her to handle even greater problems in the future.

Of course, the most significant friends we make are those who live with us. Friends and acquaintances come and go, but your children will be siblings forever. Help them be friends.

Maintaining a Sane, Safe Social Life

My friends Annette Bramsen and Virginia Vagt are both homeschooling mothers who are active in the Illinois Parents Association, a group advocating parental rights in education and other areas of life. They gave a talk recently about how our children can put into practice their family values when dealing with people outside the family. They described a range of social experiences our children face and some helpful steps we can take in preparing them for increasing social freedom.

1. The most protective social situation is when you allow your child to entertain others in your own home. It can be very instructive to see your child interacting with friends. You can assess the degree to which he is influenced by peers, or see firsthand his level of leadership. You can also use this opportunity to refresh his memory about family rules. Before friends arrive, Bransen and Vagt advise, remind your kids of the rules and have a plan for what the kids are going to do while they are in your home. Children who are poorly supervised and idle are the ones who can get into the most trouble. If a friend's visit doesn't work out well, you can have a valuable discussion with your child, asking, "How could you have handled this better or differently?"

2. Farther along the continuum of social independence is the opportunity your children have of going to others' homes with Mom or Dad. Vagt and Bramsen suggest that you remind your children of your rules and your expectations for their behavior, and if possible, find out the other family's 'rules' as well.

3. Even more preparation is needed for your children when they make visits to other homes by themselves. Don't allow your children to make such a visit unless you know the family well. Remind your children of the rules, and tell them what to do if things go bad. Suggest that they go to the adult in charge, or call you to come get them. Bramsen suggests, "It's OK to have other people mad at you because you obey your parents' rules." She points out that part of being in the world is sometimes having people mad at us for going by God's rules. Vagt has prepared her daughter for time spent independently with friends by counseling her that there are certain things they don't talk about with other people, such as horror movies or stories, or sexual behavior. She has taught her daughter to say, "I don't talk about those things." Rather, this is something she reserves for discussions with Mom or Dad.

73

The goal of guiding our children in this way is the opposite of isolation and overprotectiveness. Rather, we are giving our children the help they need in order to be safe and strong as they grow more independent socially. We can also look to friends as helpers in this process. If you allow your child to go to camps or youth groups, consider having her go with a trusted friend.

Learning Manners to Demonstrate Kindness and Respect

Why are manners an important life skill to teach at home? Psychologist Thomas Achenbach notes, "Take a look at television these days, and it's becoming almost commonplace to be arrogant and crude."[8] Good manners are an obvious work skill and interpersonal skill. The polite person will make friends easier and perform better in job interviews. But manners are not just learning which fork to use; they comprise an attitude. Etiquette instructor Patricia Gilbert-Hinz notes, "Manners are about being kind—giving compliments, team-playing, making tiny sacrifices. Children learn that through their parents."[9]

Have a family meeting in your home to create a "gentleness and politeness pact." It may look something like this:

> *A commitment of two "do's" and two "don'ts."*
>
> DO be polite—say "please," "thank you," and "excuse me," and look for chances to extend acts of courtesy.
>
> DO smile and ask, "How are you?" Expect a real answer to the question and listen to it.
>
> DON'T yell or raise your voice or be critical of another.
>
> DON'T say anything critical—of someone else or of yourself.[10]

My friend Sue, the mother of twins, reminds us, "We train and retrain in all areas." Your child will not resemble an Emily Post graduate after one training session. It takes practice and patient repetition to learn these skills. But if they are taught early, they will be remembered for a lifetime.

Act politely at the table.

The sheer volume of rules for proper dining may be overwhelming for your child. It might be interesting to discuss where all these rules originated. A U.S. Naval Institute report states:

> The modern-day use of table silver goes back to A.D. 1100, when the wife of an Italian nobleman introduced the two-tined fork into table usage in Venice, because she did not like to pick up meat with her fingers.
>
> The use of forks was not entirely satisfactory, and their use spread but slowly, even in Italy where they had the blessing of the nobility. Complete acceptance of the fork came only with the Renaissance, which also ushered in the use of the table knife to displace the common hunting knife, which every freeman carried at all times on his belt and used at the table for cutting.
>
> France and England were slower in accepting these customs, and it was not until the mid-1600s that English craftsmen commenced the manufacture of table knives and forks, and then spoons. These utensils were made of silver, and were considered a rarity.
>
> As a result of the scarcity of table silver, it fell to the lot of the English gentry to formulate the table manners of the land. It is from them that Americans inherit their table manners, modified somewhat by native American thought and customs.[11]

So how do we motivate our kids to use table manners? Ellen Banks Elwell tells what her family tried as an incentive for table manners:

> At one time our children's table manners were quite lacking,

got a pig!

so I found a little toy pig and started a pig award. It was passed around the table to whoever was found to be lacking in table manners. The pig then stayed with them until someone else committed an infraction. The person with the pig at the end of the meal cleared the table.[12]

A friend of mine has this iron-clad rule: "They have to conform to appropriate behavior or be excused from the table." Find something that works for you and your family.

To prepare your child to attend a social dinner, explain that there are three dining styles: family style—food is passed around in serving dishes; buffet style—food is placed on a serving table and guests help themselves; formal style—food is served by a server who brings dishes to each individual person at the table. Of course, you can tell your child that a good rule of thumb for any social situation is this: If you don't know what to do, watch the hostess and imitate.

Here are some other hints for your children about table practices.

- Silverware goes in one place during the meal, and another after the meal. (You might draw a table setting with your child.)
- Whether the table setting is formal or informal, use silverware from the outside inwards—salad fork first, then regular fork, etc.
- Washing hands before and after every meal is good manners and good self care.
- Unfold your napkin and place it in your lap. Large dinner napkins are opened in half, and smaller ones can be opened completely. Never blow your nose on them!
- Wait until everyone is served before you begin eating.
- Don't ever lick the knives!
- Participate in Grace by bowing your head and possibly folding your hands.

- If you don't like what is being served, say, "No, thank you," or take a small amount to be polite.
- Hold goblets by the bowl, not the stem. All other glasses are to be held at their middle.

When my husband attended officer training for the Navy, he attended a course called "Knife and Fork School." You can offer a similar curriculum to your children at home, or even to a small bunch of children from your neighborhood.

Use good manners any time you are in public.

Being out in public means being where there are people other than your family members. Something is public if it is open to the public, such as a zoo or a library. But being at a friend's house is also considered being out in public. Your children have to consider the needs of everyone else when they are out in public. They should be on their best behavior, be careful handling things, and be aware that other people may be waiting to use what they are using (for example, an exhibit at a museum or a bathroom).

What is the best approach to instill these skills in your child? Alan Kazdin, a psychologist at Yale University, believes parents should prompt their children, then praise them:

> Before the event the parent explains the expected behavior in a noncritical way: "When we visit Aunt Mary today, I'd be so proud if you could shake her hand and pull out her chair at dinner." Afterward, praise the child: "I really like the way you shook Aunt Mary's hand and offered a chair."[13]

What if the child does not comply and commits offending acts? The better approach is to blame the rules, not criticize the child. One article entitled "Can You Raise a Polite Kid in This Rude World?" suggests: "Rather than saying 'You're such a slob. Get your elbows off the table,' . . . simply state, 'Our family rule is that elbows don't go on the table.' By correcting the behavior rather than the child, you defuse a child's defensiveness and keep the correction from sounding like an order."[14]

When you are meeting or introducing people, the rules are to voice the older person's name before the younger, the woman before the man, the person in authority to the person under authority. The point is to say the name of the person of most honor in the situation. Say "I am very pleased to meet you." A boy should always extend his hand. Don't extend a hand to a girl unless she extends it first. Girls may shake hands if they desire, but are not required to do so. Men always shake hands.

Because the exercise of common courtesy seems to be becoming increasingly rare, you may want to review from time to time with your children why we do things such as the following:

♦ Open doors for others—This shows thoughtfulness and

respect, and may be of great help if the person's hands are full.

- Give up a seat on a bus or in a waiting room—This shows thoughtfulness and respect to women, older persons, or sick persons.
- Write thank you notes (or, for pre-writers, draw a picture)—These show appreciation for a gift, for special time spent together, for an invitation, or for a favor.

Also, your child may receive an invitation which says RSVP. Tell them this is French for *Répondez s'il vous plaît,* and it means please answer or respond. The party host may need a head count to know how much food to order, or how many chairs to stock. An RSVP deserves a response, whether you can or cannot attend the event.

Be a good guest at a friend's house.

Tell your child he is expected to be courteous to the parents and other family members of his friend. He should offer to help clean up after meals. He should observe the noise level in the home and try not to be too noisy. He definitely should avoid turning on the TV or stereo, or poking through other people's belongings. When he leaves after a sleepover, he should thank the friend and his parents and follow up with a thank you note. By being a good guest, he is ensuring an invitation for another visit.

Extend your etiquette education.

Have your children try some of these ideas:

- Read a library book on good manners.
- Keep a list of the bad habits you see around you for one day. With Mom or Dad, examine the list to see if you exhibit any of the same annoying behaviors. Make a plan for change.
- Host a special lunch for a grandma or grandpa, an aunt

79

or an uncle. Practice all the good manners you can, from helping a person to her seat to unfolding a napkin properly.

- ◆ Read Bible accounts of good manners in action:
    Abraham with the angels—Genesis 18:1-8
    Joseph with his brothers—Genesis 43:31-34
    Rahab with the spies—Joshua 2:1-16
    The widow with Elijah—1 Kings 17:10-24
- ◆ Read Bible instructions about good manners:
    Proverbs 25:17
    Luke 14:8-11
    Luke 6:31
    1 Peter 4:9
    1 Peter 3:8
- ◆ Make a poster of some of these Bible verses to display in your dining area.

Learning to Use the Telephone

When I walked out of the bathroom one day, my seven year old said, "Some lady called." "Oh?" I said. "Who?" "I don't know," she responded. "Did she say where she was from?" I asked. "No," she said, leaving the room.

My daughter and I can both share the blame for this incident. She was really too young to be answering the phone. In addition, I hadn't worked with this particular child on phone manners. My nine year old is a whiz in this area and frequently receives compliments. I simply hadn't worked with the seven year old yet.

Some children are too young or too irresponsible to answer the phone. Probably many people have had the experience of calling someone's house and having a child pick up the phone, promise to get the person, and then go away and forget all about the caller. So telephone rule number one is to be sure your child is ready for this job. A three year old who answers the phone and regales the caller with every detail of his life is clearly not ready to answer the phone. Likewise, the overly preoccupied or spaced-out child should not be left to this task.

Learn how to answer the phone.

The child should say, "May I ask who is calling? One moment please." Then she should go find the person, not just shout out the person's name!

Teach your older children to ask to take a message. He should find out the name of the caller, what the person wants, and how to reach him. You might even get some of those pink message pads from the office supply store and practice message taking with your child. Have him write down the message, then read it back to you for accuracy. If your child can't write, teach him to report directly to an adult after hanging up.

When your children begin to answer the phone for your family, they will inevitably encounter wrong numbers, hang ups, or prank calls. For wrong numbers, they should learn to respond politely without giving out unnecessary information. For prank calls, help them understand that strange people like to tease others on the phone and that they should simply hang up. Teach your children never to reveal too much information to callers who are strangers. They should not give out their name or phone number or location. They should not agree to buy anything, and they should never tell a caller, "I'm home alone" or "My mom is naked." The better response is to say, "I'm sorry, they aren't available right now. May I take a message?"

Learn how to make a call.

Younger children can draw a phone pad on cardboard or practice dialing numbers on an old, disconnected phone. Remind them not to press too hard or too fast. That way dialing will be more accurate. Then have them practice dialing the home number, emergency services (911), parent's work number, neighbors, and friends. When should they use "O" for Operator? When a call won't go through or when a call keeps

getting cut off. They should *not* use "O" for Operator when there is an emergency (use 911 instead), or when they need to find a phone number (use a directory, see below).

Children should always ask permission to use the phone, whether at home or away. If someone is on the phone when they pick it up, they should hang it up quietly. Let your children know it is extremely rude to listen in on calls. You should also limit the duration of your children's phone calls. If you make this a regular practice while they are still young, it will be easier to enforce when they are older.

When they are making a call, they need to wait a reasonable number of rings before hanging up. If the phone is allowed to ring more than eight or ten times, either the call will interrupt something very important, or the person simply isn't home. Teach your children that when they reach who they are calling, they need to identify themselves and state the reason for calling—for example, "Hello, this is Caitlin Field. May I speak with Sally? Thank you."

Finally, instruct your children not to call too early or too late. Unless it is extremely important or the message is time sensitive, don't place calls before breakfast or after 9:00 P.M.

Learn how to use phone directories.

Get a directory and flip through it with your child, going over the divisions into white pages formatted by alphabet, yellow pages formatted by category, and other special listings. Let them practice looking up numbers to get information, choosing first whether to look in the white pages or the yellow pages. Also direct them to find answers to questions such as the following:

- ◆ What are the library hours?
- ◆ Does the pet store sell a particular brand of pet food and for how much? How late are they open? What are the directions to the store?
- ◆ Where can you call for a weather forecast?
- ◆ What is the number of (friend's name)?
- ◆ What number do you call for movie information?

I have had my eight year old make all the calls to investigate guitar rental and pet purchases. For pets, she had to do a report complete with maintenance schedule and costs of supplies. This took research on the phone and in books.

> Have your older child study the rate structures of three long distance carriers and decide which company offers the most competitive pricing.

Learn how to make long distance calls.

Most children do not realize that long distance calls are more expensive. Showing them a bill while you write a check helps explain that point. Explain that calling at different times of the day can be cheaper.

Your children should also learn to make a call away from home. For such an occasion they could make a collect call, asking the operator to connect them, or they could use a collect call service, such as 1-800-COLLECT. They could also bill a call to your home number using a calling card. Prepaid calling cards are available for various denominations, and detailed instructions for their use are printed on them.

Learning how to handle conflict, make friends, and treat others with courtesy and respect are skills we all need throughout our lives. If, like me, you sometimes feel discouraged because you're not the greatest example at times in these things, just remember to also teach your kids that we're all in the never-ending process of learning and growing, with the Lord's help!

Life Skills Checklist

❖ Selflessness and service: Do my children know what these mean? Do they see them exhibited at home? Do we have a clear set of family rules which govern our behavior, both at home and in public?

❖ Sibling sense: Have we instilled in our children the importance of their place in the family? Do we have a procedure for resolving sibling disputes?

❖ Getting along with everyone else: Does my child understand the importance of first impressions, the meaning of true friendship, how to make and keep friends? Have we prayed about and arrived at an approach to our child's social life which preserves our family values? Does my child understand the Golden Rule?

❖ Manners: Does my child comprehend that love and respect are the underlying motivation for cultivating good manners? Do they know rules and skills for sharing meals, making introductions, showing common courtesy, and using the telephone?

CHAPTER 3

In the Home Skills

Everyone Lives Somewhere

❖ Third Maxim of Maturity

Everyone lives somewhere. We need to take care of that place and make it a haven from which to nourish ourselves and others.

❖ Transferable Skills

Ability to organize tasks and responsibilities; capacity to determine a need for order; ability to follow step-by-step processes for completing a task; and ability to maintain a routine.

My mother wanted "something better" for me than she had experienced. In the climate of the late sixties and early seventies, that translated into a liberation from the drudgery of domestic life; the young women of my generation were meant for greater things. So, while reveling in academia, I learned no domestic skills. At age nineteen in an early, ill-advised marriage, I barely handled laundry, opened a lot of cans for meals, and had a less-than-clean household. My academic training was soon completed, and so was that marriage.

My solitude as a still-young divorcée fostered an interest in home skills. I learned to cook a little better and enjoyed having the time and the freedom to organize and clean my apartment as I saw fit. Those single years were ones of catching up on some life skills that I never learned at my mother's feet. My parents died during my late teens, so there were many lessons I never got the chance to learn.

When I met and married my husband, Mark, I was more prepared for marriage and the challenges of making a home.

Raising children was the next on-the-job training I encountered. Children began to arrive, in the form of girls, and I vowed to train them to be prepared for anything God brought their way, whether careers, marriage, children, or all of the above. Whatever they do, however God calls them, they will know how to take care of themselves and their homes.

I want the same for Daniel, my fourth and final child. Because my husband has a servant's heart, I am confident our son will be equipped for anything life has to offer. He has before him the example of two people striving to do the best in their lives to build a loving home while each maintaining individual identities. We hope and trust that the children will emerge from the palette of our home with a full spectrum of life skills.

This chapter addresses shopping, cooking, laundry, and cleaning—four essential skills for making a home for themselves and others.

The Art of Shopping

Something as simple as taking your child shopping provides a tremendous training opportunity. By shopping, I don't mean the go-to-the-mall-and-buy-the-kids-anything-they-want kind of shopping. I am talking about the routine shopping involved in keeping a family properly fed. Recreational shopping is a skill they can learn another time, or indeed skip.

Prepare for your shopping trip.

Before you leave for the store, have your child help you check the cabinets at home as you make a list of needed items. If you keep a photocopied checklist of items you regularly keep, this can become the responsibility of an older child. A younger child can spend time with you in the kitchen counting how many cans of green beans are left on the shelf.

Keeping a list, whether an ongoing shopping list or an on-demand list, is not only part of wise shopping, it's also a great way to teach organizational skills. By having your child participate in making the list, you help him learn to plan ahead and organize so the home has what it needs to run. Two of the most popular shopping list methods are the envelope system and the clipboard system. In the envelope system, the shopping list is written on the outside of the envelope and coupons are slipped inside. You might star items on the list to denote which ones have an applicable coupon. I use the clipboard system, keeping my perpetual list on a clipboard in my kitchen. We inventory our stock before we shop, and coupons are clipped to the clipboard. If you tend to serve the same meals with some regularity, this will probably save more time.

Teach your children early that one of the purposes of using a list is to keep yourself from buying too much, or buying on impulse. Sticking to a grocery list can save you money and time. Children are very prone to impulse buying because they possess a lesser degree of self-control over their emotions. When they see something they want, it feels like a life and death matter to acquire that item. They don't need it, they want it. If we as parents give in to every whim, our children will never learn to control their impulse spending—something they will certainly regret as an adult.

As an extra learning tool while you are teaching the skill of grocery shopping, experiment with keeping a "Want List" with your child. Have him list three or four must-have items, then put the list away for a week. When he looks at the list again, are the feelings as intense? Encourage your child to re-evaluate whether these items are that important.

Save all your grocery store receipts for one month and have your child take a total. Compare these totals from month to month. Examine the receipts and explore ways to reduce the amount of money spent on groceries.

Work together at the store.

Once you have arrived at the store, give your children the job of pushing the cart for you if they are able. Pushing the cart makes them feel grown up. Often slightly older children can keep a younger child in the baby seat entertained quite well as you shop. Have them bring a small baggie of snacks to keep the younger child engaged. Give each child a piece of the shopping list to check off after finding the items. If your child has calculator skills, let her keep a running total of your bill as you shop.

You can use coupons as a good learning experience for your child. Cutting them out is an exercise in fine motor skills. Sorting them by product type and keeping track of expiration dates is good math practice, develops calendar skills, and is a help for parents. Once you arrive at the store, your child can search for the items depicted in the coupons. In addition to all this learning, you may even save a few dollars off your grocery bill. Some families calculate the amount of money saved by the use of coupons and do creative things with those savings. You might choose to give 10 percent of the savings to your child as an incentive for the hard work. Or you might put that amount saved aside for vacation, for going to a movie, or for having an ice cream outing with the family.

Keeping an eye on prices and looking for the best buys on products is another math exercise. Your child will use math skills for rounding off and estimating. The exercise is usually enlightening for a child, who may be unaware of competitive pricing. You might even make a formal lesson out of this: Make a list of ten common grocery items. Go with your child to three different stores and record the various prices for the items. Then discuss your findings.

Before you expect proficiency in consumer math, give your children a little lesson in unit pricing, weights and measures, and the computation of value. Teach them that liquid items are measured in ounces, and solid items are measured in pounds. Work together to figure out the following examples like those in the chart below.

Juice is sold as follows:

Two 6-ounce cans of concentrate for $1.05 (makes one quart)
One 12-ounce can of concentrate for $.75 (makes two quarts)
One 1-quart carton for $1.29
One 2-quart carton for $2.65
Which is the best buy?

Rice is sold as follows:

One 1-pound box is $ .89
One 2-pound box is $1.15
One 5-pound bag is $2.89
Which is the best buy?

Why would you ever *not* buy the most economical container? Depending upon the number of people to be fed, buying the most economical package might result in unused, wasted food. If you are buying something that will spoil quickly, economy might not be the deciding factor in your purchase. When I was very young, I went to my first farmer's market. The vendor must have had me pegged for a city girl because he sold me twenty-five pounds of fresh garlic and made me feel like I had received a bargain. As much as I love garlic, I doubt I could have used that much even in a whole year.

Check those cans.

At the store, have your child help spot and examine expiration dates. Talk about why products are marked and why you want the item with the latest possible date. Don't let your child pick out the banged up, rusty cans. They are probably quite old and less fresh. In the frozen food aisle, have them avoid packages that are very icy, as they may have freezer burn.

Bag it!

Can bagging groceries be a lesson in logic? Yes! Discuss putting frozen items together, not making the bags too heavy, not making the bags too full. There are reasons for these things, as your child will discover the first time he rips a paper grocery bag and has nectarines racing all over the parking lot.

When you arrive home, be sure to have your children help put the groceries away. Put frozen items away first, then the refrigerated ones, then everything else. Does your family do any special rewrapping or cutting or packaging before putting groceries away? Get your child involved in the process, and explain why you do what you do.

Shop safely.

Explain to your child how to carry money in public. Purses should never be left unattended in shopping carts. Money should be kept as hidden as possible so as not to be accessible to pickpockets. Backpacks and open purses slung over the shoulder are a bad idea because it is too easy for a thief to reach in and take your cash.

Stress the importance of staying together in the store. Have a plan for what to do if your child gets lost, or choose a meeting place in case you get separated. If you child is old enough, give her change for a pay phone and a watch so she can keep track of time.

Learn to shop for real value for your money.

Discuss prices, brands, and product claims with your child. When you see a commercial on television for a new and improved cleaner or for a cereal which will give you more energy (and will cost you three dollars per box more!), examine those claims with your child. Do advertisers always tell the truth? What is the purpose of advertising?

Children are never too young to learn about bargain hunting. Garage sales, outlet stores, and thrift shops are friends to the family and can be the source of tremendous buys. When using these sources, teach your children to distinguish quality items. As an experiment, give each of your chil-

dren two dollars. Make a list of what they could purchase with that money at a discount store. Then take your children to a few garage sales to see what they could purchase for the same amount of money.

Although I realize this type of bargain hunting is often a question of being in the right place at the right time, I keep lists of needed items in my purse during garage sale season. I keep the children's clothing sizes and shoe sizes, a list of needed household items, and a list of books we would like to own. When I find one of these at a sale, and most of my children's clothing and household items are found in this manner, I tell my children how much money we saved. In the long run, I hope this is teaching them to wait for things and to look for perceived needs to be met in many different ways.

Learn about consumer rights.

If you arrive home from the grocery store with a new toy that is inoperable or a spoiled container of yogurt, what do you do? One of my daughters once bought an electronic gadget with her own money, and it did not work when she got it home. I took her back to the store and had her talk to the person at the returns desk. She was nervous about doing it, but later she knew she had done the right thing—it is wrong to sell someone something that does not do what it is supposed to do.

In a more serious consumer disagreement, returning an item to the store may not be sufficient. Do you know the procedure in your area for registering a consumer complaint? Your local Better Business Bureau or State Attorney General will usually have a process in place for handling consumer disputes. If you should need to avail yourself of their services, talk to your child at length about the rights of consumers and the unscrupulous practices of some businesses. Kids may be spared some greater hardship in the future if they learn about such things now.

You and your children can also discuss telemarketers who call your home, or door-to-door salespersons who try to sell you something. Look at some of the advertising you receive through direct mail together, and examine the claims, pointing out their lack of believability or possible frauds. These few moments of informal consumer education can help lead your child to wiser financial decisions.

The Art of Cooking

The kitchen can be an area of great creativity and closeness in your family. As you reflect on your own childhood, how many tender childhood memories were made in your parent's kitchen? Don't neglect this gold mine in family training and closeness. Bonnie McCullough says, "One of the daily chore assignments should be titled Assistant Cook. The child can work alongside the adult in dinner preparations, or the adult could be the assistant to the child and do things his or her way."[1]

There are some great children's cookbooks available at almost any bookstore. These are great gift ideas for your child, as they sometimes are packaged with measuring spoons or aprons. Your local public library probably has at least ten children's cookbooks as well. We have enjoyed seeking out cookbooks which correlate with something we are studying, such as pioneer cooking, Native American cooking, or the ethnic cooking of countries we have studied. But you don't need a cookbook to start working with your child on culinary basics such as these:

- ◆ Peanut butter on bread. Use a plastic knife and softened peanut butter so your child can spread it himself. Ditto for toast and butter. Make (or buy) a shaker of sugar and cinnamon for cinnamon toast. Let him take his time and do it himself. Children won't learn without making messes first.
- ◆ Fruit salad. Have fun making this together. Even a very young child can slice a banana with a plastic knife. Let her slice peaches and drop in the raisins while you cut the harder stuff.
- ◆ Frozen juice. With a plastic pitcher and a wooden spoon, young children can mix juice. In our family, the designated juice maker has to unfreeze the concentrates and make sure there is a supply of sippy cups filled in the refrigerator for the younger children. My family consumes an enormous quantity of juice, so delegating this task saves much time. If the juice gets spilled, then we have a cleaning lesson.
- ◆ Vegetable salad. Children can tear and wash lettuce, and if you have a kitchen spray or a salad spinner, this can be particularly exciting. An older child can peel and wash vegetables. Cucumbers are good to start with because they are soft. Each of my daughters has her own peeler and participates when we have a big peeling job. (Buy good quality peelers because they are really easier to use.) We cover the table with newspaper, peel our little hearts out over a good heart-to-heart conversation, fold up the peelings, and throw them away.

Look through your recipes for things that only require a few ingredients, and get your child actively involved in cooking simpler dishes. Also, never bake alone! To do so is to squander a family closeness opportunity.

Many merchants offer child-size kitchen equipment. The only thing we have ever done along those lines was to get aprons for the children and put their names on them. Other than that, they learn on real equipment in a real kitchen. When one of my daughters was given a child's oven, the kind that makes tiny cookies cooked by a light bulb, she used it one time. Then she said, "Why should I do this when I can do the real thing in the kitchen with Mommy?"

Plan menus together.

Your children will have a greater interest in the cooking when they help plan the menus, and they will gain organization and planning skills. Try these suggestions:

- Give your children the food ads from the newspaper to study and compare. Use the sale ads to plan menus.
- Have your children write out seven breakfast menus on seven index cards, seven lunch menus on seven index cards, and seven dinner menus on seven index cards. Take your time with this exercise. At the end, your child will have a menu plan for a week. (You may use this again when concentrating on eating healthy food in chapter 9).
- Have your child plan a menu for a party. Make a shopping list and estimate costs.
- Have your child plan several menus for school lunches that they can prepare on their own.

I am not suggesting you completely turn menu planning over to your children. I am suggesting that children can be enormously helpful and resourceful, if we allow them an opportunity.

A few years ago, we had a difficult but joyous winter season. Our adopted son arrived from Korea on December 10 of that year, and on December 30 I took the older children out roller skating at a rink while Grandma and Grandpa stayed home with the baby. I fell almost immediately and shattered my arm into several pieces, requiring extensive reconstructive surgery. So, after the company went home, there I was with four children and one arm for about a five-month recovery period. My two oldest daughters were then seven and eight. We sat down and created a menu of meals that either they could prepare by themselves (something such as sandwiches), or they could get started on their own. They were troopers and rallied to the challenge, helping me through that difficult time.

Learn how to measure ingredients.

Measuring spoons and measuring cups (along with a retractable ruler) were Christmas gifts for my kids in their Christmas stockings one year. They have since learned that one cup does not mean a coffee cup, and a teaspoon is not just any spoon from the drawer. When we double or halve recipes, we have a chance to practice more math skills, and following any recipe we often come across abbreviations. Check any general cookbook for a list of abbreviations to teach your child as you cook.

Learn kitchen safety.

It is important from the very youngest age to learn about safe use of appliances and equipment and safe handling of food. Pot handles must be turned away from small, grasping hands, and stoves are to be highly respected. This is especially true of electric stoves, since the burners are a similar color when hot or cold, and some of the newer stoves with hidden heating elements. Give specific lessons on how to use the stove, blender, electric can opener, microwave, and any other appliances you may have. One lady I know says her children get a great deal of pleasure out of grinding the coffee beans. As long as you have thoroughly trained kids in an appliance's use, they should be allowed to operate it.

Teach your children not to eat any food that looks or smells the least bit strange. They can become aware of spoilage and salmonella at an early age. Teach them to clean up carefully after preparing meat or egg dishes. Here are some other safety rules to follow:

- ◆ Wash hands and tie back long hair.
- ◆ When you open a covered pan or oven, let some heat escape before putting your face near.
- ◆ Use potholders to lift hot items.
- ◆ Use baking soda to put out stove fires. Water will not work.
- ◆ Put sharp knives in a knife holder, drawer, or rack.
- ◆ Keep sharp objects out of the dishpan.
- ◆ Cover foods that might spatter in the microwave oven.
- ◆ Before lifting a hot item from the stove, set out a safe place to rest it, such as a rack, a pad, or a board.

Use recipes for learning.

As my children have grown older, we've had them copy recipes to practice handwriting. Some early favorites were vegetable soup and chicken pot pie. We made the dishes, then copied the recipes. I placed them in plastic sleeves in a notebook which has continued to grow. It has been fun to see both their cooking skills and their handwriting improve.

Encourage your children to clip recipes from children's magazines or newspapers. They can start a collection for their own children's cookbook, adding family recipes they particularly like. Bonnie McCullough shares an idea one mother used for collecting recipes. She gave each of her teen-agers (boy and girl) a recipe box for Christmas, with a promise to copy every recipe they successfully learned to make. As each child left home, they took their collection of tried-and-liked recipes with them, along with a confident feeling and a box of warm memories.[2]

You could also give your children a notebook for recording recipes. Encourage them to plan side dishes and beverages for a complete meal. They will be glad for this resource when they are on their own.

Build teamwork in the kitchen.

The kitchen is a training ground for teaching multiple children to work together. If you have several children, give the oldest child the challenge of delegating all the mealtime tasks. Have him oversee the work of the older children. Have an older child teach a younger child to do some of the tasks and cleanup involved in cooking. Also, you can institute the rule that a cooking session is incomplete until the kitchen is cleaned!

If the mess and the inefficiency of your children's cooking team begins to get to you, remember this: you are not only training them to prepare their own meals; you are training them to patiently teach their own children when the time comes.

The Art of Laundry

A speaker at a women's conference once said that laundry is like the love of God—it's *everlasting*. As sacrilegious as that may sound, it rings true for many parents. We can rely on God's unmerited love and we can always count on having lot of clothes to wash. Enlisting the assistance of your children in the laundry task is easy. Young children are enchanted with the process, and if you consciously and intentionally structure things, older children will come to realize that they must participate if they want clean clothing.

Learn to do each step in the laundry process.

Even the youngest child can sort light from dark clothes, developing categorization and motor skills. For our family, we have three bins on a rolling cart which are labeled white, dark, and mixed. You can also use laundry bags or just plain cardboard boxes. When one container is full, a load is ready to wash. If you follow this plan consistently, your children will learn that when they see a need—a full bin of dirty clothes—they must act on that need and do some laundry. Young children also can match socks and fold towels, washcloths, and kitchen dishtowels.

If you give children who are old enough their own hamper or basket, they can be responsible for bringing dirty clothes to the laundry room, sorting them in the three bins, returning cleaned clothes to their rooms, and putting them away properly. Don't expect them to do a neat job putting things away until they are about four or five. When children are learning to sort clothes, they should be taught the logic behind the sorting. Teach them why light items should be separated from dark and linty things (like towels or robes) from things that attract lint (dark materials). Children should be responsible for cleaning out their own pockets. In our house, objects found in the wash sit on a special shelf for a week, then are thrown away. If money is unclaimed, it is mine at the end of the week.

A family life educator for the University of Illinois Extension Service recommends starting to let kids of about ten years of age operate the washing machine on their own and advises putting towels or jeans, which don't require special treatment, in their first loads. She adds, "Even after the children have the hang of it, for safety an adult should still be on standby somewhere in the house while a child is doing laundry."[3] At twelve or thirteen, they should be responsible for the whole task.

This responsibility can be an eye-opening one for kids. A friend of mine says, "I taught my son how to do his own laundry after repeated attempts failed to stop him from throwing non-dirty clothes downstairs to be washed. Now he is required to launder, fold, and put away his own clothes. It's amazing how infrequently his clothes need cleaning now!"

While your children are learning, post a laminated chart by the washer with reminders about measuring detergent, setting the dials, choosing a temperature and speed, and distributing clothes evenly in the machine. Have them read laundry soap labels for detergent amounts and clothing labels for garment care. They will be particularly careful with a garment purchased with their own money! Teach them to hand wash delicate items in cold water, and discuss how to use fabric softeners and bleach.

The laundry is not really finished until it is put away, so spend some time training your children in this organizational task. Drawers should be organized by types of clothes. When my daughters are putting their laundry away, I regularly remind them to "observe the order of the drawers." If they have forgotten, we take a humorous tour of their dresser: "I would like you to meet the sock drawer!" For very young children, put pictures or drawings on the drawers, and then do the task with them several times as practice. You may even want to get some plastic carts with open storage areas. These are easier for a young child to handle than an unwieldy dresser.

Learn to take care of shoes.

Teach your children to take off wet shoes and let them dry naturally. Putting them on a heater could dry out and ruin the material. If your child has any leather shoes, let her learn how to polish them at an early age. Children generally love polishing shoes, and a special shoe polishing box makes the task especially exciting. Teach them to wash sneakers with a load of towels. A wrinkled item can sometimes be hung in the bathroom while showering and the steam from the shower lets the wrinkles get out. This is also an opportune time to talk to your children about heat, steam, water and evaporation.

Learn to iron.

Less ironing is required, of course, if clothes are hung up and/or folded promptly from the dryer. Young children are often anxious to iron, but you need to judge your own child's readiness. When you think they are ready, let them start by ironing their play clothes or handkerchiefs. Then let them try place mats or tablecloths. Teach them how to choose the correct heat for each fabric, using the care instructions on the clothing manufacturer's tag. If your child is easily distracted, you may have to remind him not to let the iron sit on one spot and burn the fabric. Teach him to use a spray bottle or fill the iron carefully with cold water for steam and to take caution when emptying the heated water. Show him how to stand the iron on its end when not in use and to unplug it, cool it down, and keep it away from younger children before putting it away.

Keep down clothing clutter.

My kids have entirely too much clothing, due in part to the benevolence of family and friends who save their outgrown clothing for us, but also in part to my love of garage sales. We have dealt with this overflow by taking a clothing inventory each season, going through the out of season clothes and making stacks of shorts, sundresses, t-shirts, etc. Then we know what we need for the next season. We write this information on a form for each member of the family (see chart). Then I note current sizes and keep the forms with me so I can check them when I run across a fabulous garage sale.

As your children exercise more choice in clothing purchases, teach them to buy classics and items of good quality. This is often only learned by trial and error, but especially if you have a number of children, a good quality garment will serve you for years.

The Art of Cleaning

Let me clarify at the outset that I am not a cleaning freak. My goal in cleaning is merely to keep the health department from knocking at my door. I don't have the time or the inclination to have a sparkling environment—I'd rather have one full of fingerprints and fun. I can clean the house when the kids are grown up.

Having said that, like most parents I have been over-

Clothing Inventory

Name: _____

Season: _____

	Have	Need	Size
shirts			
pants/shorts			
skirts			
jackets/coats			
sweaters/sweatshirts			
dresses			
nightclothes			
underwear			
shoes/boots			
accessories (gloves, hats, etc.)			

whelmed at the amount of simple maintenance required when children are running around the house. If you clean and no one ever enters your living room, chances are that it will stay clean. But if you clean with children home, your work will be destroyed within ten minutes. The scenario is discouraging, but we still have to face the fact that some maintenance is a necessary part of family life. So we try to train our children to have the attitude that if we do this cleaning thing together as a family, then we can have time to have fun as a family later. As children get older it begins to sink in that when mom is doing all the work, she doesn't have time to do the fun stuff.

How do you teach cleaning? Did you ever notice that cleaning books were written by people who assume you already know how to clean and that you merely want to improve your technique? Kids don't innately know how to clean. They surely know how to make messes, but the cleaning part requires training. I start with some general principles of cleaning. The first is that we clean from dirtiest place to cleanest place so that dirt doesn't get spread around while cleaning. The second principle is that we clean from high to low (ceiling to floor and tub walls before bathtub) because dirt tends to drop down.

Explain, demonstrate, and practice cleaning tasks.

When you want to teach some new aspect of cleaning, have a training night. We have tried, on occasion, to keep it light and fun, like a TV show. "For this evening's viewing pleasure, we will present to you the mystical, magical secrets of cleaning a toilet." Then we show them the steps, we let them watch while we do it, and we let them try it by themselves, making sure each child is ready for the task.

My friend Mary Carney sings the praises of cleaning to music. Her favorite is John Phillip Sousa marches. It's hard to stand still when the big brass band is calling you to work! Nadine Brown suggests,

> After you've cleaned a room, bring your children in and ask them if you have done a good job. For example, if you've cleaned the bathroom, point our how the towels are folded and straight on the towel rod. Have them look in the sink to see that all the telltale rings are gone. Hold up the soap dish so they can see what a clean one looks like. Let them know what kinds of things they need to check when they do a job.[4]

We have found chore standard charts especially beneficial in housecleaning. We have typed and laminated this chart, for example:

When Mom or Dad says "Clean the Living Room," I must:
1. Pick up toys and books, put them in their proper places.
2. Straighten blankets and pillows.
3. Pick up trash from the floor.

4. Do other jobs as needed: vacuum carpet, mop floors, dust,wash windows.

With chore standard charts, there is a clear expectation of what is involved in cleaning a room. Make sure to go over such a chart several times with your children before leaving them to follow it on their own. Then make sure you inspect their work and give lots of praise for a good job!

Praise goes a long way in encouraging children to keep their environment clean. Linda and Richard Eyre one day gathered their family into the den and let their children watch them clean. When it was finished, they hung a large, bright sign on the door that said PRIDE. When asked what it meant, the Eyres responded, "Pride means that I'm proud of how my den looks. . . . It means that I feel good because all my things are clean and neat."[5] This is justifiable pride in a job well done.

Anytime you can break a big job into smaller pieces, your child can learn the pieces one by one until she is proficient in the whole task. Show the order of the chore to your child and explain any logic involved in the order—you dust before you vacuum because dusting leaves the dust on the floor; you clean the bathroom sink last because you use the sink in cleaning the room. Teach the thorough cleaning of one room from top to bottom. Keep that assignment for four weeks, then learn a new room. Eventually your child will have the knowledge and the skill to clean the entire house.

As children get older, cleaning their rooms may become a battleground. How much control should a parent exert? Especially if the conflict is one over control rather than cleaning, you need to make sure it is a battle you are willing to wage. Patricia Sprinkle notes, "Apparently, growing up in a messy room does not automatically insure an irresponsible, immature adult, and growing up in a neat room doesn't make a responsible, mature adult. . . . My child's membership in my family is more important than a clean bedroom."[6]

For older children, communicate that what they do is appreciated. Heap praise upon them particularly when they do something on their own without Mom or Dad's prompting. Also let them know what to expect. What do kids hate?

> Surprises—being expected to do jobs whenever my folks ask, rather than their sitting down and telling me what I have to do all week. I feel like a servant. "Honey, will you please take out the garbage?" "Honey, will you please do dishes tonight?" I dread hearing them say "honey," because I know the next three words are going to be "will you please . . ."[7]

To avoid what kids hate, Sprinkle recommends "giving regular chores instead of occasional requested ones; teaching children exactly what each job entails, and notifying the family at once about schedule changes."

Learn to use cleaning products.

For safety reasons, try to choose more natural products. Home organization expert Emilie Barnes offers these natural cleaning recipes.

> All-purpose cleaner—Pour one-half cup ammonia and one cup baking soda into a clean plastic gallon jug. Add two cups warm water, cover, and shake. Then add twelve more cups of water. Label the jug so everyone knows it's cleaner. Use one-half cup to a bucket of water for large jobs, full strength in a spray bottle for appliances and tile.

> All-purpose nonpolluting cleaner—Add two tablespoons baking soda to one quart warm water and you have a wash that will clean plaster, tile, and porcelain. Plain baking soda will substitute for scouring powder all over the kitchen, on appliances, even in the toilet bowl. Or mix two teaspoons borax and one teaspoon liquid dishwashing soap in one quart water for a cleaning spray.[8]

With any kind of cleaning product, if you are going to do serious cleaning, have your children wear rubber gloves. If they are readers, have them read the label directions for you. Also, even if they are not sophisticated enough to understand chemistry, your children must understand that they should *never* use ammonia with chlorine products.

Learn to use the tools of the trade.

Your children will use cleaning tools all their lives. Do they know their proper function and use of the following everyday items?

Broom and dustpan
Whisk broom or small electric
    dustbuster
Sponge mop
Mop pail
Dust mop
Dustrags
Cleaning sponges
Toilet bowl brush
Scrubbing pads
Rubber gloves
Garbage cans, plastic trash bags
Paper towels
Window squeegee

Dishwashing tools: Sponge or
    dishcloth, abrasive sponge,
    scouring pads
Vacuum cleaner
Cleaning supply caddy
Dish soap
Floor cleaner
Floor wax
Bathroom cleaner
Kitchen cleaner, like Fantastik®
Glass and chrome cleaner
Furniture polish
Laundry soaps
Oven cleaners (not for any child's

As you intentionally expose your children to these things, they will often identify a favorite and become a cheerful, willing helper in that area. Washing windows and polishing furniture are my children's favorites, followed by using the dust mop to clean cobwebs out of the corners.

Keep up with never-ending dishes.

I actually enjoy washing dishes—I just don't enjoy washing tons of them each day. We have never had a dishwasher in our house, however, because we have children, so we don't see the need for a machine. Perhaps we will get one when the children have all moved away.

You can capitalize on a young child's fascination with water by allowing him to wash dishes. We were worried about breakage until we spent just a few dollars to get plastic plates, bowls, and tumblers. We store these in a low cabinet near the sink, so for most meals, the children are able to handle the dishwashing from start to finish. If they splash water on the floor, it probably needed wiping anyway.

Remind your child that the sooner dishes are washed, the better. The longer junk stays on, the harder it is to remove. If the children stray too far from the kitchen after they have eaten, it is sometimes hard to get them back to do the dishes. Show them, step by step, the order in which dishes should be washed:

1. Scrape food from plates into trash or disposal.
2. Secure the drain and pile the dishes in sink or washtub.
3. Add detergent and cover the dishes with water.
4. Wipe each item, front and back and all around. (Very dirty pots and pans may need to soak, but must be done before bed.)
5. Rinse each item thoroughly.
6. Stack items carefully on a dish rack to air dry. Items have to be standing up so nothing is sitting in water, or they will never dry. Or have a sibling or parent towel dry them and put them away.
7. Drain water and wipe off sink and counter tops.

If you have a dishwasher, teach your children to scrape the dishes, then load the machine carefully. Remind them to use only dishwasher detergent since other dish soaps could ruin the machine and cause it to overflow. Also, let dishes cool down before removing them from dishwasher.

Conquer the vacuum cleaner.

Most very young children have a love/hate relationship with the vacuum. My son, Dan, is both fascinated with it and scared to death of it. When your children use the vacuum, they should check to make sure the bag is not too full. If it needs to be changed, they should change it with Mom or Dad's help. They should never vacuum glass or items such as paper clips which can ruin the machine. They should never run over the cord with the vacuum or vacuum anything wet (this could give them a shock and damage the machine). Tell your children that most people vacuum too fast and don't give their machines a chance to do the work thoroughly. By going slowly, they can pick up more dirt.

Learn to make a bed.

Here is a task that will take many demonstrations and much practice. Rather than expecting a perfectly made bed at first, you probably want to aim at constantly improving your children's skill. Some people leave off the top sheet, especially for young children, making it extremely easy for them to make their beds. Putting a pillow into a pillowcase is like wrestling a lion for the very young, but let them try until they succeed. Make a goal of establishing bed-making as a daily habit in your child.

Schedule for success.

Why have a cleaning schedule? The reason is that parents rarely have large chunks of uninterrupted time to clean a house from top to bottom. If all family members can contribute and do a responsible job of maintaining a household, then major cleanings become almost unnecessary.

Of course, every household cleaning schedule will work best if it takes into account the personalities, skills, and time commitments of the members of that particular family. You may work best with a detailed schedule, or you may find that overwhelming and decide instead to stick to basics in yours. Here is an example of a cleaning schedule to which we loosely adhere.

Sample Cleaning Schedule

Daily:

Do general tidying
Make beds
Do dishes
Wipe kitchen counters and stove tops
Sweep kitchen floor
Take out trash

Once a week or so:

Deep clean bathroom
Deep clean kitchen
Mop floors
Dust all living areas
Dry-mop floors, ceilings, and baseboards
Vacuum all carpets
Change towels and sheets
Do all laundry

Once a month:

Wax furniture
Clean inside of windows, TV screen, mirrors
Wipe out insides of cupboards and refrigerator
Quickie-wax kitchen floor
Wash kitchen accessories
Clean the oven
Wash bathroom rugs

Several times a year:

Clean bathroom tile
Deep polish wood furniture

Dust small items
Clean windows inside and out
Wipe window sills
Wax kitchen floor seriously
Wash s hower curtains

Once a year:

Wash or clean drapes, curtains, blinds
Shampoo rugs
Defrost refrigerator, freezer
Clean lamp shades
Thoroughly clean windows and screens
Clean light fixtures
Turn mattresses
Wash walls if needed

Keeping yourself and your children on a regular cleaning schedule teaches them organization, self-discipline, and time management. It demonstrates to them that order can indeed be maintained in some areas of life and that living does not have to seem chaotic. Ultimately, it means you can have more time to do fun things together as a family!

Because everyone will live somewhere and need to take care of that place, passing on some of these very practical organizational and cleaning skills will be invaluable to your kids becoming good homemakers down the road. It will also do wonders for your own sanity right now!

Life Skills Checklist

❖ Shopping: Has my younger child accompanied me on shopping trips, pushing the cart, locating a few items? Has he helped me make and follow lists? Have I let him clip and organize coupons?

❖ Have I explained to my older child about unit pricing and food units of measure and allowed her to calculate what is a good buy and what is not so good? Can she carry money safely in public and behave with an eye toward personal safety? Has she been exposed to bargain hunting, returning items, and registering consumer complaints?

❖ Cooking: Have I allowed my child from an early age to play some role in the kitchen, or have I sacrificed teaching opportunities to avoid messes? Has my child learned the basics of kitchen safety, from using knives to identifying spoiled food? Does he know how to use the kitchen appliances? Does my child help plan menus? Has he prepared some dish independently?

❖ Laundry: Does my child sort light from dark clothes? Does she fold socks and washcloths? Has she learned to sort dried clothing by family member?

❖ Is there a system in place for putting clean laundry away and bringing dirty laundry to the laundry room? Do we have a chart of instructions for using the machines? Have we reviewed water temperature and types of clothing?

❖ Have I introduced my child to ironing? Do we have a system for inventorying clothing that makes sense? Do my children have too much clothing?

❖ Cleaning: Does my child understand that because we all live together, we are all responsible for cleaning? Does my child understand the uses of different cleaning products and cleaning tools?

❖ Have I demonstrated cleaning techniques and what is expected? After demonstrating, have I stood by, then inspected my child's work until it is satisfactory? Do my children take some part in dish washing and kitchen cleanup?

❖ Do we have a cleaning schedule for our home that is followed fairly regularly?

CHAPTER 4

Life Navigation

Getting Along in That Great Big World

❖ Fourth Maxim of Maturity

It's a big and sometimes uncertain world out there, and our children need to navigate it safely.

❖ Transferable Skills

Ability to avoid unnecessary risks; capacity for evaluating safety of a situation; ability to think and plan ahead for getting around; ability to make contingency plans.

Navigating some of life's boundaries is joyous. I recall my daughter's feeling of pride and accomplishment when she was allowed to walk to the end of the block to mail a letter. You have probably witnessed the thrill of a child being released from the limitation of training wheels. These are ego building experiences for children and sources of great pride for parents as well.

Other boundaries of life may bring feelings that are frightening and even distasteful. Who really wants to have to educate their children about strangers, drugs, and the use of public restrooms? Yet, as parents we must teach them to navigate such waters successfully, safely, and wisely.

Knowing Personal Information and When to Share It

We used some fun ideas to teach our children to memorize personal information—name, family name, home address, telephone number, parents' names, siblings' names, etc. We put some of it to music to the tune of "It's Raining, It's Pouring." The children sang, "My name is Clare Field, this is my address, (Number and Street), Wheaton, Illinois."

We then made books for each child, entitled *All About (Name)*. On page 1 was a picture of the child with the caption, "My name is _____." The next page had a photo of our house with the caption, "This is my address _____." We would read the two pages and sing the song, with our children practically effortlessly memorizing our home address. The next page had our phone number. It was put to the tune of "Twinkle, Twinkle Little Star," and it went, "Seven, ___, ___, -___, ___, ___, ___, That's the way my phone number goes." Other items in our *All About Me* books included photos of siblings, the child's favorite toy, and a swatch of his or her favorite color.

Here are some other fun ideas for learning personal information:

- Look up the meaning of your child's name and make a poster.
- Write an acrostic poem using the letters of your child's name, for example:

  C - Christian
  L - Loving
  A - Affectionate
  R - Responsible
  E - Enthusiastic

- Make a family and friends phone book.
- Draw a family tree to learn the names of extended relatives.

When your children learn their own personal information, they also need to learn *when* and *with whom* to share that information. What is safe? How much, if anything, do you tell to strangers? In general, we should prohibit our children from talking to strangers, but we should encourage them to trust and cooperate with those in authority. Have phone numbers for parents at work and emergency numbers prominently displayed. Even If your child can't yet read yet he should know where these numbers are written down, so he can direct someone to them in an emergency. You might want to make and laminate a chart of the following information:

- Home phone number
- Parent's work and pager numbers
- A neighbor's number
- Emergency contact numbers

Another idea for personal information is to cut out a cardboard house to hang on the wall with your child's personal information on it. Having it displayed in the child's room will provide reinforcement for learning these basic facts.

Handling Transportation

Transportation consists of any way of getting where you want to go, whether you are walking, biking, taking public transportation, driving, or getting a ride from someone.

Learn to walk the right way.

Your child needs to learn that there are safe ways of walking. For your neighborhood, set boundaries on how far he can walk alone. Use landmarks he can understand, such as trees in the yard, edges of the driveways, or fire hydrants. Here are some other rules for pedestrian safety:

- Walk facing the traffic.
- Learn and obey all traffic signals.
- Walk on the sidewalk, not the street.
- Look right, left, right before crossing the street.
- Don't walk or run out from between parked cars.

Talk to your children about always trying to walk on the right on sidewalks, or using stairs, or walking down a hallway. We drive our cars on the right side of the road, so even the youngest child should learn to walk on the right. Tell them not to move back and forth when they walk or to stop suddenly because the people around them will be disturbed in their path.

Learn to bike safely.

Give some thought to the type of bike your child should ride. Parents often buy bikes that are too tall for their children, thinking that they will be the correct height as soon as the child grows a few inches. This is not safe. Your child should be able to put one foot flat on the ground while sitting on the upright bike. If she cannot, try the next smaller size.

Should your child ride a lightweight, multispeed bike, or a heavier one with fewer speeds? Generally, a heavier bike is easier to balance at slower speeds. A lighter bike may go faster but requires more skill to navigate. If your child will be riding many hills, a bike with many speeds makes sense. For everyday riding around the neighborhood, most bikes are too well-equipped.

Some other biking life skills include:

- Learn the rules of the road for cyclists. Your local state motor vehicle office should be able to provide you with a pamphlet about them. Bicyclists must ride in single file to the right, and they are subject to all the same traffic regulations as a car and, in most states, must use hand signals when turning or stopping. Local hospitals or park districts sometimes offer a bike safety course.
- Even if it is not required by law, wear a properly fitted bicycle helmet as protection against head and spinal injuries.
- Avoid riding at night, but if it is necessary, make sure the bike has a reflector and a light to the front and the rear. Wear reflective clothing for added protection.

- When riding near pedestrians, especially on crowded biking paths, say something such as, "Bike on your left."
- Tape some coins on the bike with electrical tape for emergency calls home.
- To avoid theft, always lock the bike and don't leave it out overnight. See if your police department registers bicycles as a service at little or no cost. If stolen and recovered, the bike can then be identified by the police and returned to its owner.
- Never wear headphones when riding a bike. To be safe, a bike rider must be aware of sights and sounds.
- Learn to fill a tire with air or fix a flat. Also learn to keep the bike clean and make sure brakes are in working order. Oil the bike every month or so.

Learn to use public transportation.

Explain to your children that public transportation includes buses, trains, airplanes, and taxis. When your child is navigating bus or train transportation alone, have her sit by the bus driver or ticket taker. If you have the opportunity, ask this person to keep an eye on your child. Ahead of time, your child should find out the fare required, the stops made, and the schedule. Where could you go on the bus? Get a schedule and plan a trip around your town using the bus. Caution your children that they need to know the exact name of the street they are seeking. Woodlawn Street and Woodlawn Drive could be across town from one another.

For airline travel, have your children learn to read schedules and check gate numbers carefully. Talk to them about the procedure for checking baggage and walk them through it. Make sure your traveling child has extra money and a phone calling card. Many kids today have their own phones. Make sure they are trained in their use and know what to do in a traveling emergency.

Follow rules for car rides.

In your own car, it is easier to set rules such as always wearing seat belts, not sticking anything breakable (arms and feet) out the window, and not screaming when mom has a headache. What about riding in friends' cars? You need to decide at what age and under what circumstances you will allow this. Then, set ground rules for checking with you before accepting a ride. Also make sure your child knows what to do if this person drives carelessly or recklessly. Finally, your child needs to realize that she must never accept a ride from a stranger.

Practice with directions.

Learning directions can be a fun challenge for children. When you are driving, help your child start to learn street names and directions by asking, "What street comes next?" or "Which way do we turn?" Have him practice identifying right and left, then north, south, east, and west.

Ask your child to give you directions from school to your home. As soon as your children are old enough to comprehend it, make a map of your neighborhood. Bonnie McCullough gives a fun twist on the neighborhood map idea: "To help children recognize the layout of your streets, a map of your community can be drawn on a large piece of fabric with magic markers. As the children play with cars, trucks, animals and people along the named streets they are starting map reading."[1]

Have your older child take chief responsibility for planning a family vacation. He should research areas, gather maps, prepare a budget, decide what to pack, figure mileage and costs, and make necessary reservations with your assistance. Then have him keep a travel journal of the details of the trip.

Children are naturally fascinated with maps. Have inexpensive maps around for them to explore. You can pick up free maps at rest stops as you travel and even allow your child to have her own map. Your older children can decide what route to take on a trip. As they become really skilled at this, they can take a larger role in vacation planning, including making reservations and planning what to pack.

Handling Life's Emergencies

Your children must learn what constitutes an emergency and what does not. Have a discussion with them about these scenarios. For each situation, have the child choose whether to call parents, a neighbor, or emergency services (911):

- A friend fell while playing and her knee is scraped.
- A friend fell while playing and her head is bleeding a lot.
- There is a growling dog in the neighborhood.
- Someone in the house is choking.
- There is a small fire on the kitchen stove.
- A car screeched on its brakes in front of your house.
- A stranger is trying to come into your home.

Have a list of emergency numbers posted, and place them on your speed dial, if you have one. Have your children practice calling 911 on a disconnected phone. Instruct them to recite their name and address, and not to hang up until they are told to do so. When reporting a fire, they are to go outside immediately and wait for help to arrive. After calling the police for help, they should remain in the house and stay on the phone line with the 911 operator until the officers arrive.

Learn first aid.

Being prepared in life makes you feel more confident and secure. It can also help to keep you safe. Elizabeth Crary notes,

"Children who know first aid are less likely to have accidents than children who do not know first aid."[2]

As a family, assemble a first aid kit (see chapter 9 for more tips on doing this) and talk about how to use each item. Get a children's book on first aid. There are probably several in your library. At a minimum, tell your child what to do with the following:

- Cuts—For small ones, clean with soap and water and cover with a bandage. For large, bleeding wounds, place a clean cloth on the wound and press firmly.
- Bruises—Put a cold cloth on the bruise.
- Fractures or sprains—Don't attempt to move the person. Call for help.
- Fainting—Help the person lie down or bend over with head between knees. Wipe face with cool water. Call for help.
- Bites or stings—Remove the stinger, if possible. Wash with soap and water and apply ice to reduce swelling.
- Burns—For mild burns, cover the area with a cold, clean cloth.
- Nosebleeds—Have the person sit with head bent slightly forward. Pinch lower part of nose for a few minutes to stop the bleeding; then place a cold, wet cloth on nose and face.
- Choking—If person can speak, cough, or breathe, wait a few minutes. If they cannot, stand behind them with your fist placed just under their rib cage. Give four or five quick upward thrusts. Do this until the object is dislodged.
- Poisoning—Call your Poison Control Center immediately.

Make safety a priority.

Have in place clear family safety rules and review them again and again. A good project for children is to draw pictures or illustrate safety rules and assemble a family safety rules book. It should include basics, such as not touching a hot stove or playing with knives, but it must also include some rules for other situations that unfortunately are becoming more common for young children.

Here are some possible family safety rules to illustrate:

- Always wear your seat belt.
- Always tell your parent where you're going.
- Yell, scream, and kick if a stranger tries to grab you.
- Don't climb on small tree branches.
- Hold sharp objects with the sharp part pointed away from you.
- Don't poke things into sockets or electric toasters.
- Answer the door only when a grownup is home.
- Don't play with matches or fire.
- Don't touch guns.
- Don't hitchhike or accept a ride from a stranger.

Do a safety check of your home with your child. Your local fire department has materials about home and fire safety. (You could plan a trip to the fire station.) Make sure fire alarms are working properly in your home, and plan and practice an escape route in case of fire. Learn what natural disasters are possible in your area, such as storms or tornadoes, and make a plan for family safety in such an event. Survey your home for poisons and have your child clearly label all hazardous substances with poison labels. Then make sure to keep these items out of children's reach.

You could also make a scrapbook of safety signs and navigational signs for your child to learn. The safety signs might include such things as Beware of Dog; Caution; Danger: Keep Out; Exit; Flammable; etc. Navigational signs could include such things as Bicycle Crossing; Do Not Enter; Don't Walk; Stop; etc.

Have a plan for the times your children must be home

alone. They should always keep the door locked and never leave the keys in the door. If someone comes to the door and claims to be a repair person, your children should tell him to come back later. If he has to deliver something, have him leave it outside the door. (If it requires a signature, have him slip it under the door.) If someone is asking for help in an emergency, have your child offer to make a telephone call rather than allow anyone in.

Many children regularly use elevators alone in apartment buildings or schools, and they need safety rules. If they ever feel uneasy about someone waiting for an elevator with them, they should let the other person get on the elevator alone and wait for the next car. They should always look inside before they get in and then stand near the control panel. If they are already in the elevator and someone is making them nervous, they should press the very next stop and exit.

Learn to set personal boundaries.

Explain to your child that boundaries mark limits, like the borders between states or countries. Human beings have boundaries too, though the norms differ from culture to culture. Physical boundaries determine how close you allow someone near you physically. (In America, one arm's length is a good rule of thumb for a personal physical zone.)

Emotional boundaries delineate how you allow others to treat you. Your children need to know that they have a right to physical and emotional boundaries. Sometimes they are assumed, but sometimes people have to be told.

If you must, practice expressing those boundaries in the family. For example, if you have a too-affectionate uncle, have your child practice saying, "Uncle Bob, it makes me uncomfortable to sit on your lap." By all means, if someone in your family arouses these types of suspicions, never allow your child to be alone with that person. We can teach children tactics, but we are ultimately responsible for their safety, and we are remiss if we fail to do all we can to control potential danger.

What are the common lures used by child molesters to get to children? There are four, according to Michael McManus:

1. Affection—Teach your child the difference between good love and bad love.
2. Assistance—A stranger asking for help to find a lost puppy.
3. Authority—A stranger pretending to be a police officer, doctor, or priest.
4. Ego—Someone preying on a child's ego by asking if the child would like to be a model or movie star.[3]

Urge your child to tell you about any of these behaviors they might see so you can discuss it. We recently had some firsthand experience with this kind of situation. Our daughter's Sunday school teacher had some photos taken of her students and was picking up the prints at the store. As she stood flipping through them, a stranger approached her and commented how beautiful one of the girls was—my daughter! The stranger proceeded to tell the Sunday school teacher that he was a photographer who would like to meet and take more photos of my daughter. The teacher dismissed his suggestion but reported the incident to me. My husband (a police chief) and I took this opportunity to talk with our daughter about these types of potential ploys. We were grateful to have such distance from the situation to turn it into a learning experience.

Teach your children that they must be consistent when they tell people their boundaries. If they smile or giggle when they say, "Leave me alone," they send a mixed signal. They must be serious and firm and insist on their right to personal privacy. In these safety discussions, your child may become frightened. This is a great time to remind them that God, our heavenly Father, is in control. A marvelous verse for children to memorize when studying safety issues is Psalm 121:8, "The Lord will watch over your coming and going both now and forevermore."

Using the Computer Safely

The Internet is filled with great information but also reeks of rumor, conjecture, and filth. Tell your child that just because something is on the Internet, there is no guarantee that it is true, even if his school worships the technology. In addition, and even sadder, evil people try to exploit children via computers.

What parents would knowingly allow their child to communicate with a deviant? Yet, when we allow our children unsupervised access to the Internet, we run the risk of just such a scenario. How can you protect your children? Realize that you set the rules in your home. It is a good idea to keep the computer in a common area. Then, always be in the area when your child is on-line so you can check what they are doing. Investigate parental control programs that screen out violence and pornography. Do not allow your child to give out any personal information on-line, even to a seemingly innocuous person, without checking with you first.

What are some signs that your child may be at risk when they are on-line? The Illinois Criminal Justice Information Authority offers these warning signs:

- Your child spends long periods of time on-line, especially at night.
- You find pornography on your child's computer.
- Your child receives phone calls from men you don't know or is making calls, sometimes long distance, to numbers you don't recognize.
- Your child receives mail, gifts, or packages from someone you don't know.
- Your child turns the computer monitor off or quickly changes the screen on the monitor when you come into the room.
- Your child becomes withdrawn from the family.
- Your child is using an on-line account belonging to someone else.[4]

For more information on how to protect children from computer dangers, contact the National Center for Missing and Exploited Children, 1-800-843-5678, www.missingkids.com.

Handling Life Skills in Public

As a general rule, when out in public, parents have to have their children within eyesight. Tell them why this is a rule. Children are a precious gift to you, and if these precious persons were lost, stolen, or hurt, you would be heartbroken. When out in public, children must not turn a corner before parents or disappear in a doorway. In our family, the rule is we must be able to see each other. We say, "When we stay together, we have more fun." We also make sure to have a meeting place, should they get lost.

Use public restrooms safely.

If you use public bathrooms, tell your children about germs and don't let them touch anything. Make sure your child flushes. Use your foot on flush levers, and use toilet paper for suspect doors. When our children were young, they always tried to lie on the floors of bathrooms, to my disgust and dismay. When they realized how filthy such floors could be, however, this nasty habit quickly disappeared. When can children go into the bathroom alone? If you are right outside and the establishment is not too crowded, you may decide to let them go alone by age five. My husband, on the other hand, will never allow the children to go alone.

Show integrity when shopping.

When you are in a store with your children, tell them to look with their eyes, not touch with their hands. If they do pick something up, they must put it back on the shelf. If something is "taken," it must be taken back, even if it was inadvertent. And we must always be prepared to pay for broken items. What if you discover that your child has taken an item without paying? She needs to know that this is stealing. When parents brush off such behavior, they are sending a harmful message. The child should return to the store, with the parent, to return the item and apologize to the manager.

My own tough stance on being honest with stores has caused me some headaches. While shopping with three of the children a few years ago, I discovered a tuna can at the bottom of the cart after we had loaded the groceries into the car and gotten everyone in car seats. I had to do the right thing, so we unloaded the children and brought the tuna can back inside the store. Was it inconvenient? You bet. But I have used that illustration countless times with the children, and the effect has been profound.

Act with courtesy in restaurants.

This is an area where voicing expectations in advance is absolutely necessary. Tell your children what behavior is expected of them in a restaurant, and then don't back down while you are there. Your young children should never be unescorted in the restaurant. That is, you should accompany them when they need to walk out their wiggles or when they need to use the bathroom. Never allow them to roam or crawl around.

For the comfort of everyone, take care of loud noises right away when you are in a restaurant. I like the reminder one priest gave: "Crying babies are like good intentions—they should be carried out immediately."

Bring something for your child to do while waiting for your food. If your family makes a real mess during the meal, clean it up as well as you can. Tell the children it's like eating at another person's house—if you make a mess, you have to clean it up. Teach your child about tipping and why it's done. Has the waiter or waitress done a good job? A tip is a way of thanking them for good, fast, friendly service.

The easiest way to dine out with children is to try to pick child-friendly establishments. As your kids learn appropriate behavior in those places and become more skilled in handling themselves in public, you can confidently branch out into other kinds of settings.

The world today is quite different from the one in which we grew up. Our kids will be able to navigate the sometimes rough and uncertain waters of their world when they know personal information, some rules of safe traveling, what to do in an emergency, and how to set personal boundaries. These are small things that can yield big rewards.

Life Skills Checklist

❖ Does our child know his personal information and with whom it is appropriate or inappropriate to share that information?

❖ Does our child know rules for safety when walking? Does our child have an appropriately sized bike with helmet? Has she learned the rules of the road? Does she know simple bike repairs? Has our family discussed how to avoid bike theft?

❖ Are our children aware of the methods of public transportation available? If they need to regularly use one of these methods, have we gone with them a few times and taught them the routine? Do we have family rules for whose cars our children are allowed to ride in?

❖ Do our children have familiarity with directions? Can they follow simple to more complex sets of directions? Have we taught them how to read a map? Do our children have a plan for any emergency which might happen while traveling?

❖ Do we have family safety rules for our home and for when we are in public?

CHAPTER 5

Time Organization

Managing Your 7/24/365

❖ Fifth Maxim of Maturity

We are given only a certain amount of time. We have to use it wisely.

❖ Transferable Skills

Ability to manage time well, to plan and complete projects, to set goals and priorities, to establish realistic timetables and schedules; capacity for promptness and timeliness in the workplace.

While I was growing up, my father would often quote an old Irish expression: "When God made time, he made plenty of it." While having many responsibilities and stressors, my father lived with the ease and grace of a man well grounded in his faith, taking life as it came. Perhaps as a reaction to his relaxed attitude, I became the opposite. My husband used to say I was like a Windows® computer program— I could multitask. Part of that is inherent in mothering. Part of it is a nagging feeling of insecurity about whether I am doing enough with my life or my time.

I want my children to view time as the precious commodity that it is. I want them to value it enough that they will not squander it, and I also want them to savor it enough so that it will not slip away. I know, however, that cultivating such a perspective in my children is a tall order for me to fill as a parent. Author Karen Miles refers to the accelerated pace of our lives as "the frenzied family syndrome." Explaining why this is harmful, she quotes family psychologist John Rosemond:

"The frantic family loses its center, its sense of self. Family intimacy suffers and children are denied the benefits of childhoods spent in relaxed, close-knit families where they have plenty of time to absorb values."[1]

I recently heard someone say that if the devil can't make you bad, he'll settle for making you busy. It is that seductive lure of busy-ness, so sanctioned by our society, which we must teach our children to recognize.

Valuing Time

We all have the same amount of time—what I like to call our "7/24/365"—seven days a week, twenty-four hours a day, and three-hundred and sixty-five days a year. With some thought and prayer, we can learn to manage our 7/24/365 according to our values and priorities and help our children do the same.

What is really worthy of your time? If you can answer that question honestly, then look at how you are actually using your time on any given day. This will give you an assessment of whether you are walking the walk or just talking the talk. If you say that Christ is the center of your life, yet you spend no time with him, there is incongruence. If you say that family is the next most important thing in your life, yet you spend only a minimal amount of time with them, you are not being true to your convictions.

Our culture is brimming with time wasters. According to Karen Levine, University of Maryland reseachers found that Americans had almost an hour a day more free time in 1995 than they did in 1965. What do we do with that leisure time? Levine says,

> Theoretically, the purpose of leisure time is to offer psychological renewal from work, but when we spend our leisure hours at the same kind of frenetic pace as our work hours, we emerge feeling drained, not renewed. Most of us spend our weekends plowing through lists of things we need to accomplish before Monday, which makes "quality" time with our kids just another item on a "to do" list.[2]

Part of the problem is that our increased leisure time comes in short segments, just long enough to tune into a sitcom or do a little shopping. Television and shopping, two activities that consume much of today's society's time, leave us drained and disappointed. They are poor choices for relaxation because they don't truly serve to refresh spirits or lift minds to any higher level.

What is the solution to this frenzied lifestyle? At one time I waited for life to slow down, but I now realize that it probably never will slow down. Rather, I am the one who needs slowing. Marnell Jameson notes, "As life gets more compressed . . . we have to block out time to relish, time that we don't rush to fill. Time to stop doing and simply be. For that's where the quality of life is."[3] While life is swirling around me, I must capture moments of my day to treasure and savor.

I learned a great deal a few years ago from a little book called *The Practice of the Presence of God*, written by a monk named Brother Lawrence, who cooked and cleaned for the other monks in his monastery. Whether he peeled potatoes or scrubbed pots, he did it with a heart full of the love of God. "During your meals or during any daily duty," he said, "lift up your heart to Him, because even the least little remembrance will please Him. You don't have to pray out loud; He's nearer than you can imagine."[4] This book revolutionized my view of prayer and time. I realized that the seemingly mundane aspects of my day—washing dishes, car pooling, cleaning the bathroom—were actually opportunities for contemplation. I could use the time spent doing these tasks that require minimal mental energy to focus my mind on prayer, thanksgiving, and creative thought. Of course, it took considerable practice to get my brain to slow down.

When was the last time you really paid close attention to doing one thing and enjoying it? When was the last time you really listened to your child's laughter or noted the shine of the light on her hair? Have you really appreciated the exquisite beauty of the cut of your son's jaw, or the delight of his burgeoning sense of humor? These days are fleeting. Children know how to savor moments naturally, but if they don't see us doing it, they will soon lose that ability. On the other hand, we can teach our children to cherish their own children by slowing down to cherish this short, sweet time.

Understanding the Sequence of Time

Very young children have little concept of time. The flow and structure of their day is imposed from the outside. We can use the normal schedule of days to teach them about time, keeping a regular flow to their day, and talking about what happens next. The healthy baby knows that when she is lifted out of her crib, what happens next is generally feeding and changing diapers. As that child grows, the next morning activity is perhaps potty time and a cup of milk. Such predictable routines give a child not only a sense of time but also a sense of security.

Your day doesn't have to be scheduled by the hour. With small children, this is often impossible to accomplish anyway. To have a rigid schedule would also frustrate you if you were unable to meet the goals of the day. But your day should be predictable enough so that your child can anticipate what happens next. For example, after we play, we always eat lunch. After lunch we always cuddle and read a story and go to take a nap. Before supper, we always watch one television show. After supper, we always clear the table and have some time with Daddy. After that we always take baths and cuddle before bed.

We started early giving our children five minute warnings, or ten minute warnings. If they were engaged in an activity or we were visiting a friend, we would tell them how much time they had left before we were leaving or switching activities. The technique doesn't work very well at first, but children soon learn to enjoy those last five to ten minutes because they know that something different is going to happen next. This practice eases the many transitions our children are called to make each day.

Once your child has learned the flow of the day, introduce him to the flow of the week. For example, on Sunday we always go to church. Or, on Monday and Wednesday we always go to playgroup. Whatever your routine is, begin to verbalize this in conversation with your child so he is aware and alerted to what happens next. Also start teaching your child at an early age about planning ahead. In our home, we have a Saturday routine for getting ready for Sunday church. The girls choose dresses, and Daddy irons them; the children find shoes and polish them. This routine serves as an anchor in their week.

When your child is ready, introduce the calendar with activities such as the following.

1. Buy (or make) a large wall calendar for your kitchen. Each day, over breakfast, talk about the day. Mention the day of the week, the date, month, and year.

2. Talk about activities scheduled for the day that have been written down on the calendar. Point out other places where the date is noted, such as the daily newspaper.

3. On the calendar, write all the significant dates for the year, including holidays and birthdays. You could even draw a related picture to denote the holiday.

4. Teach a song to learn the days of the week. You can sing it each day as you locate that date on the calendar. As your child begins to read, write the days of the week on index cards and have her put them in the correct order.

5. Learn a poem to memorize the months of the year. Look in any children's poetry book for ideas.

6. Memorize the number of days of the months with this old nursery rhyme favorite:
   Thirty days hath September,
   April, June, and November;
   All the rest have thirty-one.
   Excepting February alone.
   Which hath but twenty-eight, in fine,
   Till leap year gives it twenty-nine.

7. After your child is familiar with the months, write the month names on cards for him to sort into the proper order. Also, try writing them in large letters on a strip of paper hung near your dining table. Practice them when you can.

When learning to tell time, capitalize on the fact that children love watches! Even before they can tell time, a simple, cheap digital watch will be a prized possession. Use the watch as a prompter to ask your child, "What time is it?" Then look at the watch together to figure it out.

1. For analog clocks, make a numbered clock out of a paper plate, or purchase a teaching clock at the store. This is a little more difficult for children to understand, but it must be mastered eventually. Take the time to teach both methods of telling time.

2. Make a time line of your daily routine out of a roll of paper shelf liner. For example, write 7:00 A.M. and draw a picture of a child getting out of bed. For 7:30 A.M., draw a picture of the child sitting at the table, etc. This gives the child a visual picture of your day and reinforces reading the times of day.

3. Make flash cards of clocks with times drawn on them. This is especially helpful in learning the analog system. If your child has trouble reading the flash cards, you can provide helpful clues such as, "This is the time we usually eat dinner." Soon she will be reading the cards without the prompts.

The changing seasons provide your child with other opportunities to learn time concepts. Here are some possibilities:

1. To learn the seasons, take lots of nature walks with your child. Talk about the current season. Discuss what came before this season. Talk about the coming season.

2. Make a collage of the types of clothing worn in each season, using saved newspaper ads. Divide one large piece of paper into four sections, and label each with a season. Let your child cut and paste items for each season.

3. Do at least one art/nature related craft each season. (I try to keep a running list of these Seasonal Savors on my web site at http://members.aol.com/MField7842.) Here are some examples to get you started:
   - Winter: Glue white cotton balls onto blue construction paper to make a snowman or other winter scene.
   - Spring: Cut out paper flowers and hang them in the window and from the ceiling with strings.
   - Summer: Collect twigs, flowers, grasses, and other bits from the back yard. Let your child make a summer collage with glue on sturdy paper.
   - Fall: Do leaf rubbings by putting leaves under a piece of paper and rubbing a crayon on the top of the paper until the image of the leaf appears.

Working on Time with the Maturing Child

As your children attain school age, get them an alarm clock of their very own. If they have a hard time getting up in the morning, their battle is with the alarm clock, not Mom or Dad. Make sure they know how to operate it and set it, then leave them to exercise this responsibility on their own.

Being on time is one of the most valuable skills we can teach and insist upon. LaVerne Ludden notes, "An organization can't operate without dependable workers. A supervisor must be able to rely on employees coming to work every day on time. When a worker is late or absent, it causes many problems. In fact, employers list absenteeism as one of the major reasons for firing employees."[5]

Of course, being on time and doing what you say you will do when you say you will do it are essential skills for any relationship. If your child has learned to value and manage time, he will be better prepared later to keep his promises to spouse, children, friends, and co-workers at church, at work, and in the community.

When planning a new semester or school year, sit down with a calendar with your child. Together, fill in all the commitments on the calendar so you both can have a concrete picture of what her schedule will look like. If it seems overwhelming, she's doing too much. On a more basic level, have your child write out what her daily schedule will look like and then her weekly schedule. Include school arrival and departure times, set times for homework and reading, regular family anchors like church attendance, and finally the desired extracurricular activities. This will give her a good idea of what everyday life will be like if she pursues all her activities. (In chapter 10 we will talk about a study schedule, which also needs to dovetail with the child's overall schedule.)

How can your child assess if he is managing his time wisely? Have him honestly answer these questions:

1. Do I turn assignments in late?
2. Do I spend a lot of time goofing off?
3. Do I feel like I can't get everything done?
4. Do I have trouble finding things I need to do my work?
5. Do I delay getting started on long assignments?
6. Do I frequently arrive late?
7. Do I rush through my work?
8. Do I feel like I am rushing to get things done?

If your child answered yes to more than two of these questions, he or she needs to take a serious look at his or her time management. Start by having your child write a few sentences in response to these questions:

1. What happened the last few times I managed my time poorly?

2. If I had been using my time well, what would have happened instead?
3. What are the biggest problems I have managing time? (Help your child to look honestly at things such as video or computer games, television time, or talking on the telephone.)
4. What are some steps I could take to improve my time management?

As parents, we can have a major impact on our children's time management style. If we model wise time management, they will pick it up. If we talk to them about their needs, we can brainstorm together to find solutions. The worst thing we can do is to criticize—"If you didn't spend so much time playing video games, you wouldn't be having school problems." This is a fairly obvious statement. But *why* is your child frittering away time? Does she need some organizational tips? Does he need some motivation to get organized? Is she suffering from some mild depression which she could benefit from sharing with you?

You can discern the answers to these questions by spending time with your young person. Make it a point to spend some individual time each week to talk about things that are important to your child. It doesn't take that long to go out for a soda. Yet, you are making an investment in your child's life.

If your child's schoolwork is suffering, you may have to step in with motivating consequences. While your children are under your roof, you have the authority to set parameters on their computer, video game, and television usage. Put them on an "electronic diet" and make a pact with them that they will be given greater latitude when their schoolwork improves. As much as children in middle-childhood years may seem to want total independence from us, they still need our guidance and counsel.

Find a time organization tool to work through with your child, such as the study schedule in chapter 10. There are also many fun, useful products on the market—day planners, assignment notebooks, calendars, etc. Take a trip to the office supply store with your child to purchase some of these tools, then take the time to show him how to use them. A day planner is of no use unless someone takes the time to plan. Spend that time with your young person today to help him organize his life. (See chart below for some ideas.)

Organization for the School-Aged Child

1. Set a goal to organize your time and space for more effective work.
2. Figure out what needs to be done first.
3. Don't put off important, long, or tedious tasks. They won't go away.
4. Don't waste time. Make a schedule and keep to it.
5. Keep a daily "to do" list in your day planner or assignment notebook. Use this for items you need to remember to bring and things you need to do. Write it down!
6. Keep your study area neat and organized.
7. Develop a file system, with your parents' help, for papers.
8. Get adequate sleep and eat nutritious foods to function at your best.
9. Take time today to plan for tomorrow's activities and responsibilities.
10. Don't forget to reward yourself periodically for a job well done.

Planning and Prioritizing Time

One of the biggest challenges for today's families is choosing wisely among too many priorities, especially in the area of enrichment activities. Mickey Rathburn, writing about sports in particular, reminds us to set priorities. "The first thing you and your child need to do is set priorities. Sit down together and list the important elements in your child's life. Explain to your child that family comes first, schoolwork second, and sports third."[6]

Parents love to rush, too. Too often we have almost a sense of pride in describing to others all the things we must do to run our children around to their activities. Have you heard yourself saying something like this? "We had two soccer games, one piano recital, a pizza party, and a sleepover last Saturday. Whew!" "Whew," indeed. You're doing too much.

What are some signals your children may be sending that they need to slow down? Your innate parental wisdom tells you that tummy aches, headaches, and trouble sleeping are red flags. So are changes in feelings and behavior, like sadness, apathy, or rebelliousness. Of course, if your child's work at school is suffering, it is time to reevaluate everyone's time commitments.

Children who are always busy with no time for play could be budding workaholics. This is an unhealthy pattern to bring to adulthood and particularly to marriage and raising a family. A focus on work to the exclusion of family concerns is detrimental to family unity, yet workaholism is accepted and even applauded in our society. "The workaholic has an ironclad argument that other members of the family can seldom puncture. It seems foolproof. 'I'm only doing this so that we can have enough money to live the way we want to live, so that we can send the kids to college, so that we can . . . '" notes Dr. Harvey Ruben.[7] It's up to parents to mentor our children in a sensible attitude toward work, so we can help them avoid workaholism in their future.

Even when we are aiming to balance work and play in our child's lives, we may still fall prey to the modern notion that our children need somehow to be busy all the time. The children themselves may be the ones pushing such an idea—when life in general over stimulates and over schedules them, they may find themselves at loose ends when the stimulation lets up, such as happens on vacations or other slower times. If children have not been given time to daydream, engage in imaginative play, horse around with siblings, and enjoy being outside, they will be cranky and bored when the bells and whistles of their lives are turned off. This is why many parents dread school breaks.

By contrast, my mother-in-law has these words to offer, "If you're bored, you're boring." I agree! Life is too exciting to be bored. If you're bored around my house, I'll give you a chore to do. With this as a consequence, my children have only been bored a few times, and they have learned to occupy themselves productively (with my guidance) in their free time.

Simpler Pursuits and Rituals during Family Time

If you find your family life is just whirring out of control, try some slowing down activities. For starters, do some things your children's way. How much conversation with your kids is directive in nature? Do you hear yourself merely giving commands and orders to your child? "No. Stop that. Listen to me. Do this. Do that. Don't forget this. Here's what I want you to do." Your younger child needs floor time. Sit on the floor with him and let him show you how he plays. Don't direct the activity, but let your child choose how to play and what to play with. Sharing these moments of childhood says to your child, "You are worth it!" Try taking your older child out one-on-one to the ice cream shop of her choice, or other similar special outings.

Playing games as a family is coming back as a popular pastime, partly, I believe, because the distraction of a game can help a child open up to talk. Some families schedule a family game night each week. Keep a puzzle set up and going in your home to work on together. Learn a new craft and teach your kids. Break a routine and have breakfast for supper or take a bike ride at sunrise. Nature walks or bike rides with no destination in mind are the most rewarding simpler pursuits for our family.

Establishing special time-related rituals can be meaningful. Dr. Mary Pipher, author and therapist, notes, "One of the things parents must teach kids is how to protect time, and the essence of ritual to me is that ritual sanctifies time."[8] Bedtime, bathtime, mealtime, and storytime are all anchors in your family's day. Your younger child counts on them to give a flow to his day. Older children may cling to these times as an oasis of peace in their busy schedules. We can make these times special and memorable with a little forethought and effort. (See some ideas for making these rituals special in chapter 14.)

Rituals or even silly traditions that we follow are the small touches that make family life special and unique—the things that sanctify our time. It gives a child a great sense of belonging and connectedness to be able to say, "In our family, we always hold hands when we pray." Or, "In our family, we always have waffles on Saturday night." Your child will remember fondly these moments of grace and celebration. And special memories of time well-spent are always good gifts for our kids.

Life Skills Checklist

❖ Do my children know the days of the week, the months of the year, the seasons? Do they know what year and season it is, and can they find the correct date on the calendar?

❖ Can my children tell time with a digital clock and with an analog clock?

❖ Does our family make decisions about commitments based on a clear picture of the time we have available? Do we say no to things when we don't have time to do them?

❖ Do we generally arrive on time and do we keep the promises we have made?

❖ Have we carved out regular family time? What slowing down activities do we use? What time-related rituals do we have as a family?

CHAPTER 6

Space Organization

Managing Physical Space and Stuff

❖ Sixth Maxim of Maturity

We all work and live in a physical space. We need to manage that space. Our children's future spouse and employer will appreciate this especially.

❖ Transferable Skills

Ability to be a good steward of material possessions; capacity to organize physical things well.

Having children means having stuff—and lots of it. The bigger they get, the more stuff they accumulate, and the sheer volume of the stuff of childhood can be overwhelming at times. Because our first child was adopted on very short notice, she came dangerously close to sleeping in a dresser drawer. The extended family, however, rallied together, and she ended up sleeping in an exquisitely handmade oak cradle that Grandpa had been secretly crafting for us during our years of infertility.

By the time the fourth child arrived, we had more stuff than we ever imagined possible, all squeezed into a tiny house—we were bursting at the seams with our blessings. In those squeezed years, we learned a lot about patience, sharing, making do, and managing our space. We now live in a house that wildly exceeds our expectations of living space. So now we struggle with the abundance of our possessions and the slippery standard of "slobbiness."

Home management expert Deniece Schofield says that a slob is anyone who is messier than you. The "slob syndrome," as she call it, has many causes.

Sometimes well-meaning parents continually wait on their children and follow them around the house picking up after them. The child grows up expecting others to take care of him and never changes his childhood patterns. Conversely, children can learn to tolerate a mess if that's what they always experience at home. Again, they bring their habitually messy environment along into their adult lives.[1]

Being able to manage and organize space is a skill that will transfer to adulthood and may make your child easier to live with as a spouse and to work with as a coworker. The image of the creative, disorganized person may be idolized on television, but it is not always well tolerated by coworkers or bosses.

In different seasons of my life I have been organizationally challenged. My first two children were seventeen months apart in age, and I had few domestic skills at the time they were babies. Our house reflected my survival mode approach to life. At other times I have been more in control. As a homeschooling mom/writer/lawyer, my life requires a fair amount of organization in order to accomplish all I seek to accomplish. But I am always striving for balance. I want my home to be orderly, but I want my children to know that people come before the orderliness of our house.

Organize by Reducing

From my time spent working in a law office and from my time spent at home, I have learned that the only secret to organizing space is to *reduce stuff*. The more you have, the more time you spend cleaning it, taking care of it, and attempting to organize it. This applies to having too many files and books in the office as well as to having too many toys and clothes at home. It's a human tendency to desire and acquire, and God has given us all things to enjoy. But Jesus said, "Watch out! Be on your guard against all kinds of greed; a man's life does not consist in the abundance of his possessions" (Luke 12:15).

141

One of the biggest mistakes we make with young children is to give them too many toys and too much clothing. At various times, each of my children's dressers have had over-stuffed drawers and I could only navigate their rooms by tripping over toys. (For a time we tried to solve the floor problem with big toy boxes, but they really didn't work. Things got tossed in, shuffled to the bottom, then forgotten and ignored.)

Let's say you just can't bear to part with some of their darling possessions. Try rotating toys. As things start adding up, we periodically pack up a box or two and put it up in the attic. After a time, we retrieve the box, and the children believe they have gotten new toys. Of course, they aren't new. We explain that the toys were were merely resting for a while. Another tactic that we try around Christmas time is this: For each new toy our children receive, they have to dispose of an old one. Such a practice can be a meaningful exercise in giving if you take the child with you to the thrift store or church nursery to donate the toy.

For each of our children, we keep one out-of-season clothes box in their closet. As stuff gets acquired or handed down, it goes into the box of the appropriate child. When we get gifts of clothing that are too large or for the wrong season, they go into the box as well. It is always an exciting time twice a year when we drag out the boxes to organize wardrobes for the season. This is also the time that we take a clothing inventory for each child so we know what we are missing, and more importantly, what we don't need. (See clothing inventory in chapter 3.)

Each of our children also has a memory box. Cardboard boxes that you can get from your local print shop work well for this. As the boxes get filled, I tape them up and put them away. My oldest (ten years of age) has four boxes thus far. It brings us great pleasure to take one out on occasion and to look at the old baby shoes and sweaters and bibs. This is a great rainy-day activity for Mom and the kids, although we sometimes become flooded with happy memories and shed a few tears.

One mom I know, who has many more children than I have, limits her children to one box each during their childhood, so the stuff they keep has to be carefully selected. I fantasize about organizing my kids' boxes into keepsake albums, but I doubt that I will complete this for quite some time. Meanwhile, things are preserved and can be found when a family member is feeling sentimental.

Setting Up a Child's Space

Our goal for young children is to have a living/playing/sleeping area that they maintain primarily by themselves. This requires a child-friendly space with elements such as the following:

- Low shelves placed around the room for toy and book storage. This way the children can reach the shelves and be responsible for replacing items.
- Personal laundry baskets and wastebaskets. As discussed earlier, even very young children can be responsible for delivering dirty laundry to the laundry room and putting clean laundry away. A lowered bar in the closet, or child-height hooks, will help them keep their closet orderly. A lightweight wastebasket can be emptied by a two year old, with a parent's encouragement and guidance.
- Labeled storage boxes. Plastic boxes with lids are great for cars or Barbie dolls. They can be labeled with pictures for prereaders.
- Plastic bags for storing puzzle pieces. Put matching numbers on pieces and boards and have a family rule that only one puzzle can be out at a time.
- Ziplock bags for storing little toy pieces, things like jacks or marbles. Place the bags in a larger box or tin.

Expanding the child-friendly space beyond their bedrooms into the rest of your household can help involve your children in your home's functioning. For example, in our kitchen, if you look for a cereal bowl, you might become confused. We

143

store plastic dishes, bowls, and cups at kid level in the lower cabinets so the children can set the table and put dishes away. By doing a few simple things like this to remove obstacles, you can actually help your child become a better helper.

Curing Bedroom Bedlam

An older child's room is a living, personal thing. (Sometimes it almost seems to breathe too.) Ask your children to ponder how they can arrange their space so it is used wisely and meets their needs and reflects their personality—within reason. Let them draw up plans for rearranging furniture. Have them measure dimensions to see if their plan is feasible.

In terms of decorating, be aware that less than permanent decorative schemes can save Mom and Dad money and time. A nine year old who is enthralled with the solar system may turn into a ten-year-old Monet aficionado. Some companies sell removable wallpapers, borders, and other decorative items. We also find Fun-Tak® very useful for hanging posters and papers. It is a gumlike substance that holds items in place, then comes off completely with no marks or stains. It is a great invention to let your child use to decorate.

Aside from decorating, your child needs to think about the benefits of being organized. Using a cause-and-effect logic, ask her what happens when she is not organized. Perhaps she is late for school because she can't find things. Maybe it takes them longer to get dressed or do homework because her room lacks organization. Your child should have one place to study or work, free from distractions and equipped for study. (This will be discussed in greater detail in chapter 10.)

Try to impress upon your children, and model for them, the benefit of being at least somewhat organized. Are you an example to them, in your own life, of the principle that better organization equals more time in your day? Or do you spend fifteen minutes searching for car keys each day? Talk to your children about your schemes for organization at work and relate these to why it is important to be organized for school.

Help your children brainstorm ways that they can be better organized. Maybe you can visit a container store, a store which specializes in storage items, and pick out some things together to help them organize their room. Just browsing one of these stores usually fills me with ideas to better use my space. Consider setting aside some time over school break to invest in your child's organization.

Taming the Paper Monster

Part of being a child is the creation of an incredibile amount of papers that parents then have the challenge of sorting. We conquer the official papers by having a file for each area of our children's lives: a school file, a medical file with immunization and other records, and files for activities such as church, clubs, or sports teams. Each file can contain phone lists, scheduling material, and papers to be signed or rerouted.

But what about all the precious artwork that your child generates? My friend Rene Jurkowski tells me, "Every few months we go through Megan's artwork and papers, throwing out the ones she doesn't want anymore and keeping a few good pieces that get added to an expandable folder for artwork we want to save." Especially with artwork, you need to put a limit on the volume of papers you are willing to save. When a designated finite space is full, that's all you will save for a particular time period.

It's a good idea also to rotate artwork on display. You might use the refrigerator or a bulletin board specially designated for artwork. Move it around and change it often. You and your children will enjoy watching their artistic progress and development. For a time, we strung a clothesline in the kitchen and used snap-type clothespins to display papers. This was especially convenient because we could take the line down if the situation warranted. Changing the artwork or papers was easy as well with this system.

We have been experimenting with letting the children keep their own photo albums. When I am updating the family albums, there are always far too many photos to use. We give these to the children to use in artwork, to send to friends, or to mount in their own photo books. They enjoy the flexibility of having photos they can keep in their room and look at any time.

Conquering Clutter

Teach your child (and yourself) to make good use of dead storage space. Think about the amount of room under beds. My children have thin plastic boxes under their beds which contain Lincoln Logs® and Legos®. As for me, I store wrapping papers in an under-bed box in my room. Empty suitcases in closets can provide great storage for out of season clothes or dress up clothes. My friend Marnie Murray told me, "I keep new garbage cans in the crawl space labeled with clothing sizes. Then when we go to garage sales, I can buy a few sizes ahead and just drop it into the can. This also works for ice skates, books, etc." With this storage method, the containers are really out of sight!

At least once a year, help your child do a room de-clutter. This will teach them to sort and prioritize their possessions. When we sift and sort, we use three containers: one for items to put away, another (a garbage bag) for items to throw away, and another for items to give away.

The older your children get, the more you want them to focus on this question: What will you want to take with you to your own apartment? As they begin to earn their own money, they can also make purchases for independent living. A few ladies I know have actual hope chests for their children which they are filling with useful items for the future. If that is beyond your means or interest, you can encourage your child to begin to stock a plastic "hope storage bin" with linens, housewares, tools, and significant books for college life or for their first apartment.

These ideas will help your children manage their room space, but what about all the items left lying around the house?

Give your older child the task of organizing the garage, basement, or attic. Ask her to draw up a plan for storage and for removal of unwanted items. Help your child to execute the plan, following her recommendations.

This was a serious problem for us at one time, and so we instituted a Confiscation Box. Anything left lying around after pick up time was placed in the box. It could be redeemed at any time for ten cents. If it was not claimed by the end of the week, it was thrown away. There were only a few items that we ended up throwing away. Just having the box is a motivator for some kids, and we found that having a system in place lent credibility to our request to, "Pick up the living room, or the toys go in the Confiscation Box."

Linda and Richard Eyre have a "Gunny Bag." Once in a while, without notice, the Gunny Bag comes out and gobbles up all the toys left lying about. On Saturday, "he spits them all up in a big pile and if they are put right away, he doesn't eat them again. If they are left out, though, he gobbles them right up, and once he has eaten anything for the second time, he never spits it up again!"[2]

If you are willing to try a more drastic measure, the Eyres have found the ultimate clutter solution. They removed everything from their children's rooms except for their beds, blankets, and one small box for personal belongings. All the toys were placed in a toy area and all the clothes were removed to a laundry area. Clothes cannot leave the clothing area unless they are being worn. Toys are "checked out" one at a time and must be returned before a new one is obtained.[3]

I have considered putting all the children's dressers in the laundry room. It would save me time and would save the children from walking to and fro, depositing and retrieving laundry, but would it teach them to manage their wardrobes?

Probably not, so for now they will continue to lug their baskets around the house.

Teaching Kids about Space Organization and their Future

Why is space organization a life skill that needs to be taught? Explain to your children that some day they will have their own home and life to manage. Do they want to spend their time cleaning and tripping over toys that no one ever plays with? An orderly home means more time to be with each other and have fun. Home should be a pleasant haven for family, not a messy mess.

Here are some suggested learning activities for older children:

- Sit with your child and ask for his suggestions while you organize your tool chest or sewing box.
- Get a book from the library on home organization and read it together, asking your child to help you implement some of the ideas. Two highly recommended books are *Clutter's Last Stand* by Don Aslett and *Confessions of a Happily Organized Family* by Deniece Schofield (both published by Writer's Digest Books, 1984).

Inge Cannon and Ronald Cannon, authors of *Mentoring Your Teen*, emphasize that the appearance of a person's work area is important. They go so far as to say, "Neatness is paramount."[4] Some people can judge very harshly. Would you want your children's other obvious talents to be ignored because they have not learned to manage space? A genius may be hiding under those piles of paper, but she may never get a chance to prove herself if someone has already judged her as a slob. If your children have learned to manage personal space while still at home, they will adjust more easily to managing space at school, at work, and in any other context they find themselves in the future.

148

Life Skills Checklist

❖ Do my children have too much clothing or too many toys or too many saved papers?

❖ Is the closet arranged so my child can hang up her own clothing? Are my child's drawers organized and not too crammed? If my child needs it, have I placed picture labels on the appropriate drawers? Do my children each have their own laundry basket?

❖ Do I have an organized place for out-of-season clothing, and do I regularly go through this storage area to keep it weeded out?

❖ Do we have a system for rotating toys so the children don't have too much out at one time? Do we periodically give away toys to somone who can use them? Do my children have a place for books and papers?

❖ Have we thought of a creative way to deal with items left lying around the house, like a confiscation box?

❖ Does my older child understand why it is important to be organized? Has he spent time thinking about the best ways to organize his room and belongings? Do I regularly de-clutter with my child, helping him to sort and prioritize his possessions?

CHAPTER 7

Around the House Skills

Fixing and Maintaining Stuff

❖ Seventh Maxim of Maturity

Things break and need maintenance. The more we can learn to do on our own, the more self-reliant we will be.

❖ Transferable Skills

Aptitude and eagerness for learning new skills; ability to remain calm, cope with pressure, keep emotions under control, and develop coping strategies to deal with new or stressful situations.

One of my husband's fondest memories is of working alongside his father on household projects, both big and small. A trip to the hardware store while holding Dad's strong hand provided an opportunity to spend time chatting and enjoying each other's company. My older daughters similarly clamor to go to the store with Dad. Whether to buy trash bags or to buy the materials for a project, they are interested and eager to be involved and help.

Some families thrive on doing home projects together. Others detest them. What if home skills are not your strength? God gifted each of us differently. Not everyone can unplug a drain or refinish a floor. But what we can do is to share what we know and be willing to learn something new. Because of the mixed blessing of home ownership, my husband and I have both been challenged to learn new things around the house. We have tried to take these moments to share with our children. It hasn't always been fun or pleasant, but we have all learned. Home ownership has taught us to:

1. Have a sense of humor. Just when you think the house is humming along pretty well, something else will go wrong. Cleaning three inches of water off the bathroom floor may not be what you had in mind, but it could be an opportunity to teach the kids about teamwork and washing the loads of towels generated by the overflow.

2. Be willing to learn. There is an assessment process that goes on each time something around the house goes wrong. We need to determine if we can handle it, or if we need to call in a professional. These are times to discuss decision making with your kids and to help them learn to make these kinds of judgment calls.

3. Be willing to ask for help. If the project truly is over your head, you can teach the children a valuable lesson by asking for help. If the money is not in the budget to hire someone, there is often someone in your church or your workplace who can help. When we can get over our pride, we discover all the other talents God has bestowed on others, and we uncover their willingness to share.

I am usually unmindful of the hazards of beginning a new household project. My husband is usually more realistic, and he's usually correct about the time and talent involved in various tasks. My image of home maintenance was set early in life when my hard-working father of eight children would take the time with me in the yard to give me wood scraps and nails for building boats. I would hammer away happily, keeping him company while he scraped and painted windows or did another of the hundreds of tasks involved in maintaining a home. So, my recollection of home projects was relatively pleasant. As an adult, I have learned that home repair projects are often grueling and unpleasant, a more realistic view.

Still, it is exciting, after almost fifteen years of marriage, to look back at the projects we have managed. I never would have believed we could redecorate or lay bricks or hang molding or put up drywall, but thanks to my husband's spirit of adventure and native home-repair intelligence, we have handled some pretty complicated repairs. Don't be afraid to try some new things. You will be setting a great example for the kids and saving a lot by not hiring outside contractors.

Who 'Ya Gonna Call?

Talk to your child about the kind of repair professional you would call for the following situations:

Furnace not working

Toilet clogged

Smell of gas coming from cold stove

Lights not working

Washing machine overflowing

Choosing Tasks You Can Do

There are things that you do every day, or week, which represent valuable life skills to teach your children. The simple tasks of mowing the lawn or weeding the garden are moments to be shared with your children, and when things go wrong with those simple tasks—the lawnmower won't start or the toilet overflows—you can set a terrific example to your kids by remaining calm, examining the situation, and trying to deal with it.

If you or your spouse is involved in the trades, you have an even better opportunity to mentor your child. My friends Marnie and Mike Murray have been able to offer their sons the benefit of Mike's work in construction. Marnie notes, "My husband has been taking my seven year old to work on side jobs. When appropriate, he can sort items, get drinks or forgotten items from the toolbox. Mike was delighted recently when Dillon helped him drywall a room—just the two of them!"

Seek out an old-fashioned hardware store. Many are run by family owners who can be extremely helpful and save you money on repairs. In these stores, you will usually find retired tradespeople who can tell you in detail what part(s) you need and exactly how to repair your problem.

Whether you visit a megastore or a small neighborhood hardware store, take the time to point out different departments to your child. Look at the displays and talk about the kinds of repairs and projects that can be done: painting, cutting and working with wood, redoing an entire bathroom, finishing cabinets, landscaping. Many larger stores offer workshops for adults who wish to tackle larger projects around the home. Take your child with you and learn and work on the project together.

Teaching Home Repairs: Ten Possibilities

Look at this list to see which home repair would be helpful and interesting to your family.

1. Fuses and circuit breakers

Before anything else, your child must understand that electricity is to be highly respected. A fuse used to be a mysterious thing to me. Now I know that it is there to protect my family. When it senses too much drain of electricity from a single circuit, it cuts off the electricity, or "blows a fuse." This usually happens when too many appliances are being operated at the same time.

The first step in this repair is to locate the electrical service box, whether for fuses or circuit breakers. This is usually located in the kitchen or laundry room. Fuses look like round, thick glass bottle tops. Circuit breakers look like a panel of black switches.

As you look into fuses, one may appear to be darker, burned, or popped out. If it is the kind that merely pops out, just pop it back in. If it is the other kind, which has a metal strip or spring, it will need to be replaced. Make sure you replace it with the same amperage fuse and your problem is solved. It's a good idea to keep a few fuses on hand in your toolbox.

Circuit breakers are considerably easier to deal with. When you open the electrical service box, one of the switches will be in a halfway position between ON and OFF. All you need to do is to shut the switch completely off and then back on to reset it to the ON position.

Of course, if you are repeatedly blowing fuses or tripping the circuit breaker, it usually means you are trying to use too many electrical devices at one time, or you have a serious electrical problem that needs an electrician's attention.

If your child is very interested in this topic, suggest the following activities:

- Read a library book about how electricity works.
- Review the electrical section of a home-repair book.
- Visit the electrical department of the hardware store.
- Observe a professional electrician at work.

2. Appliances that won't work

Try unplugging and replugging or try another receptacle. Check to see if the circuit for that area of the house had been tripped (see above). Finally, try squeezing the prongs of the plug closer together to make contact within the socket. If these ideas don't work, try a repairman.

To extend your child's interest, offer these possibilities:

- Work with a parent or observe an appliance repair person working on an appliance in your home.
- Read a book on appliance repair.
- Choose one home appliance and study consumer guides and newspaper ads to find the best brand for the best price. Prepare a report of your findings for your family to review.

3. Leaky faucets

As a short-term solution to the annoying dripping sound, drape a washcloth over the faucet or put one in the bottom of the sink. This will soften the sound so you can get a good night's sleep before attempting the repair. Some people hang a string from the faucet so that the drips will ride down the string instead of plinking in the sink.

For the truly brave, faucet repair kits are sold at hardware stores. Copy down the manufacturer's name and model of your faucet or make a sketch and head off to the store. The kits contain all the correct hardware for your faucet. As with any project, turn off the water at the supply valve before starting a repair!

The best tip I have ever received about replacing leaky faucets is to lay the pieces out on a towel as you remove them from the faucet. It's kind of like a puzzle, and you want to make sure you can put it back together in the proper order. As you disassemble the faucet, you may discover the source of the leak is a simple cracked washer. Replacement of this fifty-cent part could solve your problem. The bigger challenge is reassembling the faucet. (The less brave among us may want to go directly to the plumber.)

4. Plugged drains
With four women in our house, our drains sometimes get plugged up. The best solution to this is prevention. We try to remember to use a weekly treatment in the bath drains consisting of two tablespoons of baking soda followed by a half cup of vinegar, followed by lots of hot running water. If this doesn't work, and if you're brave enough, you can try unplugging it yourself.

First try a plunger. Sometimes the compressed air created by vigorous plunging will dislodge the clog. Next, try unwinding a coat hanger and fishing and poking around in the drain from the sink. If the clog is close to the surface, you may wiggle it out this way. Next, try a chemical solution from the store. Read the directions carefully, use with extreme caution, and clean the area thoroughly after use.

If none of those efforts work, try turning off the water supply valve and going in for a surgical strike. Usually there is a U-shaped pipe, called a "soil P trap," directly underneath the drain. Put a bucket under this and unscrew the pipe. In newer homes with plastic piping, this can usually be done by hand. However, metal pipes will require a pipe wrench or channel locks to unscrew. Then poke around with the wire coathanger to try to locate the problem. If this fails, call a plumber.

For the child who is fascinated with plumbing, work with them to:

◆ Learn to protect pipes from freezing (if you live in a cold area).
◆ Read a basic book about plumbing.
◆ Observe a professional plumber when one makes a house call to your home.

5. Stopped-up toilets
Chemicals are usually not appropriate here. Get your trusty plunger and place it right on the hole in the bowl. Plunge away until you see some downward water movement. If things are moving, try a test flush, but be prepared to shut off the supply valve if the problem persists. You may try a few plunges before calling a plumber.

6. Running toilets
Teach your child to jiggle the handle. If that doesn't work, take the cover off the back of the toilet and welcome to Toilet Anatomy 101. The jist of a toilet is to control flowing water. You want it to flow (flush) when you need it to, and to rest in the bowl when it is not in use. This is accomplished by a series of balls, wires, and arms in the toilet tank.

The tank ball is the device that plugs the discharge opening at the bottom of the toilet tank. The tank ball may be worn out or chipped, meaning it is unable to properly seal and plug the discharge opening. If this is the case, turn off the main water valve behind the toilet, flush to empty the tank and unscrew the tank ball. Get another one like it from the hardware store, screw it in, turn the water main back on and your problem is solved.

If the tank ball appears not to be frayed or chipped, the problem might be with the wire that lifts the tank ball. It may be bent and thus not directing the tank ball to squarely cover the discharge opening. Examine the wire that is attached to the tank ball directly above it. You may be able to bend it back into shape or remove the old one and replace it.

The float ball is that round ball to the right of the wire and tank ball just described above. The float ball comes into play when the toilet is flushed. Upon flushing, the water level goes down and the float ball descends with it. As the float ball descends, it pulls another wire-type thing with it, called the float arm. The float arm opens the supply valve to refill the toilet with fresh water. It also closes the supply valve when the toilet is done refilling. If the float ball has a hole in it, it won't float, so it won't be able to rise when it is called upon to shut off the supply valve. A new float valve can be purchased at the hardware store and installed.

Finally, the problem might be a bent float arm. This is the wire-type device attached to the float ball. If it is bent, it may keep the float ball from rising, or it may cause the float ball to rise too high. Try straightening this arm or replacing it.

If none of these work, call a plumber. Teach your child about evening, Sunday, and holiday pay and the differences in plumber rates. It is realistic to expect that their rates may double or triple during these times or days. In the interest of saving money, sometimes it is best to ride out the problem until the weekday. We have washed many dishes in the bathtub to avoid a Sunday service call.

7. Caulking

So many things around the house require caulk. It is a tricky substance to work with, and few of us are "born caulkers." It is an on-the-job skill.

Use a caulk remover to remove all old caulk. Scrape and wash thoroughly. I have had good luck with using rubbing alcohol to remove the last bits. Let it dry completely. Then buy squeeze tubes of caulk, as they are easier to control. Use a wet finger to smush the caulk down into the intended area. I have found this is more effective than the little tools they sell.

Some things that might require caulk are tubs and sinks in bathrooms, sinks in kitchens, and sealing around windows. If you want your child to have some experience with this substance, have him caulk some cracks in a wood project he is working on, or caulk an unobtrusive area outside your home.

8. Painting

This a great home project to do with your kids. Involve them in the project from the beginning, from measuring the room to determining the amount of paint needed, to going to buy the paint and supplies. Explain the difference between washable latex paint and enamel. Enamel is not water based and is harder to clean up. It is best for hard-use areas, such as kitchen and the bathroom. One gallon of paint covers 400 square feet of wall space. If you are using two coats, double the amount. Have your child measure the area to be painted and calculate how much paint will be needed. Then don't scrimp on the price. Paint once with good paint, or do it again in a few years with cheap paint. Also, buy good brushes and rollers. Cheap ones fall apart more quickly and often result in a less smooth job.

Show your child how to spread out drop cloth and tape windows, and explain why these steps are necessary. Children find that spackling is fun. It comes premixed and ready to use, and it's quite easy to do with a putty knife. Smoothing over with sandpaper is a satisfying experience for children. When you start painting, let your children use rollers on low areas of the walls with a tiny bit of paint. Or give them a small brush to work in corners.

If you are working with an older child who wants to try a new look in his bedroom, investigate sponge painting or rag painting. After the basic walls have been painted, this can provide an interesting way to decorate, and the project is fun to do along with your child.

9. Hanging pictures
Measure first, then measure again. Use this opportunity to teach your child how to hammer. Also look at the many different types of fasteners available to hang items. A light item might do well with a simple nail or one of the adhesive products now available to hang pictures. A heavier item might require some stronger hardware.

10. Changing light bulbs
Turn off or unplug the light before attempting. Make sure you have the right type of replacement bulb. Many light fixtures have the maximum wattage stamped into the metal bulb receptacle. Don't replace a bulb with more watts than your fixture is equipped to handle. Show your child how to replace the bulb, then check to see if it works.

Stocking the Toolbox

Give your child real tools and supervise them. I now have my own toolbox. My husband is not always home when things go bad, so I have discovered skills I never wanted to learn, and I have appreciated having the tools available to me, organized in my own fashion. We are also building up a supply of real tools for the children.

Tool Rules

1. Make sure your child knows how to use a tool before working with it.
2. Don't allow your child to use power tools without a knowledgeable adult present.
3. Keep all tools out of reach of little ones.
4. Have your child wear goggles to protect his eyes if there are chips or splinters involved.

At a minimum, the toolbox that you will use with your children should include the the following items:

A claw hammer—the hammer with the curved top used for
   extracting nails
screwdrivers—at least a large and small standard screwdriver and
   a large and small Phillips head *(To teach which way threads
   usually screw on and screw off, try saying "rightsy tightsy, leftsy
   loosey.")*
pliers with wire cutters
crescent wrench—adjustable to loosen or tighten bolts
tape measure—the retractable kind in a metal case
sandpaper—rough, medium, and fine
a power drill—for an older child
handsaw—for cutting wood
duct and electrical tape
nails and screws
plunger
good utility knife—for carpet, tile, etc.
staple gun
flashlight

To extend your child's tool tutoring, consider the following:

- Make up a game that asks your child to identify basic tools. Ask them also to show you how to handle the tools properly and care for them.
- With your child, buy or build a basic carpentry kit for making something such as a birdhouse.
- Help your child begin collecting her own set of real tools, as well as devising a suitable method for their storage.
- Let your child assist you as an apprentice as you work on household projects.

There is some wonderful teaching material on the use of tools available from Keepers of the Faith (see appendix resources for chapter 1).

Consider also teaching your older child something about repairing and maintaining autos and appliances. Explain the basic functions of the car engine and show them how to check tire pressure, air filter, and fluid levels. Teach them to use jumper cables to start or recharge a dead battery. Show them how to change a tire in an emergency. You might give your child an unused or broken small appliance to take apart and study. Toasters and radios are good small projects to try. Who knows? Your child may actually find and fix the problem. The U.S. Consumer Information Center is a great source of free or low-cost material about home maintenance and repair. (Send for a free catalog: Consumer Information Center, Pueblo, CO 81009.)

Working Outside the Home in Every Season

While learning to do the work outside, your child can spend a great deal of time with you, learning the flow of the tasks and the use of the tools. Aim to make this a time of great conversation, closeness, and fun.

Learn to care for the yard, sidewalks, and driveway.

Teach your child the following with regard to the lawn:

1. Only mow when the grass is dry.
2. Clean the yard before mowing by removing twigs and trash.
3. Walk the mower in a pattern. (My husband claimed I used to mow as if I were vacuuming the lawn.)
4. Mow as close to obstacles as possible. Trim these places up later.
5. Sweep the sidewalks and remove clumps of clippings.

In the spring do a yard pickup—even the smallest child can

pick up twigs and leaves. Then, as soon as they can distinguish a weed from a flower, your children can do valuable work in the summer yard. In the fall have a fun family time! Remember raking and jumping into leaves? While having fun, your children can be responsible for raking an entire yard. Try putting the leaves into big pumpkin bags, available at many stores in the fall. Or use leaves to stuff a "nice-crow," our family's version of a scarecrow. In the winter, provide each little person with a little shovel so they can enjoy making an important contribution to snow removal.

Learn to garden.

Gardening can be one of the most satisfying tasks to do together. Have your child analyze and chart the sun pattern in your yard. Research which plants or vegetables need sun, and which need shade. Send for catalogs and visit gardening shops. After you have purchased some seeds or plants, read the directions for appropriate planting time and spacing of plants. Give the children total responsibility for watering their plot of the garden.

My friends Sue and Craig, both landscape professionals, say,

> We love yard work and gardening as a whole family. Share the excitement of the first blooming bud or the first bulb to peek through the spring earth. Begin when they are very young—10 to 12 months! Let them touch (gently of course) and let them get dirty—it's fun! We also read fiction (*The Secret Garden*) and nonfiction books on the subject. We gave our children a pot to plant up at three years of age and a plot of garden at six.

Here are some further ideas to encourage your young gardeners:

- Learn the names and functions of garden tools.
- Learn which plants need which types of fertilizer or plant food.
- Plan out a section of the garden for the year. Decide what to plant, how much to plant, when to plant it, whether to use seeds or started plants, and how to care for them.
- Find a book in the library about composting and make or buy a composter for your yard projects.
- Keep a journal each year of your garden projects: What did you plant, and what were the results? How long did the plants take to grow and how did you care for them?
- Buy a few gardening magazines and send for as many gardening catalogs as your mailbox will hold. These are full of ideas and are also great for cutting and pasting.
- Visit a local farm or public garden.

Your county cooperative extension service is a wealth of information on gardening and care of the land. Their materials are usually free or very low-cost. Get some of their publications for your child to study. In our area, this office offers a master gardener class of several weeks duration for adults. In exchange for this excellent training, the student then offers to volunteer a minimal number of hours to assist other gardeners. If these resources are available in your area, check them out!

Even if you're not a handy repair person, remember that the goal is to help your kids enjoy the process of learning how to do things—-which keeps us as parents on the growing edge too. As we face the challenges of maintaining our homes, we are teaching our kids the coping skills they will need to face life.

Life Skills Checklist

❖ Do I have a good attitude about home maintenance and re-pair?

❖ Is my child familiar with the various trades and the type of work they do?

❖ Have I inventoried the repairs I *can* do and shared them with my child, in an age-appropriate fashion?

❖ Is my child familiar with common tools, their functions, and how to use them safely?

❖ Does my child participate in outside chores?

❖ Have I introduced my child to gardening?

CHAPTER 8

Money, Money, Money

Can You Handle It?

❖ Eighth Maxim of Maturity

Much of life involves money. Either we learn to handle it or it will handle us.

❖ Transferable Skills

Ability to set goals and priorities, be self-disciplined; capacity for keeping accurate financial records, managing a budget, establishing and maintaining accounting (accountability) systems; ability to compile financial information, interpret financial reports, monitor cash flow.

As I write this, a popular toy here in the United States is the American Girl Doll® with a price tag of over ninety dollars. Jackets of the national sports teams are must-wear apparel, at about one hundred dollars each. Expensive hand-held computer games and extensive cable television programming are standard fare in most homes. As parents in this kind of culture we need to be wise with our young consumers.

The Bible challenges us to have a clear sense of stewardship with our money and to keep eternal values in view: "So if you have not been trustworthy in handling worldly wealth, who will trust you with true riches?" Jesus asked (Luke 16:11). How we manage our children's financial consuming today will have a tremendous impact on how they manage financially as adults.

How do you view money? In our home, it is payment for our time and a means to buy food, housing, and necessities. We are very clear on the fact that our time is exchanged for money. If we were willing to invest more time, we would have more money. But since we desire to spend time with the children, our money is less plentiful. We seek to avoid acquiring money or things simply to have more money and things. These are the attitudes we try to instill in our own children.

Results of an Overindulgent Culture

My husband describes the present generation as the IDI generation—"I deserve it." He has traced much of this self-centeredness to the parental belief that caring for a child consists primarily of giving in to all of that child's demands and wants, irrespective of any regard for the future outcome of this indulgence. These children cannot help but grow up with the attitude that the universe revolves around them and that they deserve any trinket or big-ticket item that they think they want—regardless of whether they can afford it.

Lest you think we are hopelessly old-fashioned (which we are), we believe that hard times are the norm for life. Being a Christian does not guarantee a problem-free life. Overindulging our children robs them of the opportunity to learn that we must not look for all of life to meet our hopes and expectations. And it robs them of the chance to learn little by little to handle adversity; it leaves them unprepared for facing hard times when they make their inevitable appearance.

In a recent article advising employers about the so-called Generation X young person, the author notes several important characteristics about this group. They are likely to have witnessed more violence, thanks to television, than any other generation in history. They often grew up too fast, usually home alone too often while their parents strove for the American dream. They have less loyalty and commitment to the workplace than previous generations, take longer to make their initial job choices, are likely to be highly computer-literate, often question authority figures because their parents weren't around to tell them what to do, and often have unrealistic and materialistic views. "Whether from watching TV or from being spoiled by their guilt-ridden, seldom home parents or grandparents, X'ers have come to expect a whole lot for nothing. They have a strong propensity for instant gratification, wanting it all and wanting it fast," the author notes. They want the perks of work, without the hassle. "They would like their world to be filled with the same good-looking people, dressed in the latest fashions, with lots of money and prestige, and without having to work too hard."[1]

While this is a heavily negative characterization, there are many positive attributes to these young people as well. They possess good problem-solving skills and want stronger family values for their own families. They are more likely to be entrepreneurs because they are so individualistic. We should be encouraged by these things. Perhaps our children, the children of the generation X'ers, and the generation beyond, will help solve some of society's deep-seated problems.

In order to prepare them for this task, we need to carefully train and mentor them, beginning with an examination of what things are most important in life. Are relationships more important than things? Are toys more important than family? Ask your child, "If Mom or Dad or another family member died, would it be a fellow family member or a new bicycle that would bring you the most comfort?"

Children need to know most of all that the best things in life truly are free: salvation, love, family, time, hugs, doing things together. At the same time, we have a responsibility to teach them to handle money. Bob Barnes tells us that most young people are totally unprepared for the financial reality of independent living. "Because they are unprepared to handle the discipline of finances, finances are handling them. They're being forced to work harder, often at jobs they really don't like, so they can keep up with the spending."[2]

The solution? As hard as it may seem for parents to accept, children need to be given the opportunity to make financial decisions as early as possible. It is better to let them learn, experiment, and make mistakes with small sums than to wait and let them learn when they are immersed in the workforce and confronted with consumerism.

Work with your child to make a scrapbook of photographs or cut-out magazine pictures of all the things money can't buy.

Our world is full of examples of people who handle money poorly. Some believe that winning the lottery would solve all of life's problems. Yet it is fascinating to hear the stories of big winners who get divorced, lose good friends, and get into arguments with family members. In my own life, in my law practice as well as in my own family, it has been disheartening to see families fight over the assets of deceased family members. I have seen firsthand that even the closest family can become estranged over the seductive issue of money.

All of this is to say that knowing about money is important, but having a healthy attitude toward money is paramount. It may begin with our own examination of needs versus wants in our own lives. If we model for our children that there is a clear distinction between needs, which must be met rather quickly, and wants, which can be deferred indefinitely, they will learn to know the difference. By not immediately rushing to supply their wants, we can teach them planning, self-control, and discipline.

Diana Pollard notes that she doesn't allow her daughter to continually buy excess clothing, even if it's on the sale rack. In addition, the two of them volunteer one day a month at a nonprofit organization that supports the persecuted church around the world. Diane notes, "This helps her to see how materialistic we are when there are ones in prison for their faith in Pakistan who need our prayers." Intentional exposure to the suffering of the world will do much to expand your child's worldview—a view in which they are not at the center of the universe.

Teaching Children about Money

You can start to teach young children about money by teaching them to recognize coins and bills. Use real money so the children can have a real experience. Have them sort a pile of coins, then progress to a game where they show you equivalencies—a quarter is equal to two dimes and a nickel, etc.

Try playing store. Collect some empty grocery items, things like milk cartons, detergent bottles, cereal and pasta boxes, and put prices on them. A plastic grocery cart will make this play extra fun. Play candy store with real money and real candy and have the children count up the totals for candy and "pay" with real coins. Even my older children love this activity. They have devised their own scanner and ATM machine for their grocery store. You might try giving your older children a store flyer and having them find the price of bananas, a gallon of milk, ice cream, and tomatoes. Have them assemble a shopping list for one week's worth of food.

Here are some other fun money activities:

- ◆ Make or purchase flash cards with pictures of coins on one side, their names on the other. Make cards for various combinations of coins, and have your child practice identifying coins and quantities.
- ◆ To familiarize your young child with possible prices of items, use index cards to list an item on one card and its price on another. Mix up the cards, and let your child match them. Some possible items are:

car	$20,000.00
pencil	$0.25
half gallon ice cream	$4.00
candy bar	$0.75
bar of soap	$1.50
couch	$500.00
pair of pants	$25.00
t-shirt	$10.00

Making Allowances

There are many different approaches to children's allowance. Some parents are adverse to the idea, while others embrace it as an inexpensive way to teach money management. If you are considering an allowance, three things must be resolved: How young? How much? What for?

Some parents argue that an allowance amounts to paying children to do their chores. Another view might look like this: Everyone in a family makes a contribution. Those who earn wages make a financial contribution. Each family member has chores to perform and can share in the family finances, via allowances, because they have shared in the family work.

Larry Burkett and Rick Osborne share this attitude about allowance: "The family is a community: everyone in the family shares in the opportunities, responsibilities, rewards, and income of that community."[3] In other words, the income that is earned in a family is for the household and its members. Doing the jobs of the household serves everyone in the home, so all family members are responsible not just for cleaning up after themselves but for working for the well-being of everyone in the home. The family benefits when everyone works and does chores. Payment of money is a share in the monetary system of the family. It is not tied to the chores, although it may be contingent on performance of the chores. The point is that the children are doing the work as their service to the family, not merely to receive money. When the family benefits from everyone's labor, everyone should have a share in the wealth of the family.

Some families provide a means for children to earn money above and beyond their weekly allowance. One author suggests,

> Children should receive a weekly allowance. And they must be required to do weekly chores. The two aren't connected. But there's nothing wrong with having an extra job list that gives a child an opportunity to make a little

extra money. The extra job list is a list of tasks that are beyond the scope of the child's chores. The child can get paid for doing them. Each job pays a certain amount. This is a list the child can see and decide which jobs to do in order to make extra money.[4]

Such a plan gives children some control over the ways they contribute.

The best time to begin allowances is around age five or six. Prior to this you will spend more time picking the coins up off the floor than anything else. Allowance should begin when kids recognize that coins are a medium of exchange, not just something to play with. After saving and tithing, let your children make decisions about the money. If there are conditions to that freedom, spell them out. In our house, one of the conditions is that the children are not allowed to buy makeup, and any music purchases must be cleared by Mom or Dad. Otherwise, if they buy a cheap toy with their own money and it breaks on the way home, they can learn from the experience. Don't forget that library overdue fines and replacement costs of things that are broken or lost come from the child's allowance.

With an interesting twist on "matching funds," Bob Barnes has come up with a creative approach to vacations and children's spending money. He offers to "match" whatever the children have saved up until that point—money which the child can then spend on vacation.[5] My husband recalls that when he was a child, his parents would pay the program fee for Christian summer camp, but he was required to save the money he would want for spending money while at camp. These are both great ideas to help your children see that a vacation is really a reward for work, not just an expected holiday falling in their laps.

Try these ideas to increase your children's spending smarts:

◆ Some parents pay their children to practice their musical instruments, a small amount for each half hour of practice. Out of those sums, along with other monies earned, the children buy much of their own clothing and other wanted items.[6]

◆ Have your child keep a record of everything he spends for a month. Then have him brainstorm about what he would do if he had one hundred dollars. How long would it take for him to save one hundred dollars? Highlight the difference in speed with which money can be spent against the time it takes to earn it.

◆ Are your children constantly nagging you for money for vending machines when you take them to the store? Try making a rule that they have to use their own money. This will usually prevent their leaving money around the house on the floor. You can also hope that after purchasing plastic jewelry a few times from a vending machine with their own money only to see it broken within the hour, they will become dissuaded from wasting their money in vending machines again.

In the book *Teaching Your Child about Money,* Chris Snyder says that the key to using allowances for teaching money management is for the parents to stay out of it. "Once the parameters have been established—what's covered, what's not—the children must make their own decisions and learn from their own mistakes. Give advice if it's asked for, and pursue . . . consumer education . . . but refrain from making their choices for them."[7] It is when they make their own choices, and suffer consequences from them, that they really learn about money. Allowances can be a training ground for your children to practice small-scale planning, control, and feedback.

Tithing

If we believe "the earth is the Lord's, and everything in it," as it says in Psalm 24:1, then we are the stewards of what God has given us. We don't really own anything but are mere caretakers of his blessings. The Bible's teaching on tithing—giving a portion of your money back to God—is clear and unambiguous:

> "Honor the Lord with your wealth, with the firstfruits of all your crops; then your barns will be filled to overflowing, and your vats will brim over with new wine." (Proverbs 3:9-10)

> "Bring the whole tithe into the storehouse, that there may be food in my house. Test me in this," says the Lord Almighty, "and see if I will not throw open the floodgates of heaven and pour out so much blessing that you will not have room enough for it." (Malachi 3:10)

As soon as children begin to handle money, they should begin to tithe. You can set aside a special bank compartment or jar for their tithe. (More on this later.) Perhaps your church can supply you with offering envelopes, even for young children, which help make tithing a reality.

Merely handing over a part of their money to church may seem unsatisfying to your children. Impress upon them that not only are they commanded to do this but also that God will bless their giving. Proverbs 11:24-25 says, "One man gives freely, yet gains even more; another withholds unduly, but comes to poverty. A generous man will prosper; he who refreshes others will himself be refreshed."

If we really believe our material possessions belong to God, then we should thank him when he supplies our needs. Dean and Grace Merrill suggest holding dedication ceremonies when the family acquires a major new possession:

> This can be as simple as a five-minute time of prayer or as elaborate as a full evening with invited guests. . . . In each case, the prayers went something like this: "Father, we thank you for providing this. We're very happy to have it, but we acknowledge that it really belongs to you. We intend to use it for your purposes whenever we can. Help us

not to abuse it. We want to have it always ready for your call. Again, we thank you, in Jesus' name. Amen."[8]

We seek to model for our children our trust in God to meet our needs. So many times we have needed an answer to prayer or needed a particular item for our home or for the children, and we have prayed about it as a family and seen God move to supply that need for us. These memories are great reminders for all of us when we are facing a need or lack in the present.

Counting the Cost of Things

No one could argue that our culture is built on making consumers of children as early as possible. One author notes,

> Kids these days, especially teenagers, have more income to spend on non-necessities than their parents. An American study . . . showed that teenagers, who make up only a tenth of the population, buy a quarter of all clothing, cosmetics, and stereo equipment. Younger children, of course, are big consumers of candy and toys, spending their parents' money as well as their own. Television may be the largest single information source for kids. The average child in North America has watched 350,000 TV commercials by the end of high school.[9]

We can cut our children off from television, or we can use its commercialism to teach them about comparison shopping. Talk in your family about how advertisers intentionally target specific groups of consumers with marketing techniques. Have your children identify whether a particular commercial is aimed at boys or girls, at adults or children. If the product is making a claim, ask your children if that claim is reasonable. This can teach them to avoid falling prey to advertiser's wiles.

Don't neglect using your local newspaper in your life skills curriculum. It is a great source of all kinds of information about advertising, jobs, comparison shopping, housing, cloth-

Study television ads for one evening. For each commercial viewed, write down answers to the following questions:

❖ What was the product?
❖ Was the ad directed to men or women, children or adults?
❖ To what need was the advertiser attempting to appeal?
  The need to be like others—conformity.
  The need to be better than others—superiority.
  The need to be attractive to the opposite sex.
  The need to have what others have—covetousness.
❖ Was deceit, either subtle or blatant, used by the advertiser?

ing, and food costs. Have your child identify an item he wants to buy, such as a personal stereo system or a bicycle. He then should take these steps: Write down the specific item and its features; check the newspaper ads and go to several stores to check prices; look at what it sells for in catalogs. The idea is to teach them to try to find the best deal rather than just rushing out to buy the item. Older children can do this exercise with the purchase of a car. You might engage them in the family research for the purchase of a new vehicle, or have them price and compare their fantasy car.

Teach your children the importance of always reading the fine print. There are hosts of ads now for free cellular phones, or computers for fifty dollars. These types of deals usually involve committing to substantial service contracts. Study these offers and compare them with the outright purchase of a phone or computer and then finding the best deal for air time or Internet service. When something says it is free, it usually isn't. Or if something is too good to be true, it probably isn't true. Nothing is really free. (Unless it is a kitten.)

Help your children learn the differences between stores. Fancy stores usually charge higher prices, especially for clothing. Discount stores are often a better buy but offer less sophisticated wardrobe choices. Resale shops and consignment boutiques are often great sources of wardrobe items for young people.

Becoming Familiar with Wages

Where does the money come from? Who makes what? Young children have no clue about these matters, and older children need to learn the realities about wages and taxes as well. Before you give your children a negative attitude toward taxes, remind them and yourself that we live in a country with some of the lowest tax rates in the world and our level of government services shines in comparison to other nations. This is what we pay for when we pay taxes: police, fire, Social Security, schools, parks, and more.

When your child is old enough, he or she can do odd jobs around home for money. Some of the more popular pursuits are a having a lemonade stand, babysitting, serving as mother's helper, snow shoveling, leaf raking, and walking younger children to school. A young man in our neighborhood approached me recently about cutting our lawn. He used words like, "Please," "Ma'am," and "Thank you," plus he did a great job on the lawn. We normally prefer to do this job ourselves, but his services were offered in the midst of a month-long heat spell, and we indulged ourselves by having him tend the lawn for several weeks. This boy is about eleven, but I see good things in his future because he works hard and has a great attitude.

Children can also make money plant sitting, pet sitting, house sitting (also involves collecting the mail and papers), walking dogs, pulling weeds, raking leaves, having a paper route, delivering handbills, helping with a harvest, having a garage sale, tutoring or coaching a younger child, arranging children's parties, car washing, having a delivery service, or offering to be a general rent-a-kid to do anything required of them, such as cleaning out attics or garages.

In our old neighborhood, several girls circulated a flyer about a Kid's Club they were organizing for the summer. They intended to offer their services as babysitters at their home; parents could drop their children off for a few hours of play. This babysitter's club offered the added security of knowing the girls' parents would be present during Kid's Club.

Children who learn to work hard are preparing to do well in life. Proverbs 10:4-5 says, "Lazy hands make a man poor, but diligent hands bring wealth. He who gathers crops in summer is a wise son, but he who sleeps during harvest is a disgraceful son." But what about the child who works too hard, neglecting other aspects of life, such as schoolwork? If a part-time job is too taxing and schoolwork starts to suffer, stop the job first. Also be wary of the dangers of raising a workaholic— even a teenager needs time to play and reflect. Here is an area that calls out for parental involvement. Help your children identify priorities with your guidance.

With your child, try these ideas as they become interested in making money:

- List ten services from your local phone book. Are any of them ones that a young person could provide to make extra money?
- Read newspaper ads for employment. Get an idea of the types of jobs that are plentiful and what wages are prevalent.
- Go to a department store or a fast food outlet to get a job application your child can fill out as practice. Office supply stores sell stacks of them as well.

Saving and Checks

The habit of saving is the habit of delaying gratification. It is the setting aside of money today to meet needs or wants of tomorrow. In our "me first"and "I want it now" society, saving is a critical skill to develop. According to the American Bankers Association Education Foundation, personal savings have fallen steadily, decreasing about 75 percent in the last twenty years. At the same time, 73 percent of teen students report that they want to learn more about money matters, but only 10 percent say they learn about money management in school.[10] Who will teach them? We have the primary responsibility.

Children may have a hard time understanding the concept of a bank or a checking account. Deborah Carroll offers this suggestion:

> A good way to explain this is to try this illustration. The next time you give an allowance, set aside that amount in a container that serves as a bank. Write the amount on a piece of paper. Let your child keep the paper, and when he needs the money, he can trade in the paper for that amount, which is waiting in the bank. Your child will see that the money in the bank is no longer there after the check is presented, but that the paper still exists. The paper is just not worth anything after the money is taken from the account.[11]

You will also want to explain that a bank is like a store that deals in money. The bank takes in deposits from suppliers, those people who have accounts. Then it lends that money to borrowers. The bank pays interest to depositors and charges interest to borrowers. Point out that people save for many reasons. They may have future goals, like a college education. They may be planning future purchases, like a new home. Most people also save for emergencies, like illness or disability.

For purposes of teaching the young child about money, set up goals for long-term savings, such as paying for a summer camp next year, and short-term savings, things they want in the near future, like a new toy. Provide a way for them to divide their earnings or allowance into different categories. For example, their tithe could be 10 percent, their long-term savings could be 30 percent, their short-term savings could be 30 percent, and everyday spending could be 30 percent. Christian Financial Concepts sells an adorable bank with three compartments—a church, a bank, and a store. The child can allocate money into these three categories. (See appendix for information about Christian Financial Concepts.)

Before we purchased the banks mentioned above, we made our own three-compartment bank, using toilet tissue rolls. We glued them onto a flat surface, then labeled and decorated the compartments. Some families use jars for each area of savings, or paper envelopes. Another system uses plastic zipper bags designated for certain savings. This has the advantage of enabling your child to actually see the money as it accumulates.

What about those occasional large gifts your child may receive? Neal Godfrey uses these general rules with his kids: "Gifts of money under $20 go into their free money budget; between $21 and $50, half goes into savings and the other half into spending. Anything over $50 (which is rare), we work out a percentage where the bulk goes into saving, and some is available to the child."[12] You need to decide where to save larger amounts of money. As you shop for a bank with your child, you will be able to point out the different types of banks to your older children. A commercial bank is owned by stockholders and offers services to the public, both individuals and businesses. A credit union is owned by the depositors, or shareholders, and profits are shared among them. It generally provides comparable services to those of a commercial bank.

Before your child opens up his savings account, he needs to ask these questions:

- ◆ What are the interest rates offered?
- ◆ Is compounding interest paid?
- ◆ Are depositors' funds insured?

You can explain interest this way: Simple interest is figured only on the principal—the $100.00 you deposited to open your account. Banks pay compound interest. That means that at the end of a month, the bank pays the share of interest earned so far. If it is 12 percent (an outrageously high rate for a savings account, but an easy rate to explain mathematically), the bank pays one-twelfth of the 12 percent, or 1 percent. If your deposit is $100.00, then one twelfth of 12 percent is 1 percent, or $1.00. So, at the end of that first month, you would have $101.00, and in the next month, the interest would be computed on $101.00. In the second month, the starting balance would be $101.00. One-twelfth of the rate would be paid again, or 1 percent. The interest for the second month would be $1.01, and when added to the beginning balance would leave an ending balance of $102.01. So at the end of one year, the balance of your account is $112.68, representing the $12.68 in interest you received. This is called the yield, the amount of money your investment produced in one year.

You should explain the difference between regular savings and time deposits. Time deposits pay higher interest but may not allow depositors immediate access to their money. Regular savings pay less interest but allow money to be withdrawn more easily.

When you take your child to open a savings account, make sure that she knows the proper deposit amount required for a new account and that she brings her Social Security card and birth certificate to the bank. Give your child a lesson in account records. Show her how to fill out deposit slips and withdrawal slips. Your older child will have to understand ATMs and computer banking. At one point, my children believed that every machine gave money. They explained that all they had to do was ask and the machine would spew forth cash. We explained how the money gets there and the rules for obtaining money from a machine.

In addition to savings, teach your older children about checking accounts. Explain to your child that a checking account is a service offered by a bank to enable you to pay bills. Many children are not aware that there must first be money on deposit before checks can be written. Essentially, a check is the way you give the bank written permission to withdraw money from your account and give it to someone else. Checks save consumers time, they can be mailed, they provide a measure of safety, and they make bill paying easier.

As preparation for opening a checking account, give your child pretend checks and a register. Show how to write checks and keep the register. Show him your own bank statements and have him help balance the checkbook. Give him his own passbook statements to track earnings. Before opening their first checking account, your children need to understand minimum balances, free checking, and interest paying checking. They will need to know how to:

- Write a check.
- Write a check for cash.
- Endorse a check.
- Understand and avoid overdraft fees.
- Balance an account.

Also explain money orders. These can be used for occasional withdrawals from your savings account or for irregular purchases, and they are usually bought at a post office or currency exchange.

Investing

Help your children understand that investing money is putting it to work with the anticipation that it will earn a greater return than a traditional savings account. Here are some comparisons between the two:

Savings	Investments
Safe, insured, at agreed upon interest rate	May lose profit or initial investment
Can have access to money easily, except for longer-term savings	May tie up money, like real estate or jewels; stocks, mutual funds, and bonds are easier to access
Only earn agreed-upon profit or interest	Potential for greater profits or earnings

Understand how stocks, bonds, and mutual funds work.

A company sells shares to raise money for its business. Owning the shares is owning part of a company. If there are many shares issued, each share represents only a tiny percentage of ownership. Many stocks are publicly traded in a market such as the New York Stock Exchange. When stock prices rise, the individuals who have purchased the stocks make money, not the company. The money acquired from an increase in stock prices is distributed to the stockholders in the form of dividends. If stock prices fall, the investor loses money in that the value of the stock purchased decreases.

When my husband was a child, his father wanted to develop his interest in investing, so he bought him a few shares of stock. Mark watched it and graphed it each day. While doing so, he learned how the stock market and investments were positively and negatively influenced by the economy.

Explain to your child the psychology of the marketplace. It works on the law of supply and demand. When lots of people are excited about a particular company and buy its stock, the stock value goes up. As lots of people are buying the stock, others might be deciding to take their profits, so they sell off, and the market goes down. Show your child how to read the stock quotes in the newspaper. EduStock is a web site offering tutorials on the stock market and how it works: http://www.think quest.org.

A bond is a "loan" to a business or the government. It is essentially an "IOU" from the issuer. Bonds are issued with a promise to pay a set rate of interest and to repay your initial investment, or principal, in a set period of time. They are priced differently than stocks. Usually they are issued in a face value amount, like one hundred or one thousand dollars.

A mutual fund pools the money of many investors and invests it in a variety of things. The fund is managed by a fund manager. This allows smaller investors to trade in the markets and enjoy the profits which can be made in the market. Money markets can offer funds which trade in general stocks, bonds, international funds, and more. Many mutual funds offer check writing privileges, allowing the investors easy access to their money.

> Working with a few friends, have your older child initiate a pretend investment club. Each child starts out with an assumed balance of one thousand dollars in an investment account. The child must select investments, track and chart them weekly, then get together with the other "investors" to discuss their performance record.

Establishing Budgets

Since a budget is a plan for what to do with money, even a child can have a budget. As your children's knowledge and awareness increases, you might also want to increase their allowance and have them pay for their own lunches, club fees, school supplies, and trips, in addition to their regular savings and tithing. Bob Barnes cautions,

> Before your teen leaves home, make sure that he or she has spent a period of time being totally responsible for a budget. Ideally, this can take place at the start of the junior year of high school. This is a time when a budget can be set up and reviewed for all the teen's needs, from cosmetics to clothes to the after-church fast-food meals with the youth group. Once the monthly needs of the teen have been evaluated, including things such as contact lens cleaner that Mom usually purchases at the store, then it's time for the teen to live within a budget.[13]

He suggests setting up six or seven envelopes labeled for the various needs, such as church activities, cosmetics and toiletries, friends' and family members' birthdays, clothes, tithe.

Having a budget will give your child a regular spending plan to help her see where her money goes, control her spending to fit her income, and save for things she needs and wants.

In a budget, there are fixed expenses, things that stay the same from month to month—rent or mortgage payments, car payments, insurance premiums. Then there are variable expenses such as food, clothing, and medical expenses. Your child might find it interesting and instructive to learn what the average family spends in percentage of income on these categories: housing—31 percent; transportation—14 percent; food—17 percent; other—38 percent. Barbara Smith, a financial planner and stockbroker, says she has seen clients succeed with this formula: "50 percent spending money, 20 percent for short-term savings, 20 percent for long-term savings and 10 percent for charity."[14]

Try these activities to introduce your child to managing money:

- Assume a two thousand dollars per month income. Have your child figure out a budget.
- Give your younger child food ads and a budget of fifty dollars. Have him plan the family food menu for the week.
- Play the Bill-Paying game. Using a dozen envelopes and Monopoly money, count out an average salary. Then mark each envelope for each category of expense, such as $53 for the phone and $260 for the Visa card. See how far the salary goes in meeting expenses.[15]
- Have your children make a list of all the things they can do to conserve their own money. What items could they do without?
- Ask your children to make a list of the ways that the family, as a whole, can save money.

Understanding Insurance

Explain to your child that insurance is a way to share the risks of life with others. Policies are available to insure your health, your life, your home, your personal property, or your income. Early on, make them aware that this is an area where they want to deal with a well-established company. Children should know that some companies scam buyers, sell them products they don't need, and charge extremely high premiums for a long period. At times unscrupulous salespersons also attempt to prey on people's emotions and paint wild catastrophes of personal illness and grave financial circumstances in order to make a sale. Inform your children that every state has an insurance commission that they can check with for complaints and the viability of the company.

Social security is a form of government insurance that all taxpayers support with their taxes. It pays retired persons a retirement income and provides health insurance in the form of Medicaid and Medicare. Medicaid is government health insurance available for people with low income. Medicare is government health insurance available to all persons after retirement age.

Private health insurance comes in a variety of forms. Many employers provide health insurance as an employee benefit. Some people must purchase an individual policy, often at great expense. Health insurance is enormously complex. As an introductory matter, teach your child to look for the following in health insurance coverage:

- Does it cover all accidents or illnesses, including cancer, and pregnancy?
- Does it pay the total bill for all services received, or only a flat fee?
- What, if any, is the deductible amount?
- Is there a waiting period before certain illnesses are covered? (Pre-existing conditions?)
- What is the upper limit on expenses the company will pay?

Supplemental health insurance is also available, which may

pick up expenses where the primary health insurance company left off.

Talk to your child about life insurance. What is it and who needs it? It was designed to protect your family if you die by replacing your income. People with children need life insurance the most. If the breadwinner in your family passed away, life insurance would provide living expenses for your family. This is an area in which most people are underinsured.

Have your older child research and prepare a report on these types of insurance:
- ❖ Term life
- ❖ Whole life
- ❖ Credit life
- ❖ Mortgage insurance
- ❖ Group life insurance

Property insurance may be purchased for a car, a home, or personal property. In most states, liability insurance is required for automobiles. It pays for the damage you may do to others with your car. Comprehensive coverage pays the damage to others and the damage to your own vehicle. If your child is approaching driving age, have him shop for automobile insurance, checking with several companies to get their rates for young drivers. Discuss why the rates are higher, and talk with your child about how he intends to pay for his insurance.

Home insurance covers damage or destruction of a house, replaces items taken in a theft from a house, and provides medical coverage for injuries sustained by others while on your property. Renters insurance covers theft or destruction of belongings while you are renting an apartment or house.

There are various ways for older teens to learn more about money management in the real world (see the appendix for further ideas). But for starters, keeping a spending diary might be a valuable exercise for a child of any age. Have your children track their income and expenses in a format such as the chart shown on the next page.

Buying on Credit and Establishing Credit

There are three ways for young people to establish credit. They can get a credit card with a low credit limit, such as five hundred dollars, and pay it scrupulously each month. They can pay back their student loans in a timely fashion, or they can have someone co-sign for them.

Of course, there are many opportunities to buy now and pay later in our society. Your child needs to know the costs and benefits of such a practice and you need to analyze with him under what conditions it may be wise to use credit, and when it may be wiser to delay or decide against a certain purchase.

Practice shopping for credit. Make a chart of credit card terms. In one column, list the annual fee, if any. In the next, list the minimum payment. Next list the annual percentage rate (APR) and the credit limit. What do these terms mean? The annual fee is a charge you are assessed once a year to have a credit card. The annual percentage rate is the annual interest rate that the card issuer charges on the unpaid balance of the card. The minimum payment is the smallest amount you can pay each month, and the credit limit is the maximum amount you are allowed to have charged. Here are some simple examples:

Annual Fee	Minimum Payment	APR	Credit Limit
$20	2% of bal., min. $15	12%	$2,000
$40	2% of bal., min. $20	16%	$6,000
None	1/30th of bal., min. $20	12.5%	$1,000
$50	1/25th of bal., min. $30	12%	$2,500

A Spending Diary Chart

Weekly Earnings

Allowance _____
Gifts _____
Earnings _____
Other _____
Total _____

Weekly Spending

	Tithe	Snacks	Books/Music	Gifts	Toys	Other	Total
Sunday							
Monday							
Tuesday							
Wednesday							
Thursday							
Friday							

As you discuss the above examples, have your children do some calculations. While no annual fee sounds appealing, could they get a better interest rate while paying an annual fee? Other topics to address are transaction fees (fees paid for cash advances, late payments, or charging over credit limit), grace periods (the length of time you have to pay the bill before interest is assessed, usually twenty-five days), and the method of calculating finance charges (most companies use the average daily balance to compute charges).

In his book, *Ready for Responsibility*, Bob Barnes recommends giving your children experience with the use of a credit card while they are still living at home.

> This is a great opportunity for the senior year of high school. A credit card established with the lowest limit your local bank will allow is the way to begin. It's important to teach a teen that the purpose of this card is only for financial convenience. . . . The month the bill comes in and the balance can't be paid, . . . the card is taken away by the parent, to be returned only when the balance is paid in full.[16]

Because it is the credit card that gets most people into trouble, it is smart for your children to experiment with this while they are still under your control and while you can guide them in the wise use of credit.

Have your child research Bible passages that deal with borrowing and lending money.

Financial planner Barbara Smith recommends sitting down with teenagers for "the debt talk" before they leave for college. Remarking on the fact that college kids are bombarded with preapproved credit card offers, she says, "Many kids use them freely and accumulate huge debts because they don't understand how the interest adds up. This leaves a black mark that stays on their credit history for years."[17]

What about loans? Discuss these examples with your child to instruct them in this area of finance:

◆ When buying a car, two people each financed $10,000. Both got an interest rate of 8 percent. Jack's monthly payment was $203, while Jill's was $313. Why? The answer has to do with terms of loans. A larger payment will allow the consumer to pay off the debt in a shorter time. Jill will actually "own" her car more quickly.

◆ Clare is buying a computer for $1,700 and a printer for $300. She checks two stores, each of which offer financing. The first store is offering 0 percent financing for 2 years. The second store charges 10 percent for financing but will throw in the printer for free. Clare's payments at the second store would be $78.50. What are the payments at the first store? Which is the better deal? Payments at the first store would be $83, or $2000 divided by 24 months. The second store is offering the better deal in this case.

These are examples of simple loans, but be sure to explain to your children about installment loans and compound interest. Installment loans are loans paid off a bit at a time. For example, if they borrow $100 at 12 percent interest, they would pay $1 in interest, plus a part of the principal each month. The next month, the interest would be calculated on the lowered balance. It is easier to understand this if you think of it as the reverse process of what happens with your savings account. Compound interest is more expensive and is what most credit cards assess. If you make the minimum payment on a credit card, any unpaid interest is added to your balance, so you are paying interest on what you borrowed, plus you are paying interest on the interest.

Credit records will play an important role in your child's future. When she is applying for a job, some employers will check her credit history to get an idea of her responsibility and trustworthiness. This is another reason to handle the issue of credit very carefully. There are three principal credit reporting agencies: Equifax, 800-685-1111; Experian, 800-682-7654; and Trans Union, 800-645-1533). Your older children may want to check with one of these to see if they have a credit report established and to ensure that the information is accurate.

If your child is denied credit, she may receive a free copy of her credit report. Otherwise, a small fee is charged to review the report. When she checks the report, she should make sure that all the accounts listed are hers, are accurate, and are not listed more than one time. Have her check all the personal information contained as well, including correct name, address, and Social Security number.

Can't Buy Me Love

Have you caught yourself saying to your child: "Now, Danny, you be good and I'll buy you candy or a toy or a book." I've done it under all sorts of circumstances—at the store, when we're all tired; at a concert, when I want to finish enjoying the music; at Grandma's, when I don't want the children to show off their latest potty talk. I confess I've done it, and I regret it, because of what it says to my children.

This practice actually is a dangerous dance with materialism and, if used to extreme, can lead to future manipulation by children. They should behave under all circumstances because that is what is expected of them, without a monetary or other reward involved. Imagine the smarter-than-average kid who figures this out and intentionally acts out in certain circumstances, thinking he can excise some treat or favor from Mom and Dad. This practice can create a materialistic monster!

Our own kids are far too materialistic. But then, so are we. We have a modest life, but we want things, and we think we

191

need things. I think I need new books, new clothes, new gadgets, whatever captures my fancy. My kids see this, and they think they need electronic pets to care for—items that are distracting, useless, and certainly not a necessity. My children don't need an electronic toy to take care of. I have plenty of work for them to do helping me take care of all the other children!

In her own bid at preschool materialism, my four year old wanted "a Barbie car with a phone in it" last Christmas. I priced one, out of curiosity, and found it was $214. A four year old does not need this! Yet, I'm convinced that my spiritual life would be better if I had a new Bible—maybe with a nice hunter green leather binding on it. What does that say to my kids?

Tragically, the consequences of buying good behavior with material rewards do not stop at increasing materialism in our children. They cut into the whole idea of unconditional love of a parent for a child. Parents love their children no matter what. So how do we explain the attitude that says, If you are good, you'll get rewarded. If you've been a good girl, Santa will bring you the Barbie car. If you have behaved, you will be shown a conditional love by being rewarded with a material thing which can't make you happy, and which may only cause you frustration in the long run because then you will always want the next thing that you think will make you happy. This is unconditional love?

Our heavenly Parent doesn't keep lists and check them twice to find out if we're naughty or nice. God knows. He is the omniscient One—not Santa. The Bible says that when we give our lives to God that the blood of his Son washes our hearts as white as snow. That's whether we've been naughty or nice. It doesn't matter. We can all come to him and be loved unconditionally. His love is not based on whether we've been cleaning our room all year.

Teaching the Value of Serving and Giving

So, what can we do in our family priorities, including celebrations at Christmas and all through the year, to take the focus off of getting things for ourselves, and keep it on Christ—the ultimate giver, the servant who gave everything for us? Of all the skills I discuss in this book, in my opinion this is the greatest one we can teach that will create the most powerful legacy for our children: We are all here to model Christ, to be servants to one another. The Bible tells us to serve one another in love.

My marriage was fraught with power struggles until we both decided that we had to have a servant's heart toward each other. We had so many conflicts about whose career was going to come first, whose needs were going to be met first, who was going to get to do things. It was extremely destructive. My side of the story is that I changed. I submitted to my husband. I purposed in my heart to love and support him and to put my needs second. And you know what happened? It didn't happen over night, but he demonstrates a servant's heart toward me and the children now. He's not perfect, but I know now that he places his God first, his family next, and his work after that. It's evident by how he lives his life and spends his time. Now we serve each other, not in scorekeeping or out of an obligation owed. We serve each other in love.

Where do we learn that from? Not from our culture. Our culture reinforces me-first, grab-for-the-gusto, get-what-you-can, forget-the-other-guy. We learn the better way from the example of Jesus. If we could give our kids a verse for Christmas and for all the seasons of the year, it would be Philippians 2:4: "Each of you should look not only to your own interests, but also to the interests of others."

How can we help our kids look to the interests of others, amidst all the muck and materialism of our society? Here are some ideas:

1. Think long and hard about the Santa stuff while your kids are still young.
My oldest child began to figure out that Santa was an imaginary character at the same time that I became convicted about

not celebrating Santa at all at Christmas. It's an interesting clash of ideologies at this point, but if we could do it all over again, we would present Santa as an historical image of giving. Is there any wisdom in focusing on Santa at Christmas, instead of on Jesus Christ?

2. Be careful about catalogs.
My kids eagerly wait for the toy catalog to come in the mail, just as many of us may have waited for the *Sears Big Book*. They will look through it and cut out what they want. It feeds their materialistic mentality in the same way that curriculum catalogs and book catalogs feed mine. If they don't *see* a lot of the stuff out there competing for their attention, they won't think that they want it. When children's catalogs arrive in the mail, pitch them. Your children won't be missing a single thing.

3. Think about a giving project that you can do as a family this year.
We went to a playgroup at the convalescent center for a while. The residents would come to a room and watch our kids play and interact with them. My oldest still talks about the looks of joy on the faces of these ladies who would just touch their hands. Other giving projects might include stocking food baskets through your church or local food pantry, or buying holiday gifts for the needy through social service organizations. Watch your local newspapers around the holidays. There are always opportunities to give and help. Such efforts are a great way to show your children that giving brings blessings to the giver as well.

4. Model the joy of giving for your children.
Modeling is the strongest, most lasting method of teaching. Let your children know you tithe, in a positive, not haughty, way. Let them help you bundle up clothes to give away. Let them choose toys to give away to your church nursery, to local toy drives. Most importantly, let them see you serving, cheerfully and out of love, without grumbling or complaining— serving them, each other, your church, and friends, neighbors, and strangers in need.

194

Our church has tried some wonderful projects to help our children experience the joy of giving. They have had the children bring in small toys or toiletry items for missions children. They have brought in spare change to help finance the building of a playground in another country. When your church presents these minimal-effort types of opportunities, make a big deal out of them with your children. When these small sacrifices are seen as significant, then your children will be less afraid to make larger sacrifices.

For the past few years, we have modified our family Christmas gift giving. We still buy things for the children, but instead of buying a craft item for every aunt and uncle on the planet (and there are many!) we have given a large gift to our adoption agency, Bethany Christian Services, and presented the relatives with tasteful cards indicating that the gift had been made in their name. As a family, we have found this much more satisfying than the last-minute rush for gifts.

Handling Family Finances: To Tell All or Not

Larry Burkett says, "It's important to let our kids know about, see the workings of, and get involved in family and household finances."[18] In my time growing up, money and sex were taboo items. Neither we kids nor our parents talked about either. Such an approach is unhealthy because, in essence, it denies children critical life skills and sets them up for failure later in their teenage and adult lives.

Avoiding family discussion of finances is cheating your children out of marriage preparation. Many marriages dissolve over money issues, and personal bankruptcies are at an all-time high. Children need to be critically and knowledgeably aware of the cost of living. I don't think we need to share every single bill or check stub with them, although some families do make bill paying a family affair.

Children also need to be aware of the importance of wills. They don't need to know specific details in a will, but they should know they will be cared for and what will generally happen to them if you die. Older children may want more details. Also talk to them about your life insurance coverage and where important family records are located.

In closing, either money will manage us or we will manage money. The skills needed to set financial goals and priorities and to manage a budget are teachable over time. Enjoy the process of learning about money issues with your kids, so they will learn to handle money well.

Life Skills Checklist

❖ Have you studied biblical concepts of money and finance with your child?

❖ Can your young child identify money, count money, make money transactions?

❖ Have you developed an allowance system?

❖ Is your child aware of the cost of things? Have you done comparison shopping with your child?

❖ Does your child understand the concept of wages and earnings?

❖ Have you developed a savings/spending/tithing plan? Do you have your child consistently tithe?

❖ Have your older children studied the cost of living independently?

❖ Have you opened a savings or checking account?

❖ Can your children write a check, endorse a check, keep a checkbook balanced, and stop payment on a check? Do they know how to avoid and handle a bounced check?

❖ Does your child have a budget? Do you have a proposed budget to play with?

❖ Have you taught your child about the cost of credit?

❖ Does your child appreciate the value of giving?

❖ Have you and your spouse resolved how much family financial information you will share with your child?

CHAPTER 9

Healthy Habits

Self-Care Skills for Your One and Only Body

❖ Ninth Maxim of Maturity

Each of us has only one body. We have to take care of it.

❖ Transferable Skills

Capacity for self-discipline and self-awareness; ability to keep impulses under control; ability to make changes in lifestyle for health.

Our bodies are wonderful creations and it is important to treat them well. As our children grow, we need to help them learn ways to stay healthy and to prepare them for the critical, life-changing physiological changes ahead called *puberty*—a word dreaded by many parents. I believe the greater ease with which we as parents deal with our own bodies, reproduction, and growing older, the more comfortable our children will feel when faced with these matters.

But how do we discuss these sometimes awkward topics? Sometimes in quiet moments with my children, I will bring up some feeling or experience from when I was their age. I might say, "You know, when I was nine, I was really worried because I had to wear glasses and I thought everyone would make fun of me." The wide-eyed child will generally respond with a shocked, "Really?" Usually this will lead to a discussion of what might be bothering them, be it a fear of new braces or another anxiety about their changing bodies.

There are also many materials available now to help us talk to our children about the changes ahead. With diseases so rampant, we must educate our kids. We cannot rely solely on our schools to teach them about AIDS or STDs. James Dobson's book *Preparing for Adolescence* (Regal Books, 1989) sets the gold standard in resources for preparation for puberty. We came across an audio presentation of this work and have enjoyed listening to it with the children. There also is a workbook for the child to supplement the text.

For girls, the American Girl Library has a book called *The Care and Keeping of You* (Pleasant Company, 1998), which my girls particularly enjoy. It discusses everything of interest to preteens to prepare them for their future. My daughter Caitlin matter-of-factly informed me that she had restructured her bedtime routine in light of what she read in this book because she was getting older and her old routine "wasn't working for her."

Some parents have enjoyed taking an adolescent weekend with their child, to watch a video or listen to helpful tapes. In the relaxed atmosphere of a hotel or resort, parent and child can listen to the presentation and take time to talk and pray about the subjects raised.

Establishing Hygiene Habits

Children either love or hate baths. Either way, you can seek to make this regular hygiene activity a time to reconnect with your children. We have enjoyed lots of different toys in the bath, and I have read many books to the children while they bathed. If your children hate bathing, try an incentive program using a chart with stars or hearts for each time a bath is taken without complaining or tears.

What makes the experience a positive one for your child? Most children enjoy having their own special washcloth, towel, and soap. Our younger children especially love the small soaps in different shapes available at craft stores. They can help turn on the water (Teach them about adjusting the temperature on the faucet, but *never allow your younger children to do this themselves*). They can also learn how to drain the water when they are done. As a fun twist, we often ask our kids to

help us by washing down the walls of the tub while they are bathing.

To encourage hair care, give your children their own set of hair care tools. A nice set is often an important possession, for a young girl especially. If your child's hair is longer, teach her how to work on tangles a section at a time. Teach your children about choosing shampoo for particular kinds of hair and about making sure not to use too much shampoo and not to leave any shampoo or conditioner in their hair. Also work with your child to find a hairstyle that is flattering and easy to care for. Look at a book of child's styles and choose something appropriate together. Let your child experiment with using a hair dryer, with your help.

When we trim all our children's nails, we are cutting some eighty nails. We recommend getting a soft nail brush and showing children how to scrub with it. Get them used to the feel of filing when they are four or five so you can smooth out rough edges with an emery board. To encourage hand washing, ask your children whether they would feel comfortable seeing their food cooked by someone with dirty hands? How about going to a dentist who has dirty hands?

There is evidence to suggest that frequent handwashing could prevent the spread of colds and bacterial infections. Some handwashing "to dos" are as follows:

- Wash hands with soap and hot water, front and back.
- Dry hands completely.
- Keep fingernails short to make cleaning them easier.
- Wash hands after using the bathroom, after touching something dirty, after sneezing, before and after eating.

Most very young children hate having their face washed. We struggled with most of the children until we figured out that we could give them a damp, warm washcloth while they were still in their high chair. If they played with that damp, warm washcloth for a few minutes, they would end up washing most of their face themselves, without the battle with Mom or Dad. All we had to do was a quick touch-up and they were done. For older children, remind them that their face is the first thing that people see. To help your child learn proper face washing, try holding a face washing demonstration; make it light and humorous, and they are more likely to remember. Keep track of conscientious face washing for one week and reward your child with a special soap.

Choosing and Caring for Clothes

Talk to your child about wearing clothes appropriate for the weather. As an art project, you could make a chart of the seasons and cut out pictures of children wearing appropriate clothing. For children who like paper dolls, get one of their favorites and have them make different seasonal clothing for the paper doll. As you check the weather for the day, ask your child to pretend to be a special weather forecaster, advising children what to wear to suit the weather. For example, "Since our forecast for today is wet and windy weather, I recommend that all children wear long sleeves and long pants, and take their raincoats and umbrellas when they go outside."

Discuss suitable clothing for the occasion. Ask your child, "Would you wear your church clothes to play in the mud?" Then talk about the difference between play clothes and church clothes, or sports clothes and school clothes. Your older children might find it interesting to get a book from the library about the history of clothing. They can have fun finding out what children wore to play in Victorian England and what Puritan children wore to church.

Using word pictures, or actual drawings, introduce your child to Mr. Messy Dresser and Mr. Neat Dresser. (Or Miss Messy and Miss Neat.) What does Mr. Messy wear? His shirt is untucked, maybe some buttons are unbuttoned, his shoes are untied, his hair is messy, and he only has one sock. Mr. Neat Dresser, on the other hand, has neatly combed hair, shiny shoes, and clean, freshly pressed clothes. Ask your child what he thinks of each of these dressers. This might be a good time to discuss the difference between seeking to look our best and thinking our worth is based on our looks or judging others on what they wear or their neatness.

Seeking Health and Dental Care

Preventive health care is one of the most important lessons we can teach. Make sure you get regular exams (after baby checkups, these should occur at two, five, ten, fourteen, and eighteen years), and follow your doctor's recommendations for follow up and treatment. It is also never too early to talk to children about gender disease prevention that could save their lives. Some examples of this might be mammograms and pap smears for young ladies and prostate health screening for young men.

If you ask people, they will usually categorize going to the dentist as a negative experience and equate it with pain. We chose our family dentist because he was known for his gentleness and ease with children. His hygienist treats us like family members and tries to make the experience as light as possible. Start off your children with a good attitude toward dentists by

preparing them—meet the hygienist first and explain what your children can expect. Most dentists recommend an initial visit by age three.

Make sure your child understands why visiting the dentist is necessary. One of our children asked, "Why do I have to go to the dentist when I don't have a toothache?" We explained that they help us keep our teeth clean, check for cavities, make sure our gums are healthy, and see that new teeth are growing in properly. Here are some other ideas for preventive care:

- ◆ Try to avoid the sticky snacks such as jelly beans. If your child does eat them, encourage tooth brushing as soon as possible after indulging.
- ◆ Have your child use one of his stuffed animals to practice brushing. Dentists recommend that brushing take at least three minutes. Time your child with brushing his bear and with brushing his own teeth.
- ◆ Ask you dentist for disclosing tablets. Have your child brush and floss, then chew a disclosing tablet. This will leave red stains on any plaque remaining on the teeth. Is your child surprised by the disclosure? It mean she must brush more carefully.

- Teach proper flossing techniques. Dental floss is now available in grape as well as mint flavor!
- Investigate having your child's teeth sealed. It is a new method to prevent cavities. Ask your dentist for more details.

Your dentist probably has some colorful, printed material to share with your child. If you'd like more information on dental care for children, you can write to: Public Information Department, American Dental Association, 211 East Chicago Ave., Chicago, IL 60611-2678 (312-440-2806; www.ada.org).

Staying on Top of Hearing, Vision, and Immunizations

We play lots of hearing games with our younger children. We have them practice whispering, shouting, singing, imitating sounds, seeing how far away they can walk before they cannot hear us. There are lots of creative things you can do with music as well, such as playing very soft music and playing very loud music and having your child move around in time to the music. If any of these fun activities alert you to a potential hearing problem in your child, take action immediately.

Hearing should be tested by age five or earlier and again in early elementary school. Likewise, your child should have a vision screening around age five, or earlier if the child shows symptoms of vision problems. Some symptoms of this might be complaints about headaches, squinting, or holding printed material very close to the face. Immunizations are the subject of some controversy. Consider all sides of the issue before deciding what to do. See the appendix for more information about audiologists, vision screenings, and immunizations.

Familiarize your children with all the people who help you take care of your health. Make sure they know the difference between a doctor, a nurse, and a physician's assistant. Have them meet and greet your local pharmacist and explain his role. If your child needs a prescription, take the opportunity to talk with her about following the doctor's orders. How often is the medication to be taken? Should it be taken with water? With or without food? Show them the medicine labels and explain what some of them mean.

Forming a Healthy Body Image

There are lots of sizes and shapes of children, especially in puberty. Your child needs to know that puberty can change his body type, and that it may not be permanent. A child who gets chubby in puberty may end up being a different body type in later teenage or adult years. Don't let your children go on radical diets or see you going on a radical diet. If you have a healthy body image, your children are more likely to have a healthy body image. Too much focus on body size or type when children are young can lead to anorexia or bulimia or other disorders in adolescent years. If your child is involved in an activity such as gymnastics or dance and she is obsessing about body size and weight, you may want to reevaluate your child's participation. Teach your children the importance of good health over any other effort at beauty.

> Have your older child begin a scrapbook of newspaper and magazine articles about health. Discuss ways the articles agree and disagree.

Feeling Fine through Fitness

The American Dietetic Association notes that during the past decade the number of overweight children has more than doubled. Physical activity of children has drastically declined. The same paper notes that 48 percent of girls and 26 percent of boys do not exercise vigorously on a regular basis. Participation in school-based physical education classes is declining, from 42 percent of students in 1991 to 25 percent in 1994. Along with this decreased activity, children are watching more television, an average of four hours per day.[1]

Of course, both children and adults need exercise, and the best way to encourage this is to be good role models as parents. Make family fitness a priority by taking nature walks and hikes or biking together. Consider the following ideas:

- Teach your children swimming early, either by yourself or through one of the plethora of swimming classes available.
- Make a habit of going to play at the park. Throw a ball or a frisbee.
- Limit the amount of TV your children watch. Television and snacking go together, and the more TV your kids watch, the more they snack.
- Do physical chores together—shoveling snow, raking leaves, etc. Weed and dig a vegetable garden. Besides giving everyone a workout, you will get the job done faster, have fun, and build teamwork.
- Give fitness-related gifts, such as sporting equipment. Rather than a video game, buy a good pair of skates or a new soccer ball.
- Try some exercise videos the whole family can do together.
- Jump rope. It's low-cost and can be done anywhere.
- Get some books from the library about exercise and fitness and research other ideas. Talk to your children about the three components of a good fitness program—it increases flexibility; it increases strength; and it increases endurance. Evaluate individual exercises together to see if they meet these requirements.
- Try walking together!
  —Learn some warm-up stretches.
  —Commit to walking four days a week for one month.
  —Keep a family diary of distances walked, routes taken, and weather conditions.

—Research walking shoes. Does it really make a
    difference what you wear?
—Learn to dress for the weather.
—Find out all the places you can walk that are within
    one or two miles of your house. Vary your walking
    routes.

Will it be hard to get started? Ann Douglas gives these encouraging words: "While you may find it difficult to schedule time for family fitness initially, it won't be long before that Saturday morning trip to the swimming pool or that Tuesday evening walk around the block becomes second nature."[2] In other words, it will be an anchor in your family time. In addition you will be helping your child establish the important life skill of keeping physically fit.

Be positive about physical fitness. If you don't complain about exercising, chances are your children won't approach it negatively. Find a fun way to keep track of your family fitness program. Perhaps your children could put a star on a chart for each day they engaged in exercise. Or keep track of the number of minutes exercised or miles walked and when a certain total is reached, plan a family treat.

Being Wise about Nutrition

The American Dietetic Association (ADA) reports that 91 percent of children aged 6 to 11 years are not consuming the recommended minimum of 5 servings of fruits and vegetables per day, but are merely averaging 2.5 servings each day. In a broader group, the percentage of 2 to 19 year olds who do not meet recommendations ranges from about 70 percent for fruits, grains, meats, and dairy to about 64 percent for vegetables.[3]

Use the Food Guide Pyramid.

The Food Guide Pyramid provides several fun, interesting ways to introduce our children to a healthy eating style. To refresh your memory, at the base of the Food Guide Pyramid are grains. We are advised to eat 6 to 11 servings of grains each day—bread, cereal, rice or pasta. The next level shows fruits and vegetables. The ADA suggests 2 to 4 servings of fruits and 3 to 5 servings of vegetables each day. The next level consists of dairy products and protein. We are advised to have 2 to 3 servings of milk, yogurt, or cheese and 2 to 3 servings of meat, poultry, fish, dry beans, or eggs.

Try this activity for encouraging healthy food awareness. Draw a large pyramid on poster board and have your children cut out pictures of foods from the food groups and paste them in the appropriate sections of the pyramid. Even young children can enjoy this project. If you have a budding artist, have her draw her own selections in the food pyramid.

To have fun tracking the family's adherence to the Food Guide, try this experiment. Post a large Food Guide Pyramid in the kitchen along with lots of sticky notes. Every time a meal is served, fill out a sticky note for each food group represented and place it in the appropriate space in the pyramid. At the end of the day, calculate how well the family diet stacked up. Talk with your children about simple ways that you could replace a few of those unhealthy sticky notes with wiser choices. Kids of all ages can have fun with this project and can contribute to choosing a healthier diet.

You can also give your child a list of items, perhaps bagels, tuna, peanuts, grapes, soda, milkshakes, carrots, eggs, macaroni and cheese, crackers, olives, watermelon, bananas, and onions. Then have him place them in the correct food group. Or, challenge your children to list thirty different fruits and thirty different vegetables. If they have trouble coming up with this number of items, research different varieties at a well-stocked produce market.

The ADA presents a Family Food Challenge (see appendix for details) to encourage families to get their day off to a healthy start. This is a competition in which parents and children compete to earn the most points for following the food guide and exercising each day. One point is awarded for each

The Food Guide Pyramid

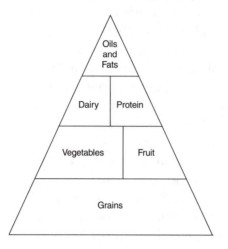

food group represented at your breakfast, and one point is awarded for each activity performed for more than ten minutes each day. At the end of the week, whoever has the most points wins the competition.

The Dole Food Company has a 5-A-Day Adventure Program with some colorful materials at their web site (see appendix). One consists of keeping track of the number of fruits and vegetables eaten by pasting their fruit photos on a strip. It would be fun to do the same thing with stars or other stickers on a strip of paper on your refrigerator. This bright visual reminder can help everyone to eat five a day.

Here are some other fun health reminders:

- ◆ Emphasize that water is essential to good health and life. Keep a chart near your sink or water dispenser. Have family members place a check by their name on the chart each time they drink a glass of water. Are you drinking sufficient water? Try replacing juices or sodas with water.
- ◆ Get your children a pocket calorie counter. Determine the amount of calories they need per day, based on their age. Have them look up the foods they regularly

consume and get an idea as to whether their calorie intake is adequate or excessive.

◆ Have your children keep a diet diary for one week. See the suggested format below. Discuss their food intake and whether, overall, it is a healthy diet.

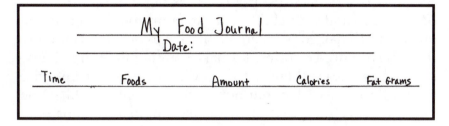

My Food Journal
Date:

Time	Foods	Amount	Calories	Fat Grams

Learn with food labels.

Reading food labels can start at an early age. I remember studying cereal boxes at the table when I was a child and indeed learned a great deal of my reading skills in this manner. But nutrition education is much more serious stuff. Food labels are now extremely informative. They tell you the nutrient content per serving of that food, and they list the ingredients used to make that food. Teach your children that the ingredients are listed in descending order by weight. They may be surprised to learn that some of their favorite corn or wheat cereals list sugar as the first ingredient because the weight of the grain may not exceed the weight of the sugar.

I recently began a food program that disallowed the use of any product with sugar ingredients in the first, second, or third position. If it was fourth or beyond, it was acceptable. My reading children became my source of accountability as they scrutinized labels and assisted in keeping me on track. Make sure your children know that "sugar" can mean sucrose, dextrose, lactose, molasses, corn syrup, honey, invert sugar or fructose. Make label reading a fun part of your shopping. Go "sugar spotting"—tell your children to find as many products as they can with sugar as the first ingredient; then put them back on the shelf!

On every food label is the serving size, the number of servings per container and calories per serving, and the amount of protein, carbohydrate, and fat per serving, as well as an analysis of the percentage of the recommended daily allowances fulfilled by the serving. Most people are unaware of actual food serving sizes. If a cereal is one hundred calories per half-cup and your child pours an enormous bowl containing two and a half cups of cereal, they have consumed far more than one hundred calories. To make your family aware of serving sizes, measure them out for a while. Get an inexpensive food scale and see what four ounces of chicken looks like. You might be very surprised at the actual number of calories in your diet, once you have begun counting calories based on accurate serving sizes.

> Save food labels from the foods you commonly eat. Cut them out and place them in a basket. Spend an evening or two reading labels and discerning their nutritional value with your children.

If you want your children to be healthy eaters, involve the whole family in planning the menu for the week. Using the Food Guide Pyramid, get them all involved in menu and shopping list preparation. Chapter 3 gives an idea for family brainstorming to plan meals for seven days on index cards (see page 94). Show your child how to check these cards for healthful foods and make a shopping list from them. As your children get older, they can take on this task themselves.

Eating Healthfully

"I can't get my kids to eat healthy foods!" many moms cry. Remember that food preferences are *learned behaviors*. If they learned some less than optimal behaviors, they can also learn some better behaviors. Even if they don't like broccoli, keep exposing them to it. Provide a healthy, varied diet and don't nag. The American Dietetic Association notes, "With a minimum of eight to ten exposures to a food, children will develop a real increase in preference for that food."

Let's say you are convinced that you need to change things around for your family to present them with healthier food choices. Where do you start? A trip to the health food store is intimidating. The nutrition section of your bookstore is a blur.

Cheryl Townsley's book, *Kid Smart! Raising a Healthy Child,* is a great place to start (Lifestyle for Health Publishing, 1996). Townsley had a fast-paced lifestyle, poor eating habits, and too much stress when she reached a crisis point with her health. Her own experience on a journey back to wholeness inspired her to begin her organization, Lifestyle for Health, and she has written many encouraging books about getting started on a healthy lifestyle.

Townsley gently reminds us that health is a process, not a destination, and that we must look at wellness over the long haul of our family life. Then, rather than giving the standard list of things to avoid in a diet, she suggests that health begins first in the addition of healthy foods, such as more fruits and vegetables, more whole grains, pure water, and supplementation. Only after these elements have been added does she recommend subtracting substances that detract from health— processed foods, hydrogenated fat products, white sugar and flour—and minimizing meat and canned produce.

Here are some activities for older children who want to learn more about healthy eating:

- Get five different diet books from the library. Make a chart of their recommendations. Show whether each plan corresponds with healthy eating on the Food Guide Pyramid.
- Research the six basic nutrients: carbohydrates, proteins, fats, vitamins, minerals, and water. What are they? What foods contain these nutrients? How much of each is required for a healthy diet?

- Look up bulimia and anorexia. What are they and how are they caused?
- Do a grocery store scavenger hunt. Have your child find specific brands or products meeting specific calorie requirements. Use nonperishable items only, please!

Teaching about Poor Health Habits

Modeling has the most significant value for teaching in this area. Your children will not listen to your message if they see you engaging in unhealthy behaviors. A second major influence in this area is that of peer pressure. Take on the challenge of building your children's inner strength and nurturing their security and you will help them to resist such pressure.

What is a habit? It is something you do without thinking. Talk to your child about the fact that there are good habits and bad habits. They probably have many good habits. Ask them to make a list: washing their hands, reading their Bible, exercising every day, etc. They also have the potential to develop bad habits. Talk with them about why they want to avoid bad habits—practices which are not good for them, once begun, are hard to quit. The best approach we can have to these bad habits is to never give them a foothold in our life.

Understand the dangers of smoking.

Tobacco is referred to as a "gateway drug," meaning that a child who first experiments with smoking will build up courage to try other substances. Michael McManus reports, "Kids who smoke are six times as likely as nonsmokers to experiment with cocaine and three times as likely to get drunk."[4] Since most smokers start between the ages of ten and thirteen, it is never too early to talk about smoking.

We have taken advantage of the abundant antismoking advertising to discuss this topic with our children. These powerful, often humorous, ads are great conversation starters. Ask your child to look at some cigarette ads, perhaps those featured in your favorite news magazine. Have them describe the people in the ads. Then ask them these questions about the cigarette models:

- Do you think they have a healthy heart and lungs?
- What does their breath smell like?
- Are their teeth really pearly white?
- Would you allow your baby to be around these people while they were smoking?

Most people who smoke express a desire to quit. Ask your child why. If smoking is as glamorous as ads claim, why do smokers seek to quit? Talk about nicotine and its addictive nature. Many people who smoke are actually addicted, and quitting would involve great pain and sacrifice to them. Stress to your child that even casual experimentation can lead to addiction.

Have your older children do some independent research:

- Have them look up the diseases and health problems associated with smoking.
- Have them prepare a report on the effect of second-hand smoke.
- Have them find a book about the effect of smoking during pregnancy.

Steer far away from drugs and alcohol.

As parents, we are especially dismayed by the extent of teen alcohol consumption today. "The surgeon general reports that 10.6 million of the nation's 20.6 million seventh-through-twelfth-graders drink. Eight million do so weekly; one million, daily. Half a million teens consume fifteen drinks per week."[5] In addition to the personal tragedy this can represent, it contributes to general health deterioration and eventually costs many dollars in the workplace. One statistic notes that substance abuse costs U.S. businesses more than $100 billion each year in lost work time, employee sickness, poor performance, and workplace injury.

Schools play an important part in substance abuse education, but you cannot totally rely on your child's school to teach about drugs and alcohol. There are many resources available to help parents open up the discussion in this area. To introduce the subject to younger children, talk to them about prescription drugs, ones ordered by a doctor for the patient to take for a specific purpose or illness. Explain that there is another category of drugs, often obtained from friends or strangers, which are harmful and deadly.

Children who become involved with drugs and alcohol are often told that consuming these substances will make them feel good. Talk to your child about the endless possibilities for feeling good in life—being part of a family, loving and obeying God, playing sports, singing, drawing, camping, etc. Make sure your child has enough pursuits and ideas in her life to feel good about so she doesn't see the need to look elsewhere. Also stress to your children the consequences of smoking and drug or alcohol use, including medical, emotional, psychological, and legal problems.

To introduce the subject to older children, ask first what they already know. Most older children know more about this than their parents, so often we must prepare by educating ourselves. Here are some research ideas for older children:

- Find out at what age people can legally purchase alcohol in your state. Also discover the criminal punishment for the possession of alcohol before that time.
- Determine what criminal charge can be brought against you if you are present in a vehicle where alcohol is being consumed, even if you are not yourself drinking.
- Find out what level of alcohol in the bloodstream is

considered legally drunk in your state and list the criminal and civil punishments for drunk driving.

- Determine the age at which people can legally purchase cigarettes in your state. List criminal charges that can be brought against a person who buys cigarettes for an underage person.
- Find out the criminal penalty for possession of marijuana and of cocaine. Determine the potential prison time and the maximum fine that can be imposed.
- Prepare a report on one or more of the many drugs that have helped people, such as antibiotics and aspirin.

"Growing Up Drug-Free: A Parent's Guide to Prevention," a brochure available from the U.S. Department of Education, draws the inescapable conclusion that, "Children who decide not to use alcohol or other drugs often make this decision because they have strong convictions against the use of these substances—convictions based on a value system."[6] Where do they learn this value system? From their parents.

Take teachable moments to talk to your child. If you see an obviously drunk person on the street or read a story in the paper about a drug arrest, an accident involving alcohol or drugs, a baby being taken from his mother because of her drug abuse, ask your children what they think of this. Observing the folly of another person is often a valuable conversation starter.

Make sure you are involved with your children's activities and know their friends. Peers and friends are typically the ones who introduce or suggest these unhealthy behaviors. While your children are under your roof, you have more control over these influences than you may imagine. What if you have used drugs, alcohol, or tobacco in your past? While I certainly would not advocate lying, you only need provide the information your child is seeking. Determine what and why your child is asking. Point to the negative effect it has had on your life or on the lives of others who have abused such substances. Emphasize that your use was a mistake and that you want to help them avoid making a mistake too.

Handling Other Self-Care Skills

Teach your children self-care for minor injuries, such as how to take care of a cut so it does not become infected. Expose them to the basic specialties of medicine, such as pediatrics, cardiology, allergy, and internal medicine, so they know what type of doctor to see for what ailment. Consider exposing them to nontraditional approaches to health and healing, such as acupuncture and homeopathy. As these practices become more mainstream, they may become a greater part of your child's life.

Make a family project of assembling a first aid kit. Get a book from the library on first aid and read it together. Many hospitals and park districts offer classes in first aid for children, and first aid and CPR for adults. Consider taking one of these with your child. Your family first aid kit should contain the following: bandages, gauze and adhesive tape, rubbing alcohol, an eye cup, a mild soap, peroxide or iodine, tweezers, calamine lotion, cotton swabs and balls, aspirin, ice pack, ipecac syrup, smelling salts, small scissors, matches and candles, and first aid antibacterial cream. Put it on your family calendar to restock the contents and dispose of expired materials once a year. Prominently post a listing of phone numbers for the police and fire departments, for your doctor, and for the poison control center. Review these numbers periodically with your child.

Building Healthy Self-Esteem

We explored earlier in this book the misguided self-esteem movement. We can clearly see the results of an unbiblical, inflated sense of self-esteem in people who are selfish, self-absorbed, and lacking a servant's heart. Yet a healthy, balanced sense of self-esteem is important in all areas of life. In marriage, a well-developed sense of self and a realistic esteem will allow each partner to serve the other without feeling threatened. Healthy self-esteem also contributes to a person's work life:

> According to research, employers want employees with positive self-concepts. Higher morale, more motivation and greater productivity are indicators of a positive self-concept. Because productivity, work quality, creativity and flexibility are based on self-concepts, a positive self-concept affects your job success.[7]

We don't want our children to think too highly of themselves, but we want them to have a realistic self-esteem, based on their security in the Lord and their gratefulness for his blessing them with individual talents and abilities.

Here is a great idea for something you and your child can do to foster the goal of building healthy self-esteem. Sondra Forsyth suggests having your child keep a notebook—"not a scrapbook in the traditional sense, . . . a reflection of who she is and who she is becoming in the context of the world around her."[8] Into the notebook would go pictures of your child stepping forward and doing things, such as being in a skit or playing an instrument. The notebook would also be a place for lists of interests and the possible career choices they might point to, lists of her favorite and unique things, a list of what is "right" about herself, wishes for her life, things she likes to do to make herself feel good (like hot baths and tea), and more.

Think of the possibilities if you expand this idea with Christian values in mind. It could include thoughts on marriage, the qualities of a good spouse, steps to raising good kids, etc. This notebook could become a significant part of your child's dreams, plans, and aspirations.

Slowly building a knowledge of healthy lifestyle habits is an invaluable part of your child's life skills education. We only get one life, and as Christians, we have the duty and privilege to serve and honor the Lord with our one and only bodies.

Life Skills Checklist

❖ Do we have an honest, forthright plan for puberty and sexual education discussions?

❖ Have our children developed good hygiene habits? What hygiene areas do we need to work on? What creative ways can we use to encourage good hygiene?

❖ Is our child on a regular schedule for physical exams, dental exams, and eye exams?

❖ Do we encourage a healthy body image? Does our family exercise together? Do our children exercise?

❖ Have we examined our family's diet? What can we do to get our children involved in planning healthier meals and eating habits?

❖ Have we discussed drugs, alcohol, and tobacco early and often? Have we chosen and obtained materials to help us with this?

❖ Do our children know how to take care of themselves? Do they know when to see a doctor and what types of injuries can be cared for at home?

❖ Do we have a family first aid kit and does each member of our family have some basic first aid knowledge?

❖ Have we discussed and fostered healthy self-esteem?

CHAPTER 10

Your Mind's Life

Using Your Marvelous Brain

❖ Tenth Maxim of Maturity

A brain is a valuable thing. We should aim to make it work at peak performance.

❖ Transferable Skills

Ability to understand ideas and assimilate new information; ability to remember information and details, and follow instructions; capacity for examining underlying assumptions, formulating questions, analyzing problems, and defining situations with clarity and accuracy.

What is a mind worth? Our minds are tremendous gifts from God and he has gifted each of us differently. One child might be musical, another a voracious reader. As parents, we need to become aware of each child's gifts and encourage their use. In one sense, we can see this task as good stewardship of God's amazing gift of children to us.

While teaching our children to value their minds, we need to remind them of their worth as heirs of the kingdom of God, no matter what brain power, talents, and achievements they have. As a licensed attorney who practiced law for eight years before becoming a full-time mother, I found the transition from a career identification to the loss of that identity extremely difficult. Similar transitions occur throughout our lives with loss of jobs, disability, retirement and other changes. If your children have invested too much of their identity in what they *do* rather than *who they are,* they will be shaken if that identity is taken away from them.

Clearly the value of a mind has an unmistakable financial aspect—the more education one has, generally, the greater that person's potential income. Yet, people with a broader view of how God wants them to live may make choices that fly in the face of conventional financial considerations. I have seen many parents make considerable sacrifices to send their child to an Ivy League school. The child may have entered college with aspirations of a fast-track, well-paying business career, but at the end of four years, his heart has changed and he now wants to dedicate himself to the eradication of urban poverty.

Whether God leads a person to serve in some career on a generous salary, or to serve in some kind of ministry on a modest one, he or she can and must learn self-sufficiency. Our role as parents requires us to perform the fine balancing act of instilling in our children that one's mind and life is not measured by how much money he or she makes, and encouraging them to work hard and achieve their potential.

Using Your Mind at School

A child's mind grows at a phenomenal rate right from birth. Much of this growth and learning occurs naturally, thanks to the provision of our marvelous Creator. One of the biggest joys as parents is watching these little tiny people take giant steps in learning without self-consciousness or fear or any idea of the miracle at work in them. At school age, however, children's learning may become something less natural. Insecurities and fears may begin to surface, which can have a substantial impact on their academic training. As parents we can do much to encourage our children to get the most out of their opportunity to learn at school.

The most important thing we can do is to have a good attitude about school ourselves. One mother notes, "My attitude is crucial. If I'm excited and encouraged, it rubs off!" When our children have a good attitude, they will approach their schoolwork with confidence and gain more from it. Ask your children to identify which of these statements best describes their attitude towards learning:

If I work hard, I will do well.	I'm stupid.
I can do things when I try.	I can't do anything right.
I do as well as other children.	I'm the dumbest kid in class.
I remember when I review.	I can't remember anything.
Math is OK.	I'm terrible at math.
I do well on tests when I study.	I always do poorly on tests.
I can do it.	I give up easily.

For children to do well in their schoolwork, they must exert effort and they must have a good attitude. If either of these ingredients is missing, their work will suffer. As you discuss the above statements with your children, try to discern their level of motivation and effort.

If you sense a lack of effort, work with your child to implement the good study habits discussed in this chapter. If you sense a less-than-positive attitude, help your child become aware of his negative thinking. Have your child write down all his negative comments about himself for a day to see how much bleak self-talk it amounts to. At the end of the day, have him write a positive thought for each negative comment. Have your child track the things that go well in the school day. Looking back on a day of small successes can encourage a child to try harder.

The fear that some children have about school makes it impossible for them to learn. If they run from this fear, it seems to expand, making them feel helpless. It's better to learn to face school fears and overcome them. Your child may fear she is the only one in class who doesn't understand some things. Explain that if she speaks up and asks a question, she may actually be helping other students who don't understand. Talking about fears is one of the best ways of reducing their power. Don't neglect to approach your child's teachers and other school personnel for help.

If we, as parents, profess that we value our children's education, we must be prepared to spend some time and energy on what we say is important. For younger children, this takes the form of reading and studying with them and being excited about learning with them. For the older child, it may mean investing substantial time and energy to determine what will positively motivate your child. Talk to your child about the value of asking questions, getting involved in class discussions, doing collateral reading, or doing an extra project to increase his interest in a subject.

One more suggestion: teach your children that the physical act of taking notes is a tremendous study aid. For some reason, involving your hand and your brain helps you remember things. Janet Winkler, in a book about study habits for children, notes, "Your hand has a memory. . . . Scientists have found that the act of writing can help you remember something much better than you would by reading alone."[1]

Learn in bites.

We teach our children chores by breaking down the tasks, and the same approach can be taken in their learning anything new. We learn new things, even complex concepts, by breaking them down into smaller bits or bites. Sometimes something new is learned by combining it with something old. For example, we teach subtraction by demonstrating that it is the inverse of something we already know how to do—addition.

Concentrate on reading.

Much of learning depends upon reading. There are concrete things we can do to ensure that our children will love and enjoy reading. Elaine McEwan tells us there are four common elements in the homes of children who learn to love reading:

1. Reading took place in the home. Parents read to chil-

dren regularly. They themselves read. Reading was a part of the family lifestyle.

2. A wide range of printed materials was available in the home. Magazines, books of all kinds, and newspapers were part of the interior decorating scheme.

3. Children had lots of contact with paper and pencil. Children were able to produce their own scribbles and scrawls and do their own "writing."

4. Finally, all of the adults in the environment responded to what the child was trying to do. They took very seriously his attempts to make sense out of the written and spoken word.[2]

One of the biggest gifts we can give our children is frequent contact with words throughout childhood. Make this really a family pursuit—if you have several children of varying ages in your home, try having an older child tutor a younger child or having your older child offer to read to younger children at home, in the neighborhood, or at church.

Finding the Best Way for Your Mind

If you want to help your child study more effectively, try to discern whether she is a visual, verbal, or kinesthetic learner. Armed with this information, and with ideas for study methods tailored to her particular style, your child is on the road to becoming a successful life-long learner.

A *visual learner* learns by seeing and watching demonstrations. Elizabeth Crary notes these characteristics of the visual learner:

> Remembers faces, forgets names; writes things down. Takes notes and looks at them. Deliberate; plans in advance; organizes thoughts by writing them; lists problems. Quiet; does not talk at length; becomes impatient

when extensive listening is required. Uses words such as see, look, watch, etc.[3]

For promoting visual learning, learning style expert Cheri Fuller suggests these strategies:

- Provide him with lots of slides, maps, diagrams, and charts.
- Give him opportunities to draw, paint, and build with a variety of materials.
- Use visual objects to represent abstract ideas or concepts. When he is learning geography, for example, a game like "Where in the World?" (which uses brightly colored shapes of countries), or a multicolored map or puzzle will help him relate the name of countries with specific colors or shapes.
- Buy flash cards and use make-your-own-study cards for any subject.
- Avoid disorganization. Visual learners are easily distracted by clutter.[4]

A *kinesthetic learner* learns by doing and having direct involvement with his subject material. Some identifying characteristics of this kind of learner may include:

Remembers best what was done, seen, or talked about. May take notes and not look at them. Attacks problem physically; impulsive; often selects solutions involving greatest activity. Gestures when speaking; does not listen well; stands close while speaking or listening. Uses words such as get, take, made, etc.[5]

For kinesthetic learners, Fuller recommends these strategies:

- Buy a big chalkboard or a large white chalkless board with markers for the child to use to practice spelling words, math, etc.

- Encourage lots of drawing in preschool years; let the child dictate stories and make them into books.
- Make use of multisensory reading and writing materials (like sand on a cookie sheet to trace letters).
- Use concrete materials found around the house (like Cuisenaire rods, beans, muffin cups) for the child to count, add, subtract, and multiply in order to learn and practice his arithmetic.
- Allow the child to bounce a basketball, clap his hands, or march around the room while practicing rote materials such as math facts or multiplication tables.
- Make up a cheer for spelling words.
- Provide a puzzle map for the child to take apart and reassemble to learn geography facts.[6]

In our own family, one of our kinesthetic learners simply could not grasp the concept of subtraction, no matter what I did to explain it to her. We tried counting blocks and pennies, but nothing seemed to work. In desperation, I placed a line of masking tape on the floor and drew numbers on it. I had her jump forward on the line to add, and jump backward to subtract. This child needed to involve her whole body in the process of learning a new concept.

A *verbal or auditory learner* learns through verbal instruction, either from others or self. This child might benefit from tape recording what needs to be memorized. He can read it once into the recorder and play it back hundreds of times. I used this method upon completing law school and studying for the Bar Exam to obtain my law license. I read my review notes into the tape recorder and listened to them on my personal stereo.

Some characteristics of the auditory learner may include:

Remembers names, forgets faces; remembers by auditory repetition. Talks problems out; tries solutions verbally, subvocally; talks self through problem. Enjoys listening but cannot wait to talk; descriptions are long and repetitive. Uses words such as listen, hear, tell, etc.[7]

For promoting auditory learning, try these strategies:

- Talk with the child as much as possible.
- Provide her with lots of opportunities for storytelling and books, records, and tapes of the spoken word and music.
- Create opportunities for writing pen pals, keeping a journal, helping get stories and poems published in children's magazines, and making books.
- Quiz orally on material to be learned or use a fill-in-the blank tape for review.
- Have the child play a card game like "Concentration" in which pairs of vocabulary or study cards are turned face down and then correctly matched as the game progresses.
- Play "Memory" and other games that develop visual memory skills.[8]

Another helpful study hint is to use a timer. One of my homeschooling friends says that her kids study in short bursts of ten to fifteen minutes. She comments, "Our brains remember the beginning and ending of material better than the middle. Studying or reading for shorter periods creates more beginnings and endings. Students aren't rewarded for hard work (studying for hours); they are rewarded for right answers."

Studying in short bursts allows for frequent breaks that can refresh the mind and actually make the studying process more efficient. Try having your child alternate the subjects to be studied. Do history reading for ten minutes, then work on an English writing assignment, then do math problems for ten minutes, then begin the cycle over again. This works great for the child who has trouble sticking with one subject for a long period of time.

Organizing Time for Studying

To help your children organize their work for now and into

the future, show them how to use checklists and assignment sheets. Have each child write down the assignments as he gets them at school. Give him a notebook specifically for that purpose. Train him to immediately ask for clarification of an assignment that he does not understand. Then he must bring the assignment book home and use it.

If your child has a big assignment, such as a long science chapter to read, or a several-page paper to write, help her learn to break it down into smaller segments. If she reads ten pages a day, she will have finished fifty over the course of a week. And if she invests a little time in writing each day, the paper will not seem to be such a mammoth task.

Work out a weekly schedule and daily schedule for studying. The process of charting on paper how one uses time is often surprising. Ask your child to chart his time for a few weeks to see how the hours are actually spent. If he complains he doesn't have enough time to do homework, this method will usually uncover several hours of the day which could be put to better use.

Make several copies of this chart, and over the course of two weeks, help your child to analyze how his or her time is spent. (You might want to do this kind of a time evaluation for yourself too!)

My Time Record

Mon	Tues	Wed	Thurs	Fri	Sat	Sun
7:00 a.m.						
8:00						
9:00						
10:00						
11:00						
12:00 p.m.						
1:00						
2:00						
3:00 (etc.)						

Your child can use colored highlighters to outline the hours usually spent in school, and then pencil in all the things she does on a weekly basis, such as soccer practice or piano lessons. For the first week, your child should fill in regular events and unusual events, like the skating party scheduled for Thursday at 4:00 P.M. Also don't forget Sunday worship time and regular family time.

Examine your child's time record and try ideas such as the following:

- Are there short gaps of time that can be used for study bursts? For example, if your child has one hour available between school and soccer practice, allocate fifteen minutes for a snack and one-half hour for reading, studying spelling words, or practicing the piano.
- If your child has doctor appointments scheduled, have him pack a study bag to take with to work on while waiting.
- Help your child to honestly account for the hours or half-hours spent watching television, playing games, playing on the computer, or talking on the telephone.
- Investigate studying at different times. If your child usually tries to do all her studying in the evening, encourage her to slot a half-hour of time in the morning for study, rather than cram it all in at night.
- In addition to this daily planning for your child, make sure your family has a large family calendar where everyone's schedule is written. Take a few minutes each week to go over the schedule and make special arrangements for transportation or trips to the store for needed items. Ten minutes a week to coordinate the family will make the week go smoother for both parents and children.

The advantage of charting and analyzing how your child spends time is that you and your child have the opportunity to make a better plan if any part of your current plan isn't working.

Organizing Space for Studying

Your first step in helping your child learn to physically organize schoolwork is to carve out a designated study space. Make it a special place, perhaps unlike anyone else's. It could be the bedroom, the kitchen table, or a card table set up for the purpose of doing homework. Does your child share space with a sibling? Make sure each has a portable box to put items and books in to move them around so materials are always ready when it is time to study.

Some people say study space should be facing a blank wall because windows are for dreaming. Windows are also for watching, creating, and getting inspired. If your child is easily distracted, you may want to consider a less stimulating place. But there is no doubt that your child should not be expected to study anywhere near the television. Much has been written about studying with appropriate music. Some children, however, find any music too distracting. You are the best judge of your child's needs in this area.

Does your child have a desk or table with a chair? Nowadays there is a great variety of children's furniture available, but furniture from second-hand stores and old card tables work just fine. When I was a child, I sat on the couch to study and used an old drafting board which sat in my lap. I always knew where it was and always put it to use when it was time to study.

In choosing a space, don't neglect good lighting. The quality of light can have an impact on your child's work, as poor lighting can lead to fatigue and eyestrain. Cheri Fuller comments,

> Three elements that impact over 70 percent of children's learning are light, design, and time of day. Some students need bright light to concentrate and learn difficult or new information. For others, however, bright light causes headaches, makes it hard to concentrate, and increases

hyperactivity. These students read and concentrate best in low light. Formal design means standard straight-backed school desks in rows. Informal design might be beanbag chairs for reading times or carpet squares to sit on while writing. Some kids learn best in a formal, structured setting, and some in a more informal classroom design. We all have peak times of the day when we focus, concentrate, and learn the best. The time of day affects the achievement of many students. For example, when offered a choice of courses and times of day, it is better to take the hardest subjects at one's peak time of day.[9]

Take time to help your child determine what is the best lighting, design, and time of day for her studying.

What supplies should be on hand in the study area? In addition to the obvious paper, pens, and pencils, children should have an age-appropriate dictionary, even if they also have one available on CD/ROM. Dictionary skills are still important to learn, and it is often easier to grab a book than to boot up a program. We allow each child to have a bulletin board in her room for special flyers and projects. We also have a larger bulletin board in our family room for the work we want to share with the whole family.

Any study area will face the subject of clutter. We like to use copy paper boxes from the printer for storage. We keep old schoolwork in them as well as files for ongoing research or projects. You might also wish to provide your children with a smaller box to save special greeting cards and pen pal letters. Help them to label their boxes so they can have easy access to the materials later. Get your older children a box of file folders. Show them how to label the individual folders for soccer practice schedules, church youth group news, etc. For a few dollars spent on folders, you can help your children organize their lives—a skill that will last a lifetime.

Try expanding this organization effort to another component in school success—negotiating the morning rush hour. If you are like most families, it is a substantial challenge to get out of the house in the morning. The best way to minimize this crunch, with all students prepared for the day, is to have a central place for backpacks to be emptied, and for putting items to be returned to school. Some families use boxes or dishpans. When permission slips are signed and homework is completed, it is returned to the box for the next day.

For older children enthusiastic about using computers to help them organize their learning, try these ideas:

◆ Have your child research the effectiveness of computer learning. Who benefits the most from computers: young children, middle children, young adults, or adults? What types of resources are available for computer learning?

◆ If you have access to the Internet, help your child assemble a directory of fifteen to twenty sites useful for research or help with homework assignments.

Being Honest about the Hard Work of Learning

As I've said earlier, in our home we believe only a boring person gets bored. The human mind is sufficiently wired to keep a person engaged for a lifetime. Often we observe the education establishment is in the business of edu-tainment. My husband and I have both taught at the college level, where we have observed students who require instruction to be entertaining or they tune out the teacher. What these students are missing is the understanding that much of real learning is simply hard work.

Marialisa Calte laments kids growing up "with a debilitating need to be constantly entertained." She advises,

> Let's give kids the straight dope on life: that it requires hard work and tenacity, and that not every minute of it is jam-packed fun. That students can—independent of teachers—challenge themselves. That kids should be actively involved in educating themselves, rather than allowing themselves to be passively "bored" by the performance of others.[10]

We only do a disservice if we allow our children to refuse learning because they find it boring. Taking on the challenge of motivating themselves may be one of the most important life skills we can teach them.

Exploring Careers with Your Child

At about middle school age, your child will need to begin to think about careers, if not before. The *Occupational Outlook Handbook* (OOH) published yearly by the U.S. Department of Labor provides detailed descriptions of several hundred common occupations. It can be accessed free on the Internet (http://stats.bls.gov/ocohome.htm), or it may be viewed at your public library. The *Dictionary of Occupational Titles* (DOT) contains detailed information about specific occupations, such as skills required, knowledge and education needed, job responsibilities, work activities, average pay, etc. It can be accessed free on the Internet (http://www.doleta.gov/progams/onet/) or viewed at your public library.

Make it a family project to research one career a month. This can be book research, or your child can interview various people. If asked, many professionals will allow children to work alongside them.

1. What is the job description? What does this person do all day? What skills do they use? What is their work environment?
2. What education or training is required for this job? How long will training take, and what will be its cost?
3. What are the pay and benefits of this job?
4. What are the advantages and disadvantages of this job?

Of course, we need to keep what our kids *do* in perspective, and focus on the kind of people our kids are *becoming*. Author Nadine Brown reminds us:

Contrast career choices with a life commitment. My husband has shared with our boys many times one of the distinct memories from his childhood. As he grew up he went through the typical stages of wanting to be a policeman, a fireman, a carpenter, etc. Whenever he shared with his mom what he was going to be when he grew up, her response was always the same, "Son, it doesn't matter what you do in life . . . as long as you are a Christian!" Be sure your children hear more about being a Christian than about being anything else.[11]

We must teach our kids how to use their minds and maximize their learning abilities. Yet, it is also very much in our hands to guide and encourage our children to pursue the path that God has for them, whether or not it fits in with what their friends are doing, what society seems to value, or even what we have dreamed for them all of their lives.

Life Skills Checklist

❖ Have we instilled in our children the value of their mind?

❖ Do our children have tools for succeeding in school?

❖ Do they understand the value of class participation, asking questions, getting involved?

❖ Do we as parents have a positive, encouraging attitude to-wards school?

❖ When our child learns something new, does he or she know how to break it down into steps?

❖ Have we experimented with some study tips that work for our child's style of learning?

❖ Do we have an regular, orderly, quiet place for our child to study?

❖ Does our child have a system for recording and completing assignments?

❖ Do we have a designated place for all the papers and books that fly in and out of our home?

❖ Have we started to discuss, even in a very preliminary fash-ion, potential careers?

❖ Are there things we can do to offer our children, younger and older, exposure to career interests?

CHAPTER 11

Spiritual Habits

The Wellspring of Life

❖ Eleventh Maxim of Maturity

If God is not at the center of your life, it will ultimately be unsatisfying.

❖ Transferable Skills

Ordered priorities; respect for authority; ability to keep life in balance; capacity for surviving life's vicissitudes.

Like many couples, we found that having children was the turning point in our spiritual lives. Children force you to confront your own personal beliefs and practices in a most intimate way. We knew we had to set an example, and we knew we wanted our children raised in the church. The happy coincidence of reconsidering "religion" came about because of the children, and we are enriched both individually and collectively by our spiritual journey.

David Heller, author of *Talking to Your Child about God*, notes, "Since you are the interpreter of your child's significant life experiences and the adviser on his or her difficult questions, you are also your child's most influential guide to religious beliefs, practices, and the spiritual process."[1] This is an area that is impossible to "subcontract" out. Church leaders and Sunday school teachers may work with you, but you are the child's first teacher of spiritual truths and habits. Sally Leman Chall puts it this way:

We have only now to make God real to our children. . . . Well, you say, that sounds easy enough. We'll just take them to Sunday school and church, perhaps enroll them in Christian schools, involve them in youth groups, send them off to church camp, and make sure they say their prayers before meals and at bedtime. But it doesn't work that way. Our society teaches us that if we want our children to learn to swim, we need only enroll them in swimming lessons at the YMCA. If we want our children to learn to play the piano, we must find a great piano teacher. If it is early learning we are interested in, signing them up for the best preschool in town fulfills our responsibility. But this theory falls short where the spiritual well-being of our children is concerned. The activities the church has to offer may truly enrich our children's lives, but the responsibility for teaching them about God is ours![2]

Deuteronomy 6:4-9 tells us that we must first love God with all our heart, soul, and strength, and then we are to teach God's commandments to our children throughout all aspects of their lives. The injunction for us as parents is to first have our own spiritual house in order. Then, and only then, can we honestly seek to teach our children spiritual truths.

Knowing What You Believe

Sometimes we go to church and practice our religion but don't really know why. A couple of classic books to read to clarify your own beliefs are Paul Little's *Know What You Believe* (Victor Books, 1985) and *Know Why You Believe* (InterVarsity Press, 1988). Books like these will help you understand and stand more firmly in your own faith—the best position from which to influence your children. I read these books a few years ago when my children were beginning to ask questions that left me fumbling around for answers. They gave me the confidence to discuss some of life's weightier truths.

My friend Sue instills spiritual habits in her girls by taking devotional time by herself first thing in the morning. She notes, "If the children arise early during my time, they can interrupt to say good morning, but they have been taught to be quiet and play or read to give me time with the Lord."

If the way that we conduct ourselves as parents differs from what our religion dictates, our children will be confused. Make sure they know that sometimes one's personal ideas don't fit exactly with specific religious customs and that there is always an allowance for religious individuality. This is not to endorse hypocrisy, however. If your beliefs differ to that extent from your denomination, perhaps you need to re-examine your affiliation. I am referring here to variations in practice, such as handraising, head coverings, and the like.

The practice of Christianity varies widely. While we want our children to have a solid, intimate relationship with Jesus Christ, we don't ever want them to think that we have all the answers about how faith should be practiced. Rather, we believe that we should not allow ourselves to become what I commonly refer to as "cookie cutter" Christians. Just as we are gifted with different talents, we can worship God in individual, creative ways. To fail to let our children see the grand diversity of God's children would only foster intolerance in them and ultimately divisiveness within the body of Christ.

A fundamental truth to teach our children is that God is about love and that his love should be expressed in all our relationships—inside the home and outside as well—to Presbyterians and Methodists and Catholics, Jews and Muslims. There is a firm difference between Christian acceptance and blind tolerance. We are called to love those who may differ from us the most. Didn't Jesus minister vigorously to sinners and those quite different from him? Yet, in our religiosity, we sometimes are so judgmental of others that we cannot extend Christian love.

Teaching your children spiritual habits can be simple and natural, or complex and strained. With very young children, take advantage of the beauty of nature and creation as a natural way to talk about God's world. Who made this beauty? How did it all come about? This is a natural lead-in to the Creation story in Genesis and the Old Testament. The wonder of the human body is another introduction to an ingenious God. Have your child wiggle toes and fingers, and discuss how God built us to take messages from the brain, down the nerves to the muscles to make movement. Even though we are technology-wise, we can't accomplish anything nearly as wonderful!

Elise Arndt says, "It is so important that a mother should talk about God to her children as easily as she talks about food, clothing, or the weather. As she does this, the reality of God becomes easier for her child to grasp, and he naturally begins to apply the Scriptures to his surroundings."[3]

Knowing What the Bible Says

As parents we must know what the Bible itself has to say about life's issues. When we have a firm familiarity with its teaching and wisdom, we can consult it for everyday problems and disputes in our homes. Most study Bibles have a concordance in the back listing topics and several references. If your children are speaking unkindly to one another, for example, you could direct them to look up the word *tongue* in their concordance. They would be directed to read passages such as Psalm 34:13 and James 1:26, among others. These verses talk about the need to keep careful watch over what we say to others because the tongue has great power to hurt.

We have found two topical studies relating to parenting to be very useful. *For Instruction in Righteousness: A Topical Reference Guide for Biblical Child-Training* by Pam Forster (Doorposts, 1995), available from 5905 S.W. Lookingglass Dr., Gaston, OR 97119, and *Proverbs for Parenting: A Topical Guide for Child Raising from the Book of Proverbs* by Barbara Decker (Lynn's Bookshelf, 1995), available from P.O. Box 2224, Boise, ID 83701.

Psalm 119:11 tells us, "I have hidden your word in my heart that I might not sin against you." Even at a young age, you can work on Scripture memory with your child. Many churches offer clubs for children (such as AWANA), which involve fun nights of games and prizes with the goal of helping children memorize Scripture. Here are some ideas for working with your children at home on Scripture memory:

- Learn the books of the Bible.
- Memorize significant passages, not just isolated verses.
- Keep a Bible time-line to go with your story reading.

Renee Jurkowski is putting together some Bible memory cards to memorize together with her daughter:

Each index card will have a picture on one side and a corresponding verse on the other. I want these images to be everyday things so that when she sees them during the day, these verses will come to her mind. For example, one will be a picture of her, with Psalm 139:14: "I praise you because I am fearfully and wonderfully made." When she looks in the mirror and sees herself, I hope it will give her positive self-esteem.

Making the Word Come Alive in Your Home

When the apostle Paul writes to his young helper Timothy, he reminds him of his long familiarity with biblical truth: "From infancy you have known the holy Scriptures, which are able to make you wise for salvation through faith in Christ Jesus" (2 Timothy 3:15). The stories of the Bible are so good that children are naturally interested. As soon as children can hold a book, they should have their own Bible. They can begin by looking at the pictures of a well-illustrated Bible. There are also many video and audio tapes available of dramatized Bible stories to captivate young viewers and listeners. To add a truly personal touch to audio tapes, make a tape of Mommy or Daddy reading the psalms or a Bible story for your child to listen to at bedtime.

If your church provides materials for kids to bring home, be sure and read the Sunday school papers together. These can be a wonderful source of spiritual food to your child between meetings. Have a review of the lesson midweek using the take-home papers. Make a chart of the verses your child is working on for Sunday school. Award special stars on the chart when verses are memorized.

Everyday life presents many opportunities to use object lessons to teach our children:

- When gardening, teach the parable of the sower from Luke 8: 5-15.
- When taking a bath and washing feet, teach the story of Jesus washing his disciples' feet from John 13:1-17.
- During a thunderstorm, talk about the power of God and how Jesus calmed the sea from Mark 4:35-41.
- When playing with building blocks or passing a construction site, talk about the house built on a rock from Luke 6:46-49.
- When preparing the morning toast with honey, read from Psalm 19:9-10 which says that God's rules are sweeter than honey.

Parents sometimes stress learning the shall and shall nots and neglect training their children toward a relationship with an indwelling God. While we may memorize verses and have devotionals, remember that we are trying to reach the hearts of our children, not just their intellect. All the verses of the Bible parroted back will not matter if your child does not feel the loving presence of the indwelling Abba, Father God.

Teaching Children to Pray

Our children pray in private and public devotional and worship time. The examples we set will help them to develop a rich prayer life. One of the most basic things we can do is to take time to pray during the day. Give God thanksgiving for blessings, or seek his help when you are in a stressful situation. Many times I have let my children in on my private, frantic prayers: "Dear Lord, help me to know how to deal with this child!" On a more positive note, my friend Marnie Murray relies on "spontaneous prayers of joy and thanksgiving during the day." Whether you are praying thanksgiving or intercession, let your children hear you!

So often, young children get the impression that God is a vending machine. We go to him to ask for a new toy or a baby brother. It is quite natural for children to do this, but as they mature in their spiritual understanding, they must learn that God is not their personal vending machine. Prayer entails much more than asking for things. Teach your children that we should all pray not just for those people we like, but also for those we dislike. We should offer prayers for those who have harmed us or who are not at peace with us. The prayers of a small child can mend relationships and heal brokenness.

"Realize that words are not always necessary when you pray," says Norman Vincent Peale. "Think how good God is, how kindly, and that he is by your side guiding you and watching over you."[4] We need not focus so much on what words our children should say when they pray. Instead, they can focus on God himself. Prayer can be listening prayer. Often we are so busy we don't have the time to listen for God. Can your child sit still and be silent? This is great training for the practice of listening prayer.

My daughter Grace and I have a funny tradition. Every night before bed, she says her memorized prayer, "Now I lay me down to sleep." Then we brainstorm together to say thanks for something obscure, like pancake syrup. I am trying to teach her that God is the source of everything in our lives, even warm socks in the winter.

Help your children to sit still for fifteen minutes a day. They may think or pray quietly, but they may not play with toys or listen to music. This is great practice for individual devotions and for sitting still in church.

Make your child a "wordless prayer book" like the ones available from Child Evangelism Fellowship. Include four colored pages and talk about what they symbolize: Black, for our sin (read Romans 3:23); Red, for Jesus' blood and sacrifice (read John 3:16); White, when our sins are forgiven (read Isaiah 1:18); and Gold, for our heavenly eternal home (read Revelation 21:21). Then share this lovely old poem:

> Once my heart was black with sin,
>   until the Savior came in.
> His precious blood, I know,
>   has washed it whiter than snow.
> And in his Word I'm told,
>   I'll walk the streets of gold.
> Wonderful, wonderful day!
> He washed my sins away.[5]

If your family has a group prayer time, write out the things you are praying about on three-by-five-inch cards. Pass the cards around the table so different people can pray for different requests. Intersperse praise cards between the requests, praising what you appreciate about God. When a prayer is answered, write the answer on the reverse of the card and praise God for that!

Praying for Your Children

Many parents keep a prayer journal to keep track of prayer requests and answers to prayer. Kent and Barbara Hughes use a loose-leaf notebook as a prayer journal, divided into various sections for meditation, confession, and petition. The petition section is their family prayer list. They suggest mounting a photo of each child and using sticky notes to change the petitions. The areas of prayer for the children include their spirituality, character, friends, health, protection, problems, future spouse, and praises for answered prayer.[6]

Moms in Touch programs offer another opportunity for

parental prayer. These are groups of mothers who meet, usually once a week, for the express purpose of praying for their children and their local schools. It is not a social gathering, but a time for serious prayer and intercession. All denominations participate, whether their children are in public schools, Christian schools, or home schools. Moms in Touch was started fifteen years ago by one woman, Fern Nichols, who felt a burden to pray for the tests and temptations her children would face in school. The group's vision comes from Lamentations 2:19: "Pour out your heart like water in the presence of the Lord. Lift up your hands to him for the lives of your children." (To find out more, call 800-949-MOMS or contact their website: www.europa.com/~philhow/moms_in_touch.html).

Bill Carmichael puts this area into perspective for me, "We parents spend a lot of time worrying about what kind of world we are leaving our children. Maybe it's time to be more concerned about what kind of inner strength and traits of godliness are left to our children. After all, we cannot change world conditions, but we can influence our children."[7] And praying for our kids and with our kids is one way to encourage their spiritual growth.

Sharing Our Faith and Serving

All Christians are ambassadors for Christ, and so our children need to feel comfortable speaking the Word and living the Word. Help your child be alert to opportunities to share his or her faith in simple ways with other children. Does your child know a neighbor or school friend who has been injured, lost a bike, or whose grandparent recently died? If your child promises to pray for that friend, it could open the door for the two of them to have a discussion of what it means to pray for someone. Prayer is the cornerstone of our faith, and praying for someone is often a powerful introduction to the faith for nonbelievers.

Work with your child to develop her testimony. How and when did she become a Christian? How has her life changed since then? What Bible verses can your child use to lead another to Christ? Some books for parents to read to encourage evangelism are *Out of the Saltshaker* by Rebecca Manley Pippert, *How to Give Away Your Faith* by Paul Little, and *Answers to Tough Questions* by Josh McDowell.

As you teach your child spiritual habits, don't neglect to foster the habit of Christian service, following the example of Christ, the greatest servant of all. Why don't more children serve in their communities? "Urban teens say there are a number of factors keeping them from participating in community service projects: No time: 25 percent; Peer pressure: 21 percent; Apathy: 17 percent."[8] We can deal with such obstacles by making service a family priority.

Brainstorm ways with your children that you can serve others. Start with ideas such as visiting nursing homes, working with young children in church nurseries, making meals for families in crisis, helping an elderly person with yard work. The list can go on and on with ways you can spend time together and bring joy to others at the same time. Use these ideas and questions as a springboard to teach about service:

- ◆ What are some things Jesus did to serve others? Find five examples from the Gospels of Christ's service.
- ◆ What does the Bible say about our attitude toward serving others? Have your child look up Philippians 2:14 and Matthew 25:34-40.
- ◆ Encourage your child to find ways to serve at home without being asked. Talk about initiative and give young children some ideas on how they can practice initiative. Initiative can be defined as doing an act of service for others without being asked—picking up toys, getting a drink for a sibling, wiping up another's spill.
- ◆ What methods of service are discussed in Matthew 25: 34-40?
- ◆ What project could you do, as a family, based on the ways of serving listed in that passage?

◆ What kinds of needs do people have? They need food, money, clothing, companionship, prayer, friendship, knowledge of the gospel. As you brainstorm these needs, ask your children to think of ways they can meet the needs of others in their Christian service.

Emphasize to your family that Christian service takes many forms, only some of them are formal and organized. A few people serve by running a large church program or a community charity drive, but all of us can have a lasting impact by serving every day with the simple gifts of our time and talent.

Celebrating Biblical Holidays

Most of us will honor Christmas and Easter, but what about the other rich biblical feasts? Studying and celebrating these holy days can help our families to become more deeply rooted and grounded in the teachings of the Bible. Robin Scarlata and Linda Pierce have written an impressive volume called *A Family Guide to the Biblical Holidays*. In their discussion of reasons to study such feasts, they ask what would be known about the Pilgrims if we did not celebrate Thanksgiving? Similarly, biblical holidays serve as reminders—"a shadow of the things . . . to come" (Colossians 2:17).

Consider a study with your family of such Old Testament holidays and events as Passover, eating of Unleavened Bread, Day of Firstfruits, Feast of Weeks, Feast of Trumpets, Day of Atonement, and Feast of Tabernacles. "Each of the spring holidays is a picture of Christ's first coming. Jesus was sacrificed for our sins on Passover, buried on Unleavened Bread, and arose on Firstfruits. The fall holidays are a picture of his second coming and the beginning of the messianic reign."[9]

Hanukkah is the Jewish festival of lights celebrated in December each year, which commemorates the historic event of the defeat of Syrian Greeks by the Maccabees in 165 B.C. and the rededication of the temple of Jerusalem. A tiny container of oil found in the temple was said to be sufficient to burn for eight days, so in celebrating this festival, a nine-branched candlestick called a menorah is used. One candle is lit each day and children receive gifts at this time.

Passover occurs in spring and commemorates when the angel of death "passed over" the Hebrew children as the first-born Egyptians were all killed. A ceremonial meal, called the Seder, recalls the experience of slavery in Egypt and the hasty escape or Exodus. The meal consists of unleavened bread (because there was no time to prepare leavened bread), bitter herbs, eggs, lamb, and wine, each with a particular historic significance.

Rosh Hashanah is the Jewish New Year and marks the beginning of a period of high holy days, commencing with the sounding of the shofar, or ram's horn, symbolic of the ram placed by Abraham in place of his son Isaac. The feast of weeks is called Shavuot. It is celebrated in the spring and commemorates the giving of the law, the Torah. The feast of booths, Sukkoth, is a fall harvest festival. Yom Kippur, the Day of Atonement, is the most important holy day, coming ten days after Rosh Hashanah. At this time, sins are confessed and amends are made. The shofar is again heard at the end of Yom Kippur.

Studying these practices will add a rich dimension to your child's understanding of the Christian salvation history.

Denominations

Are you familiar with the traditions, regulations, and practices of your faith? If you are not, don't expect your child to blindly embrace them. Educate yourself. Most churches have denominational literature and may have members classes to familiarize people with their tenets of faith.

If your child is interested in learning about other churches and other faiths, make the learning process a family project. Visit some other churches and read about their practices, comparing with your own. Get a book on comparative religions and read it together, making a poster of the various religions and beliefs. As your kids come across these topics in their school studies, it would be a natural time to discuss these things.

One good resource for information on denominations and religions is the Commission for Church and Youth Agency Relationships. This offers a variety of denominational workbooks to aid Boy Scouts, Girl Scouts, Camp Fire Girls, and 4-H members for earning items toward completing a study of their faith. Call or write for their brochure: Programs of Religious Activities with Youth (P.R.A.Y.), 8520 MacKenzie Road, St. Louis, MO 63123 (314-638-1017).

Sometimes people will say, "I'm a Christian, but I don't go to church." Your child will probably run across people who shun organized religion, yet may have a genuine relationship with Jesus Christ. In our family, we don't play the game of speculating whether or not someone is really a Christian. We figure only God knows for certain, not us mere mortals. To presume that we can determine whether someone's faith is genuine is destructive and leads to religious superiority, which we seek to discourage in our children.

Facing Hot Issues in Christianity

Christians in society are sometimes challenged to defend their beliefs, particularly on certain hot topics. Are you prepared to discuss and defend your position on these issues? Your children may be exposed to a variety of teachings on these. What does the Bible say about these following difficult areas, and how will you present them to your children?

1. Premarital sex—A fairly recent statistic notes that "More than a million teens become pregnant each year and almost half that number have abortions."[10] As Christians, we believe sex is reserved for the sanctity of marriage and that sexual activity outside of marriage is immoral. For Scripture study, see 1 Corinthians 6:9-10, among other passages.

2. Abortion—We believe that conception marks the beginning of life. The secular world regulates abortion relative to the trimester of development. The older the fetus, the more the state can regulate abortion. Scriptures to study on this topic are Exodus 20:13, Jeremiah 1:5, Ecclesiastes 11:5.

3. Bioethics—While medical science is making enormous strides in the preservation and, in some cases, creation of life, an argument can be made that this is God's province. For Scripture study on ethical issues such as infanticide, see Psalm 127:3, Proverbs 24:11-12, Jeremiah 22:3 and Matthew 25:37-40; on euthanasia, see Genesis 9:6, Exodus 20:12, Leviticus 19:32, Deuteronomy 30:15-19, Psalm 8:2, Proverbs 16:31, Isaiah 3:5, and Matthew 18:10.

4. Homosexuality—The Bible is clear that homosexuality is a perversion. For Scripture study, see Leviticus 18:22-23, Romans 1:26-27, Genesis 1:27, 1 Kings 14:24, 1 Timothy 1:9-11, Jude 7.

5. Capital punishment—This is the taking of a life by the state as punishment for a wrongdoing. Scriptures dealing with the death penalty are Genesis 9:4-6, Exodus 21:12-15, Leviticus 24:17-21, Numbers 16:9-34, Deuteronomy 21:22, Ecclesiastes 8:11, Luke 23:40-41, Romans 13:3-4.

Consider having your older child take a position on one of these issues and write a paper supporting the position, using the above Scriptures as a springboard to his or her research.

Encouraging our children's spiritual growth is one of our greatest joys and privileges. If we believe that the purpose of life is to know and enjoy and serve God, then we must pass that truth on to our kids. Having a strong faith will give their lives meaning and provide an anchor through all the ups and downs of life.

Life Skills Checklist

- ❖ Are we as parents clear and firm in our own beliefs?
- ❖ Do we have a ready, user-friendly resource to use to consult on Bible topics, such as a concordance or other resource?
- ❖ Do our children have their own Bibles?
- ❖ Do we pray aloud, regularly and often?
- ❖ Does our family memorize Scripture?
- ❖ Do we have a family prayer journal?
- ❖ Are we familiar with biblical holidays and their significance?
- ❖ Do we know where we stand on premarital sex, abortion, bioethics, homosexuality, and the death penalty, and why? Are we prepared to discuss this with our children?

CHAPTER 12

Decision Making

Practice for Every Day of the Rest of Your Life

❖ Twelfth Maxim of Maturity

We must make lots of decisions in life. The more decisions we make, the better decision makers we will be.

❖ Transferable Skills

Ability to review different points of view or ideas and make objective judgments; competence in evaluating possible courses of action in a critical way; aptitude for using imagination and thinking of new ways to get a job done; ability to learn from experience and apply this knowledge in other situations.

Decisions. We all have to make them every day. Some are big, some are inconsequential. But all require some ability to examine a situation and make wise choices. Have you known people who would not or could not seem to make a decision about anything? (Maybe you are one of these people.) They stayed in the same job rut because they were incapable of choosing from other options. Maybe they studied car models for the entire year, unable to settle on a purchase, until it was time for the new model year's offerings. We often miss opportunities for growth because of fear of making a decision, or fear of making the wrong one.

Being able to make good decisions involves discernment and, for Christians, a dedication to abiding by the Word of God. A good decision conforms to biblical values and is one that we can cling to strongly because it is the right thing to do.

A good decision is a defense from the pressure of peers or the difficulty of situations. We need to be showing our children how to become good decision makers.

Making good decisions at its essence involves wisdom, which is a function of maturity and experience but also a gift available from God. If we can train our children, at an early age, to seek God's wisdom in their decision making, they will make godly decisions. His Word promises us, "If any of you is lacking in wisdom, ask God, who gives to all generously and ungrudgingly, and it will be given you. But ask in faith, never doubting, for the one who doubts is like a wave of the sea, driven and tossed by the wind (James 1:5-6, NRSV). It goes on to say that the person who doubts God's direction or wisdom is double-minded and unstable in every way.

Defining Areas of Choice for Early Childhood

Gaining what is necessary for the skill of decision making begins early in life in a gradual fashion. When my children were very small, I chose which outfits they wore—laying out dresses, socks, and shoes for the next day's activities. It was largely my choice of what we ate, where we went, and what we did. As they grew a bit older, they were given limited choices, such as wearing the green dress or the blue dress, or having pancakes or waffles for breakfast.

To the young child, the array of life's choices can seem overwhelming. A few years ago, we entertained houseguests who were the parents of a three year old. They would ask, "What would you like to eat, son?" Feeling the pseudopower of unlimited possibility, he would make outrageous requests like marshmallows and chocolate candy for breakfast. When his unwise choices were rejected one by one, he was thrown into a physical and emotional fit of frustration. How much better it is for everyone when *parents lay out the choices*—"You may have cereal or toast, or you may wait for lunch." The child can then make a reasonably healthy choice yet retain a sense of independence by having actually made a choice.

Parents sometimes sabotage these early decision-making sessions. We tell Suzy that she may buy a trinket at the store. When she gets there, she makes several requests that we have good reason to deny. She can't have the bubble gum because it will rot her teeth. She can't have the inexpensive doll because the head will fall off by evening. Poor Suzy has been led to believe that she will have real choice, but then her parents put so many conditions on the choice that she is left feeling frustrated, manipulated, and controlled. Better to preface the shopping trip with a limit of genuine choices: "Suzy, you may have a coloring book or a small candy." The entire store is not up for discussion. She can then freely look at things, enjoy the experience, and know what her limits are.

At some point, we may widen the choices sometimes and risk letting a child come home with the inexpensive doll whose head falls off that night. By doing so we are letting her learn a lesson about consequences: when we buy cheap things, they don't last. As she gets older, she may decide to save that dollar until she has five dollars and can purchase something of greater value.

Giving defined areas of choice has many applications in the everyday life of childhood. Because my first three children were girls, we frequently fell into the trap of having fashion fights. "What would you like to wear today?" I would naively ask. Two hours later, with the contents of the closet and dresser strewn about the room and with a tearful daughter in the middle of it all, we still hadn't chosen an outfit for the day. The better solution for us has been to present a choice of two outfits. "Which of these two would you prefer?" I ask. A choice is made and, generally, that decision is closed for the time being.

The solution to the clothing monster is simple. Designate an area of the closet for school clothes, one for church clothes, and one for play clothes. Allow your child to choose for the appropriate activity. If she fails to choose, you get the choice. If she chooses inappropriately, after being instructed on what is appropriate, then a consequence is imposed, such as no snacks that night.

In the early years, then, helping children make decisions is really a process of helping them to focus on defined choices that are under the parent's control. As they grow and have greater exposure to the world, the array of choices expands exponentially, making decision making skills essential. Bob Barnes says, "If we want our children to be decision makers, . . . if we want them to be leaders rather than peer followers, we need to teach them to make decisions . . . by giving them decisions to make."[1]

Your children know that adulthood requires some serious decision making. As they get older, ask them to brainstorm with you to make a list of all the big decisions they will be called upon to make over the next ten to fifteen years of their life: college, what they will study, career, car, apartment, marriage, children, where they will live. The sheer number of items on this list may impress upon them the importance of learning wise decision making.

The stakes for a lifetime are high. How can we prepare our children? In his book *Teaching Your Child to Make Decisions*, Gordon Miller notes, "Children commonly follow one of three patterns when it comes to making decisions." They may take a quick reaction approach and so choose the first thing that comes to mind. This is really more a form of acting on impulse than making a decision, and it rarely leads to a satisfactory result for the child. Or the child might take a "me first" action, selecting the course that leads to immediate gratification. (It makes sense to think of a child acting this way, but how many adults still operate from this decision-making model?) Finally, the child might look only to the immediate consequences without any consideration of what could happen over the long term. This is often seen in the teen years.[2] Perhaps you see one or more of these patterns in your children.

Sadly enough, children today are surrounded by examples of poor decision making. My husband bemoans the hastiness that is prevalent nowadays. In one of his recent articles he quipped that many people have a great "exercise plan"—that of jumping to conclusions. Referring to the law enforcement community, he notes many are guilty of "rushing to judgment and breaking the formidable rules of logic without even breaking a sweat."[3]

Sometimes it is simply maturity that stands between your child and logical conclusions. A young child may have a frightening experience with an aggressive dog and conclude that all dogs are mean. Or another child in kindergarten might be chastised by a teacher for giggling in the hall and then conclude that laughter is prohibited in school. Our children need maturity, good examples, and opportunities to practice in order to become good decision makers.

Working with the Maturing Child on Decision Making

For the younger child, the parent's role is to give defined areas of choice with set boundaries, and then allow them to use their limited freedom to exercise decision-making skills. As the child moves out into the world, she is called upon to make more complex decisions. Not only must she continue to choose clothing and meals, but she must exercise discretion in the area of deciding on activities, making friends, and selecting from a whole host of life's possibilities.

At this stage more than ever, I believe we must stress the existence of consequences with our children. Whatever they do, whatever they choose, has a consequence. Miller writes, "Any action you take has something of a ripple effect. There isn't just one consequence; there's a flow of consequences."[4] When we shield them from experiencing these consequences, we are cheating them out of a necessary stage in the development of their character. When their actions have no consequences, they believe they can do anything with impunity.

This will cause unspeakable problems for them and those who work with them throughout life.

When children make decisions and are allowed to live with their consequences, they begin to have faith that they are capable of making decisions. As they mature, this confidence can help ensure that they won't be overly swayed by the opinions of others or even their own emotions. Peer dependency and raging hormones are powerful entities for your maturing young person. Beginning to work with children early on these skills may help to tame some of these influences.

My friend Sue, mother of eight-year-old twins, says, "We talk through options, pray for wisdom, and sometimes put space or a time period in between so we don't make a rushed decision that they may regret. And when they've made the wrong decision or a poor choice, we may talk it through, comfort the tears, and encourage a possible better choice for next time."

Your children already make a multitude of decisions. To prove that fact to them, and to inspire their confidence that they can indeed make decisions, have them list all the decisions they made throughout the course of one day. They had to decide what to wear, what to eat, where to sit, what route to take to school, who to walk with, and much more. Ask them to evaluate which decisions were good and which were not. This exercise should give them confidence that they can be decisive.

Decision-Making Tactics

Here are some simple tactics or techniques you can use to help your child make decisions.

Just give me the facts, ma'am.

"I can't possibly join the youth club at church this year," your daughter sighs. "They make you memorize the whole Bible and all the other kids have been doing it for years so they are way ahead of me. I guess I'd better just forget it." Sensing an opportunity to expand your child's biblical knowledge, you don't want to let this thought pass without a complete discussion. "Do you know that for sure?" you gently ask. "Well, that's what I heard," she responds.

And so begins the opportunity to teach your child the value of *getting all the facts before reaching a conclusion.* Children, and many adults, are quick to draw conclusions based on incomplete information. This is how prejudice, in its many ugly forms, first develops. When your child seems to be reaching a conclusion without all the facts, work with her to research the issue before its closure. In this case, encourage her to phone the youth club coordinator, visit a meeting, or talk to a child who is already involved.

Getting the facts can be a good tactic for dealing with a variety of frustrating situations. Let's say your child is overwhelmed by the prospect of writing a four-page paper on elephants in the next five days. Sit down with him and break the work down day by day: perhaps he can write an introduction, visit the library for his research, write the next few pages, do some more research on the computer, and finally complete the assignment. His temptation will be to procrastinate and throw up his hands at the thought of a challenge. Help him to meet it, bit by bit, by setting out the facts.

How do we get all the facts? There are several ways— through other people, through direct observation, through reading and research, through experience, through self-examination and prayer. You might talk to experts, parents or friends—but friends are not always the best source of unbiased information. If one of these ways is neglected in a big decision, that decision is probably based on incomplete information.

Brainstorm for results.

In my own life, the ability to think creatively and generate ideas is a marvelous gift from God. I have found brainstorming, or freely allowing my brain to mull over a problem, extremely useful in a variety of situations. Whatever the choice or problem encountered by your child, she can benefit from brainstorming in two ways, by generating ideas and options and by exploring thoughts and feelings.

Let's take a simple idea. Your child needs to choose a science project. He has no clue what to choose. He doesn't know where his interests lie. Take a piece of paper, write the word *science* in a cloud in the middle and begin the brainstorming. As you discuss the branches of science, begin to draw a brain burst, such as this:

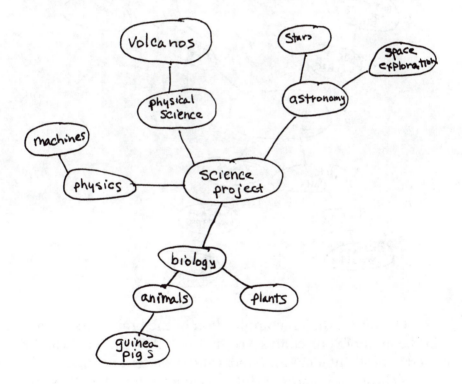

Voilá! His chosen science topic turns out to be the care and feeding of guinea pigs. He approaches the project with enthusiasm and a sense of ownership.

In this instance, your child used a simple technique to

uncover a forgotten interest or passion. This technique can also be used to solve other types of problems. Let's say it is the beginning of the school year and your child is partnered for a major project with a schoolmate with whom she simply cannot get along. You can use the brain burst to explore her options in trying to fathom this relationship:

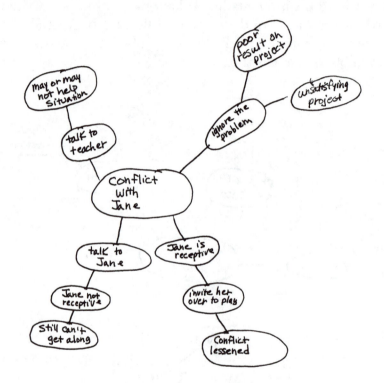

Of course, the final application of the brain burst idea is in the area of your child's writing itself. A brain burst can be used to flesh out ideas for papers and projects, and once a subject is chosen it is a wonderful vehicle for filling in details and nuances. Try it!

List pros and cons.

Let's say your child has to choose between playing soccer and taking ballet lessons. Try making a simple, logical list of the pros and cons of each alternative to help her reach a decision.

Soccer		Ballet	
pros	**cons**	**pros**	**cons**
exercise	competitive	exercise	costs more
fun	weather	fun	long drive
increase	dependent	chance to perform	
coordination		increase coordina-	
close to home		tion and poise	
		wear pretty outfits	
		doesn't depend on	
		weather	

When you are analyzing this data, ask your child to articulate her priority in choosing an activity. In a close decision like this, the priority for either is probably the chance to get exercise and have fun. After establishing the priority, ask your child to express her feelings about each option. Careful, reflective listening will help to reveal the child's real preferences and desires.

We faced the above soccer versus ballet decision at our home recently. While my two older daughters really enjoyed playing soccer, our discussion of their feeling revealed that ballet was more important and of greater benefit to them. Although soccer was appealing, ballet won because of its emotional significance to them.

This technique is used a great deal by adults who are facing major life decisions. The value of putting the positive and negative ideas on paper is that we tend to bandy about these thoughts in our heads and at various times give more weight to one over another. By placing them on paper, one can tangibly see and then weigh and prioritize the various associated issues in a much more well-defined way. As your child grows older, he can use this process to sort out the pros and cons of college choices, career goals, study opportunities, and other life choices. If he learns it early with simple decisions, he will use it wisely later when the stakes are higher.

Linking Priorities and Decisions

Of course, all decisions are going to be influenced by priorities. What is important to you? Chances are you are conveying to your children that certain things are important, and they will grow to place priority on these things as they grow older. Are your priorities to be wealthy and powerful? Don't be surprised if your child learns to make decisions with these priorities as a back drop. Are your priorities your faith in God and your love of your family? Your children will pick that up as well.

Bob Barnes talks about the importance of establishing priorities:

> Many individuals spend a lifetime battling guilt, feeling that they are not managing their life properly and that important considerations are being neglected. That's because they have no life manager. Without placing one of these areas in a priority role, life will boil down to "oiling the squeakiest wheel." The job world and its demands will scream as the bills and debt seem to beg for primary attention. Lacking a sound philosophy of life, a young person can respond by giving his job top priority without giving a thought toward his personal and private lives.[5]

Even at a young age, your children can begin to clarify their priorities. Have them do the following exercise and talk about why they made these choices:

List these items in the order of their importance to you:

faith	_____	friends	_____
family	_____	career	_____
money	_____	a nice car	_____
respect	_____	inner peace	_____

a good job	_____	fame	_____
nice clothes	_____	the well-being of others	_____

Why take the time to discuss these things now? you may be thinking. As parents, we have the awesome joy and responsibility of sharing worthy values to live by with our kids. And we need to do it while we can. Look at these disturbing statistics reported by Michael McManus:

> When pollster Louis Harris questioned five thousand children in elementary, junior, and senior high schools, he found only 16 percent said they made moral judgments based on "what God or Scripture tell them is right." A fifth say they take an adult's advice, but that number drops as kids get older. By high school, kids turn to peers for advice. Nearly half (45 percent) said their moral compass was their "own personal experience." Students were asked, "If you were unsure of what was right or wrong in a situation, how would you decide what to do?" Some 18 percent said they'd do "what makes me happy"; 10 percent would do "what would get me ahead."[6]

As children get older, they become more and more influenced by peers. One perceptive writer for *Teen* magazine warned teenagers to "think through the consequences—try to avoid snap decisions, and if you feel pressured by someone else, stop. A good motto: When in doubt, don't."[7] Many of us pray that our children will have that wisdom when it comes to the peer-related decisions of their lives. If we have spent the time and energy in helping them form values and order their priorities, they will stand a better chance of choosing wisely.

Individual and Group Decisions: Who Decides What?

Do you know people who worry about everything? They consider it their personal responsibility to bring peace to the world. If neighbors are quarreling, they take all steps possible to resolve the quarrel. Children also sometimes take on more burdens than are rightfully theirs. Such children agonize over every personal decision and try to decide more than they really have to. We all must make personal decisions, but often our decisions are influenced and sometimes even controlled by others. To illustrate this to your children, have them make a list of who, at this time in their lives, influences their decisions. The list might look something like this:

- Myself
- My family
- My friends
- Others in authority
- God's Word

Next, give them a list of decisions and discuss with them who is involved in making those decisions:

- Whether or not to go to school
- What subjects to study
- What to wear to play
- What kind of haircut to get
- When to do homework
- How much allowance to receive
- What to do with free time
- What movies to see
- What time to go to bed
- What to eat for dinner
- Whether friends can come to visit.

Your children will see that very few things are solely at their discretion. They may decide on their own what to wear to play, but they will have to consult you as to whether their friend can come to visit. Deciding what to study at school is largely out of their control, especially in the younger years. Deciding how much allowance they will get can be a more collaborative decision, made by the parent and child. Children learn from this exercise that very few decisions are made in a vacuum. They influence and are influenced by others.

Make a PACT

As Christian parents, our primary job is to teach our children how to live as Christians. That is the light which illuminates the rest of our tasks with them. Whatever your children face, you can help them choose to live a godly life and to make God-honoring choices. They can do this by making a PACT, following these steps:

> **P**—Have they *prayed* about the decision? Does the Bible speak to this area of life?
>
> **A**—Have they asked for the *advice* of trusted others? Have they considered what impact their decision will have on others? (Have your child make a list of trusted people to whom he could go for advice when making decisions.)
>
> **C**—Have they considered the *consequences* of their actions? Have they reviewed any possible alternatives?
>
> **T**—Have they *taken action* on their decision?

As maturing Christians themselves, they can make a pact to honor God in all aspects of their life.

Decision-Making/Problem-Solving Models

Problem solving and decision making are direct job skills. LaVerne Ludden notes, "Problem solving is a highly marketable skill. Employers are looking for people who can think on their feet. Learning to solve problems is important to your success on the job."[8] You can see that the small steps you take now with your child are giving him significant training for the future. The world needs decisive people who are not afraid to make God honoring decisions.

Elizabeth Crary tells us that effective problem solving has several parts: define the problem, gather data, consider many options, evaluate ideas and make a choice, and plan, implement, and evaluate.[9] Let's apply these steps to a problem your child might be having. Let's say you recently moved, and your child is having trouble making friends at school.

1. Define the problem: Your child has trouble making friends.
2. Look for possible solutions: Review the material on making friends in chapter 2 of this book.
3. Examine the good and bad outcomes of each solution: Your child may be rejected by some potential friends but may be embraced by others.
4. Select the best solution: Your child will try to smile at more kids in the hall, will join one after-school activity, and will stay on the playground for ten minutes longer after school to try to mix with other students.
5. Take action: Your child tries this plan for one week.
6. Review the action taken.

Use these steps to brainstorm possible solutions to these hypothetical problems:

- Your child's math grade slipped a half a grade
- Your child accompanied a friend to the store, and that friend failed to pay for a candy bar.
- Your child's best friend has started to hang out with a group of kids whom your child has observed smoking and drinking.

Children learn to solve problems by solving small problems. Have you ever watched a parent playing blocks with a child? If the parent is achievement oriented, chances are he will be constructing a skyscraper. Junior, meanwhile, sits passively by and watches, soon losing interest in the whole process—precisely because the parent has focused on the product, not the preciousness of the process. Instead, if Dad sits back and lets Junior build and share his ideas and thoughts with him, Junior has a satisfying experience and feels connected to Dad.

We often do the same with art projects. If the craft isn't going right, we jump in to take over for our child. I attended several Mommy and Me classes when my children were young. Most of the time, the mommies sat at the tables meticulously completing the craft project while the children wandered off to more satisfying, self-directed activities.

We often make the same mistake with decisions. We want to rush in to protect our children from a poor decision. But while the consequences are still small (such as, gum versus toy, not premarital sex versus courtship), we can give them a great gift by allowing them to practice the process to strengthen the skill. As your children get older, the decisions will become tougher. Help them today to prepare to meet tomorrow with confidence.

Negative Models: Threats and the Blame Game

How many times have you given your child an ultimatum, such as: "If you don't stop kicking the chair during dinner, you won't be able to finish eating." I've used this, unsuccessfully I might add, with kicking, whining, and other undesirable behaviors. When we threaten our child, we give him two choices: he can comply with our request or he can choose to disobey. We are really acting out our insecurities as parents. Our children, on the other hand, want to know that their parents are in control and that there are standards for their behavior.

It is better to give an unequivocal command, such as "We don't kick the chairs during dinner." This removes the element of choice inherent in the threat: "If you don't stop kicking the chair, then I will . . ." It's extremely important for us to communicate our expectations unambiguously when it concerns behavior. Set the standard, "In our family, we don't say unkind things about others." This sends a much different message than saying, "If you're not nice to Jimmy, then I'll . . ." The more closely these unambiguous standards are tied to biblical standards, the more closely we can expect to see our children walk with the Lord. We need to set high expectations for our children. One more example—Is it effective to say: "If you don't have your devotions today, I'll . . ." Or is it better to say: "In our family, we honor God first"?

It is popular in our society, rather than to assume personal accountability and responsibility, to blame someone else for everything. I saw a cartoon once of a man lying on a therapy couch. Above his head was a big wheel with an indicator. When spun, the wheel could land on slots indicating one's parents, the environment, the education establishment, and the like. The therapist encouraged the patient to spin the wheel of blame to see who was responsible for his problem. Of course, the patient himself was not represented on the blame wheel.

Childhood abuse, TV violence, and alcoholic parents have all been used to excuse adult behavior. When I worked in the criminal justice system as an attorney, I believe I heard them all. How refreshing it would have been to see a defendant come to the bench and say, "I did it. I am ready to accept my punishment."

We must teach our children to take responsibility for who they are, their decisions, their choices. While they may never find themselves criminally accountable for their behavior, in the eyes of the Lord they will be held to account for their lives. When that day comes, there will be no one else around to blame. If they make good decisions, there will be no need to lay blame. There will be no need for excuses. We must let them practice for that today by not accepting excuses from them.

Ethics and Decision Making

A full discussion of ethics is far beyond the scope of this book.

Yet even for children, decisions frequently have an ethical component. LaVerne Ludden offers these basic guidelines for making ethical decisions:

1. Is it legal?
2. How will it make you feel about yourself? . . . What you're really asking is: Am I at my best? Most of us want to do our very best. We want to look at ourselves in the mirror without feeling guilt.
3. How do others feel about it?
4. How would you feel if the whole world knew about it?
5. Does the behavior make sense?
6. Is the situation fair to everyone involved?
7. Will the people in authority at your organization approve?
8. How would you feel if someone did the same thing to you?
9. Will something bad happen if you don't make a decision?[10]

Michael Josephson of the Josephson Institute of Ethics has a three-point checklist for making ethical choices that he calls "The Bell, The Book, and The Candle." Does a bell go off in your head to alarm you to a bad choice? Will your choice withstand scrutiny in light of the Good Book? How will your choice look in the light of day?[11] Try walking your child through one of these models for ethical decision making.

Allow Children to Change Their Minds

It may be difficult to admit a mistake, but it is more difficult *not* to admit it. When I was a child, I begged to play the violin, just as one of my daughters later begged to play the piano. I hated the violin. My daughter grew to despise the piano. We were each separately aware of the disappointment we would cause, but even more mindful of the misery we would endure if we did not disclose a change of heart.

Sandra Lee Smith, author of *Coping with Decision Making*, says it takes courage to change your mind.

> The courage to change your decision takes the same self-confidence and sense of purpose and values that give you the assertive power to make a decision in the first place. People may be unhappy with the fact that you admit you were wrong. They may be inconvenienced with the new changes you made. You need to look at the overall picture and weigh their momentary inconvenience with yours. Will it be better in the long run to live with the poor decision or exert the effort to make the change?[12]

If we allow our children to change their minds about playing the piano, perhaps they will more readily admit when they have chosen an unwise friendship or harmful association. If they have confidence they will not be condemned by you for a poor decision, they may be less likely to stick to the decision out of sheer stubbornness.

When Decisions Are Still Difficult

Your child's emotions about a particular decision may need to be tamed. He may have agonized and fretted himself into an impasse. Encourage him to let some time pass for him to calm down. Wise decisions are made with a peaceful mind, not a tormented one. You may need to simply give it a rest. Your child may be exhausted from the process of trying to decide. Let him sleep on it. This is one way I personally use to discourage impulsive behavior. When a decision does not require an immediate response, teach your children to mull it over.

Finally, make sure your children know that no decision/person/situation is ever perfect. Jesus was the only perfect one to walk the earth. The rest of us struggle with our sinfulness and silliness. Living with imperfections and uncertainties can strengthen your children's faith. Here are some ideas for sharing some of your own past experiences while encouraging them to make good decisions:

- Teach your children to pray for guidance when making decisions.
- Tell your children the story of the best decision you ever made.
- Tell your children the story of the worst decision you ever made.
- Do a Bible study on the will of God, guidance, or wisdom.

As parents we must remember that our children are always watching. Bob Barnes comments,

> Our children need to be able to watch us live in such a way that there is the least amount of confusion. They need to see us live and make decisions by a philosophy of life that helps us to live so consistently that their little eyes don't miss what we're doing and why. Children don't hear us with their ears. Children hear us with their eyes.[13]

The greatest gift we can give them is our faith, and "it must be a faith in something bigger than feelings. A faith that consistently gives answers to life's difficult decisions."[14]

Decision-Making Scenarios

Daily life with young people will suggest to you plenty of opportunities to practice decision-making skills, but let's look at some ideas to spark discussions with your child:

- Daniel has made a promise to rake an elderly neighbor's leaves. That same afternoon, he receives a last minute invitation to a basketball game. What should he do?

- A new girl at school seems cold and unfriendly. All the other kids say she is a snob. Your daughter isn't ready to dismiss her as a snob. What should she do?
- Your son is passionately interested in karate and gymnastics. He has taken a few classes in each. The new park district schedule arrives and karate and gymnastics are offered on different nights. Your son could sign up for both, but he also has a church youth group on Wednesdays and an after-school activity on Mondays. What should he do?
- The schedule for summer enrichment courses arrives in the mail. Your daughter shrieks with excitement when she sees an American Girl® workshop offered, along with a craft class on rubber stamping. Her reading comprehension scores have slipped a bit this past school year and her Sunday school friends are expecting her to go to Christian camp with them for two weeks. What should she do?

Making decisions is something we do every day of our lives. We can help our children grow into mature decision makers by teaching them how to pray about situations, how to evaluate the pros and cons of a decision, how to see different viewpoints and options, how to be creative in brainstorming a possible course of action, and how to live well with the consequences of their choices.

Life Skills Checklist

❖ Have we practiced letting our young child choose between two choices?

❖ For all children, have we stressed that every decision has a consequence?

❖ In making decisions, do our children know how to gather all the facts, brainstorm for ideas, list pros and cons?

❖ Do our children understand that every decision is based on priorities?

❖ Do we know our children's priorities?

❖ What can we do to influence them to have good priorities?

❖ Have our children prayed about important decisions and sought the counsel of trusted others?

❖ Have we protected our children too often from their own poor choices?

❖ Have we avoided letting our children place blame when their decisions have proven unwise?

❖ Do we allow our children to change their minds when warranted?

CHAPTER 13

Creativity

Leaving a Little Beauty Behind

❖ Thirteenth Maxim of Maturity

All of life involves creativity. From artists to accountants, we can all develop and nourish that creativity.

❖ Transferable Skills

Ability to use imagination and intuition, to generate new ideas and find new solutions to problems; capacity for conceiving new interpretations to ideas or information, making connections between seemingly unrelated things; ability to reshape goals to reveal new possibilities; knack for using wit and humor effectively.

One of my fondest images of parenting revolved around a creative activity. I was sitting on the couch knitting one day. My two oldest daughters were sitting with me, working on their pretty latch hook rug kits. One of the girls turned her beautiful face to me and said, "Isn't this neat, Mommy?"

Any time we can contribute a little bit of beauty to the world, it *is* "neat," as my daughter meant that word. From something as simple as a smile or a well-chosen word to something as complex as an artistic masterpiece, we can create beauty with paint or fibers, wood or pliers, human interaction or musical sounds.

Renowned Christian author Edith Schaeffer says,

A Christian, above all people, should live artistically, aesthetically, and creatively. We are supposed to be representing the Creator who is there, and whom we acknowledge to be there. It is true that all men are created in the image of God, but Christians are supposed to be conscious of that fact, and being conscious of it should recognize the importance of living artistically, aesthetically, and creatively, as creative creatures of the Creator.[1]

As creative creatures of the Creator, we invest a bit of ourselves into creating something beautiful, and that creation reflects our praise to him. How do we nurture this desire to create in our children?

Sharing Your Passion

Several years ago I wrote my first book, entitled *Coming Home to Raise Your Children*. My daughter Caitlin was about five when the book came out, and she would spend many hours at the kitchen table drawing and writing, some of it decipherable, much of it not decipherable at all. She was working on her book, which she said explored her love for animals. She called it *Coming Home to Raise Your Pets*. It gives me great happiness to see my older children enjoying writing and often composing stories and poems totally on their own initiative, as well as for schoolwork. They have seen the great satisfaction that I receive from writing, and they seek to model the same.

What do you love? Is it growing flowers in the spring? Give your child a trowel and let him dig beside you in the garden. He may catch your passion and soon possess a greener thumb than you. Earlier in the book I mentioned my friends Craig and Sue, landscape architects who delight in working the earth with their daughters and have done so since their children were very young.

Do you sing? Sing to your children and let them sing with you. You are making a wonderful memory and may be encouraging a skill. A few families I know have incredible vocal talent and enjoy singing together at home as well as for others, at places such as church, convalescent centers, and other group meetings.

Do you play an instrument? Teach your children. You can

at least teach them the basics before you turn them over to a professional teacher. Some would disagree and argue that you will only inculcate your bad habits in your pupil, but this is an effective and frugal way to explore areas of musicianship. When you know for certain that your child is interested, then invest in the lessons. One of my children has taken piano for almost two years, and it is a good match for her. Another daughter has tried piano, violin, and guitar. These have been somewhat costly experiments. I am hoping the next instrument she chooses will be something I can play, but she has hinted at wanting to try the drums.

These are some musical adventures which are virtually free:

◆ Expose them to a variety of musical styles.
◆ Study a different composer each month.
◆ Look for CDs and movies in your public library about the lives of composers.

Do you have a budding actress? Most communities have many opportunities for children to dance, sing, or act. Check your local papers for community theaters, which often offer children's productions. In addition, our local park district has at least two full-scale productions each year that use children from the community. For the past few years, our girls have participated in the *Nutcracker*, sponsored by a local ballet school. This is a professional dance troupe and the ballet requires the presence of many, many children, so children from the area are invited to audition. The children get to be in a real show and get to watch professional dancers work, as well as older children who are a little more mature than they.

Many churches offer summer Vacation Bible Schools with a drama or music theme. In a Christian, noncompetitive setting, this is gentle way for them to explore their gifting. We have participated in a few of these and the children have wonderful memories of meeting new friends and practicing for the big show night.

Exposing Children to the Arts

When we had two preschoolers who were seventeen months apart in age, we went to a local concert offered by a prominent children's singer. What an opportunity, we thought. The kids will love this! The ordeal of travel to the theater and waiting for the performance proved too much for them. Ten minutes into the performance, they melted down, and we had to leave the building.

Was one of their first exposures to "the arts" a failure? Absolutely not! Rather, it was misplaced expectations on our part. Even at my ripe age, I am not sure I could sit through a six-hour opera. Instead I would work up to that by listening to some light opera and shorter works at home before tackling any live performance.

We need to know our children's endurance limits. A child of ten can sit enthralled by a performance for several hours. Prior to seven or eight, children can handle only shorter periods; for this reason, we rarely take the younger children to costly live performances, relying instead on free park concerts and quality recordings. Don't set your expectations too high for museum visits either. I could spend days wandering around an art museum. The limit for my children is about an hour and a half.

What about the visual arts? Many method books are available, and classes for kids are everywhere. With regard to children's art, don't focus too much on the end product. Don't correct your child or compare her work to that of another child. To encourage artistic expression in your home:

- Display your child's work—perhaps on a bulletin board in the kitchen.
- Give your child enough supplies and a variety of supplies. Don't be stingy with paper.
- Give your child undirected time to create. Skills need time to develop. My daughter Clare sometimes draws the same image over and over until it satisfies her.

Encourage drawing and painting.

Is your child constantly drawing and begging to paint? Here are some ideas to encourage their creativity:

- Try different media: paints, crayons, pastels, chalk, felt markers charcoal, colored pencils.
- Learn the primary colors and mix them to make other combinations.
- Get a drawing and painting book from the library. Explain and experiment with shading and perspective.

Try photography.

For the child who is intrigued by photographs, try these ideas:

- Borrow or buy a camera.
- Learn the differences between types and speeds of film.
- Learn to load and unload film.
- Take nature pictures and some pictures of people.
- Get a library book about photography as a hobby.
- Get a library book of photographs by a famous photographer. Try to discern what makes the photographs good.

Experiment with sculpting or ceramics.

Does your child love to get his hands into clay? Start with these ideas:

- Get a book from the library about ceramics or sculpting.
- Use Play-doh® and different types of clay from the craft store to feel the differences.
- Learn about kilns. Try to find a place to get a piece fired. In my area, there are drop-in ceramics shops where, for about ten dollars, my child can paint a ceramic piece and have it fired.
- Use the coil method to make a piece of pottery.

- Visit a potter's or sculptor's studio.
- Collect photos of beautiful pottery or sculptures.
- Find a library book with professional photographs of pottery and sculptures.

Work with textiles.

The textile arts are enjoying a renewed popularity, with sewing classes, sewing clubs, and even sewing camps being offered for children. You can also find wonderful publications available for children, some of which are mentioned in the appendix.

A sewing kit you lovingly assemble is a great gift for a your child: Collect different threads, assorted needles, good scissors, thimble, needle threader, measuring tape, pin cushion (make one together), and some buttons. One easy sewing project is to quilt a nine-patch pillow. Any quilting book from the library will have directions for this. It can be hand sewn and stuffed for display in your child's room. If they enjoy this, they can make pillow gifts for Christmas.

Consider all the different kinds of needlework: embroidery, crochet, knitting, just to name a few. Try to locate a guild in your city. This is an established group of crafters that will welcome new members, even beginners. Inquire at your local craft store or county cooperative extension service. I only recently started to cross stitch, which can be easily learned. Start with a simple project, like an ornament, and choose a large cloth weave, such as size 11, which children find easier to use. They can even practice with yarn on plastic canvas to get a feel for cross stitch.

Latch hooking is an easy finger craft for young children. They can begin with a simple design kit and progress to latch hooking a rug. Have your child commit to finishing a project, and hold him accountable to working on it ten minutes a day. This will teach both finger skills and perseverance. Weaving is another great finger craft. You can make a pattern for coasters or placemats out of heavy cardboard. Any children's weaving book from the library will show you how to make the pattern. Your child can use leftover yarn around the house to make a belt or a purse. When you are certain of your child's interest, a lap loom, priced at about forty dollars, will enable her to tackle bigger projects.

Explore other crafts.

Some children like to try almost any craft, while others find one they particularly like and stick with it. Calligraphy kits with instruction booklets and pens sell for about ten dollars. If your child is interested, check to see if your park district offers classes. Rubber stamping is another possibility. If you want elaborate stamps, try a stationery store. Your children can use the stamps to make their own greeting cards and stationary.

You could also try pressing flowers. Build a press from two pieces of wood and some wing nuts. Layer lots of paper and cardboard in between the boards, and you are ready to press. Instead of making a press, you can also use heavy books. Place the flowers to be pressed between pieces of paper, then place in a book under other heavy books. The item will be dried and pressed in about two weeks. We have used dried flowers to decorate cards and to arrange in a lovely framed wall hanging.

Perhaps your family would enjoy woodworking. In our area, the Home Depot stores have children's classes. Each week they feature a different simple project for the children. We are taking a less structured approach to this. We regularly visit our local lumber yard to pick up scraps. I have also bought the children some lightweight, but real, tools and nails and screws. Totally on their own, they have made chairs and nightstands for their rooms. It was a process of experimentation as they learned that a two-legged table won't stand, and then they reworked the design and put together some pretty nice little tables. Our next project is to sew some tablecloths.

Extend this interest with these activities:

◆ Read about Dorcas in the Bible (Acts 9:36-42). She had

some special skills she used to glorify God. What could your child do with his creative skills to glorify God?

◆ As a family, commit to hand crafting all your gifts this Christmas.
◆ As a family, commit to hand crafting all your greeting cards for the year. Use pressed flowers, rubber stamps, etc.

Choosing Hobbies

Your child can choose from a *doing* hobby, such as the activities mentioned above, or a *collecting* hobby. They each require creativity, organization, care, and thought. Hobbies often are avocations, but, for your older child, consider that there may be career possibilities related to his hobby. For example, a child who enjoys making jewelry might become a jeweler. A child musician may pursue music as a career.

Before beginning any hobby, have a discussion with your child about these questions:

◆ Is this activity pleasurable and enjoyable?
◆ Can I afford this?
◆ Do I have the space or time to pursue this hobby?
◆ Can I find others who share this hobby?
◆ Do my parents approve?

To begin any hobby, whether making a collection or doing an activity, first find a library book about the hobby. Locate any adult or children's magazines about the hobby and try to find a club or organization in your area that supports your child's interest. In my area, stamp clubs meet once a month. The club usually provides a bin of stamps that visitors can have for free. Getting hooked up with a stamp club is an inexpensive way for a child to gather information about this hobby.

Here are some possible collecting hobbies, followed by some common doing hobbies:

- ◆ Collecting: rocks, coins, stamps, seashells, postcards, dolls, sports cards, recipes, stickers, tapes or CDs, movies, autographs.
- ◆ Doing: board games, card games, chess, biking, fishing, singing, playing an instrument, team sports, gardening, reading, bird watching, cooking, photography, sculpting or ceramics, woodworking, fiber arts.

What if your child doesn't know what to pursue? Begin this exploration by asking about her subjects in school. What subjects yield the best and worst grades? Which subjects does she like best or like least? What are her favorite things to do in or out of school? Does she favor energetic, team activities, or quieter individual pursuits? How does she spend her free time? Taking a look at what your children are already doing may lead to an expansion of those interests.

Also, consider with your children what they receive the most praise for. Certainly our children should not be driven by the opinions of others, but if they are frequently complimented for their voice or drawing ability, this is a sure clue for them to follow for a creative outlet.

Nurturing Creativity in Children

In *Growing Creative Children,* Marlene LeFever says that creativity training begins in the home.

> A creative person doesn't necessarily invent anything new, although this is possible; but, working with the material available, she or he amplifies it and arrives at a new pattern or new way of looking at known facts. . . . A truly creative person can be happier, freer, because he is bound only by God's restraints and principles.[2]

Take advantage of everyday activities to ask "What would happen if . . ." or "How else could you do this?" Do spontaneous things with your children, and change routines around.

Engage in a lot of verbal play with your children. They love silly rhymes, puns, and jokes. My brother-in-law Bill would reverse the words in nursery rhymes to amuse his daughters. Little Bo Sheep had lost her peep. The wolf said he would huff and huff and hoe their blouse down. This helps them have fun and make phonetic connections between words. Keep your house stocked with lots of materials for non-directed art; have your children paint with different materials, such as marbles, string, or medicine droppers. Give them scraps to make free form collages.

Don't forget to leave time for free play. Free play stimulates creativity. Most children have too many toys that can only be played with a certain way, so less creativity is required on their part. Open-ended toys, such as simple dolls or blocks, encourage children to make their own game, rather than following the suggestions of a toy manufacturer.

Why should we nurture our child's creativity? It's part of being human. It adds depth and color to life. In addition, creativity is needed by all the professions, whether artists, doctors, lawyers, or parents. Without creative thinking, some of the greatest medical breakthroughs would not have been made. Without creative minds, corporations would not succeed. Without using creative brain cells, parents would not survive.

Nurturing creativity starts with your own creative approach to life. LeFever observes, "If you have a fresh outlook on life and are willing to experiment, if you can express yourself and relate to others, if you are the fullest person you can be, your child will have a far greater start toward creative adulthood than all the textbooks, methods, and creative toys dumped on him could ever have."[3]

Is your parenting dry and tired? Are you lacking the enthusiasm you once had for being a parent? You need only ask the Lord to renew your spirits. Sally Leman Chall reminds us, "I am convinced, from personal experience, that the God who never ran out of ideas or power when He created the universe, the God who is Himself a Father, can give us the ideas and strength we need to parent our children creatively and individually."4 Let your prayer be to become a family of creative creatures of the grand Creator.

Life Skills Checklist

- ❖ Have we shared our passion with our children on a meaningful level?
- ❖ Have we exposed them to the arts, beginning with community concerts and theater?
- ❖ Have they read a library book on a skill of interest?
- ❖ Can they visit someone who does what interests them?
- ❖ What gifts and cards can we make together as a family?
- ❖ When can we visit a craft fair or exhibit to get ideas and enjoy others' creativity?
- ❖ Have we helped our children analyze their interests?
- ❖ How can we approach life with an eye toward being more creative?

CHAPTER 14

Celebration Skills

Finding Joy in the Everyday

❖ Fourteenth Maxim of Maturity

Rejoice and be glad! This day is all we have.

❖ Transferable Skills

Ability to enjoy the present; capacity to live a life without regrets and what-might-have-beens.

Parenting is serious business. I have observed the drawn, tired, and stressed-out faces of other parents and wondered, "Isn't this supposed to be fun?" Maybe fun is too flippant. How about joyous? Sometimes we take our parenting so seriously that we squeeze all the fun out of it. Noted Christian author Richard Foster says, "The carefree spirit of joyous festivity is absent in contemporary society. Apathy, even melancholy, dominates the times." He then concludes, "Celebration is at the heart of the way of Christ."[1]

We need to be reminded to celebrate. If we exhibit an attitude of thankfulness and joy and strive to accentuate the goodness and fullness of life, in spite of a negative world that tends toward crassness, our children may learn to delight in the daily joys of life. Henry David Thoreau wrote about the art of enjoying the present: "It is something to be able to paint a particular picture or to carve a statue, and so to make a few objects beautiful, but it is far more glorious to carve and paint the very atmosphere and medium through which we look—to affect the quality of the day—that is the highest of arts."

Reasons for Rejoicing

What does the Bible say about joy and rejoicing? Psalm 118:24 says, "This is the day the Lord has made; let us rejoice and be glad in it." Not when the kids are older. Not when the baby sleeps through the night. Not when the kids have made it through middle school. But rejoice in *this day*. We can be happy in the Lord today. And next to knowing and loving the Lord, I believe that parenting possesses the potential for the greatest joy because it holds the hope for the greatest family closeness.

Do you know how lucky we are to be parents? My husband and I particularly appreciate our blessings because we struggled with infertility for several years before adopting our first child. We did not know if the Lord had a family planned for us. But our prayers were answered, and after our first adoption, our biological child was born seventeen months later, and we subsequently adopted two more children. We have never taken the privilege of parenting for granted, and we rejoice in the fact that children are a heritage from the Lord.

Why should we celebrate? Because the season of childhood is short. The on-call, twenty-four-hour-a-day parenting passes quickly. The joy to be found in these days may be in the fact that they are gone in an instant. Once preschool days are over, they're over. Once young adulthood has passed, it's gone. We have to savor these days.

I was at a Pioneer Girl party at my church with our three daughters recently. They were acting wild, having consumed far too much sugar and had too much excitement. An older lady came up to me and said wistfully, "You know, the time when my children were young was the best time of my life." I looked down at their cookie-smudged faces, and I said, "You're right. This is the best time of my life."

In Elise Arndt's wonderful book called *A Mother's Touch*, she says, "If ever there was a need for family celebration, it is today. The family which celebrates is bound close to each other in a sense of unity which sociologists find missing in so many families. A celebrating family is a happy family; they are celebrating the very act of living."[2] We can rejoice in our children and in their childhood, just as God rejoices over us. I love the passage from Zephaniah 3:17 that says, "The Lord your God is with you, he is mighty to save. He will take great delight in you, he will quiet you with his love, he will rejoice over you with singing." Can we say that about our families? Do we delight in them and rejoice over them with singing?

As I close this book I would like to share some ideas for celebrating and having fun. I don't want to overly focus on activity because there is great value in just being together. But the small things of life, the little exchanges we have with others, are the things that make and maintain connections between us. Do you know that feeling you have when your spouse brings flowers for no reason, or leaves you a little note? It's the small gesture that makes you feel special. Similarly, the small gestures of kindness and fun we have with our families make them feel special. If we intentionally create these times with our children, they will strive to do the same with their children, and they will inherit generations of blessings.

Jerry and Patti MacGregor, authors of *Family Times: Growing in Fun and Faith* speak of one obstacle many families encounter:

> A few years ago Patti and I decided we'd had enough of the expectations of our culture. We started saying no to things, stopped attending extra meetings, and made a conscious effort to do something fun with the kids a couple times a week. We don't even call it "family time" because that would suggest we are doing some type of program. All we do is have fun. We play games, visit places, talk about life—all the things you keep telling yourself you're going to start doing someday, as soon as your schedule lightens up. You see, we realized that our schedule was never going to lighten. The culture was keeping us so busy, we weren't able to do our jobs as parents.[3]

So how do we counter that culture of overactivity to slow down and savor time with our families?

Remembering to Celebrate: Idea Savers for the Scatterbrained

I have a terrible memory. Ask me what I did this morning, and I probably won't be able to recall. So I make lists and keep files so that I never run out of ideas. Sometimes, if we make a list and post it on the refrigerator, we can look at it when we are at a loss for something to do. If we have ideas, in our brains or on paper, we can turn the daily minutia into something special. We can practice the life skill of celebration.

Ask your kids what they like to do. If you have fifteen minutes to spend, do they like to play a game of hopscotch with you? Take a short walk, play catch? If you have thirty minutes to spend, play a game or work a puzzle? If you have a few hours, go to the park or go shopping? The point is this—when you have a few smidgens of time, it is very easy to just turn on the TV. If you have a list, however, you will have a ready plan for how to spend this time memorably.

Another idea is to have a "special time basket." We wrote down some of the kids' favorite activities, such as baking cookies or playing a game or taking a walk, and folded the papers and placed them in a pretty little basket. When it was time for some special time, the child or children would draw a paper, and we would enjoy that activity together.

I also keep an idea box in which I collect articles, recipes, and patterns. You can use an accordion folder labeled for the months of the year, or a separate file folder for each month. Into each folder go all the seasonal fun ideas we find in magazines or handouts from places we would like to visit on a field trip. We also have what we call our "magic closet." Into this cabinet go the papers, glitter, pipe cleaners, and Styrofoam egg cartons that we hope to use for a project some day. When the kids want to do something artsy or make a collage, we dip into the magic closet for some free-form art fun.

As we focus in on celebrating our families, I challenge you to think about this: What do you remember from childhood? The little things! The small things of my childhood are the things I cherish. The pictures burned in my memory are those of crowding around the table at mealtime, of getting special attention from my mom when I was sick, of hearing Peter Rabbit stories at bedtime from my father, and of taking long walks with family members. We didn't take fancy family vacations or have elaborate celebration rituals. Our life was rather simple. But it was rich and full.

Richard Foster says, "God's normal means of bringing his joy is by redeeming and sanctifying the ordinary junctures of human life. When the members of a family are filled with love and compassion and a spirit of service to one another, that family has reason to celebrate."[4] What are some of the ordinary junctures of your life, and how can you sanctify them?

Make mealtime fun.

Do you have a hard time with the children around mealtime? When our first two children were very young, our secret weapon for handling this was a predinner bath. It worked like magic. It calmed them down, and it calmed me down. It was also a chance to sit and read them a story to smooth that arsenic hour at the end of the afternoon.

Do you hold hands while praying? If you don't, this is a nice thing to try. Try to learn some different ways to give thanks. You can learn some new prayers. Pass a squeeze around the table. If I forget, one of the kids reminds me. It's also a good time to let your kids practice praying out loud. They need to practice and be comfortable with it at home so they will do it elsewhere. Mealtime can be a good time for having devotions, either before dinner or after. It's a time when you are all together, and if your kids are old enough to sit without squirming, this can be the best time.

Dinnertime can be the ideal time for manners training. Practice them. Pretend you are at a formal banquet and only the most proper behavior will be tolerated. Review the manners material in chapter 2 and practice these simple rules of civility.

Make placemats and cover them with clear contact paper. You can illustrate a place setting with the proper placement of dishes and utensils, or you can make charts or diagrams to work on things you are trying to teach your child. We have been using a clear, plastic table covering at our everyday table. Under the covering we put a world map, multiplication tables, capitalization rules, or a leaf identification poster. Try this with any pieces of information you are trying to get the children to remember.

We like to have the kids tell us things around the table. We will usually ask them: (1) name something good that happened today; (2) tell us one thing that you learned today; or, (3) tell us one thing you are thankful for. Usually our kids are not quiet, but when they need some conversation starters, these questions are great.

Have you ever had a country night? Maybe you can tie this in with a geography or history study, but choose a country, research a recipe, find some music or maybe a movie such as a travel video, and color a flag of the country. If you want to plan far in advance, you can write to travel bureaus and ask for literature and posters, and you can research the country's dress and make or put together an outfit. Of course, if you are studying a language, this is the perfect culmination to a period of time in foreign language study.

Finally, try this one: Tell your kids that tonight the family is having a monastery meal. Give them towels to wear as hoods over their heads, and tell them that they are not allowed to speak for the entire meal. Tell them about the religious orders that have vows of silence, and see how long they can keep it up. A few moms I have spoken with have had hilarious results with this.

Aim for bathtub bliss.

Daily baths are another one of those ordinary junctures of life that can be a pain or a pleasure. When our stress level is high, we are often tempted to go through the motions in bathing the children. Yet, bath time presents an opportunity for real fun and closeness. You can do amazing things with sponges and Styrofoam™ meat trays. You can cut out shapes or letters and stick them on the walls. You can make boats out of them. Provide the kids with little sticks and pieces of fabric for sails, and let them have fun sailing. Make sure the meat trays are thoroughly washed with soap and water before giving them to the children, of course.

Once in a while, I will let the kids have a cheap can of shaving cream. They have so much fun! And the beautiful part is that it just rinses off. Let them have paintbrushes, too, and they will clean your bathtub walls for you. My daughter used to cover herself from head to toe in shaving cream and pretend that she was dressed as a bride. I have a few photos of this that I have promised never to display to future suitors. One summer I let them use the shave cream on the front picture window. It was a blast and attracted several neighborhood kids. Afterwards, we just rinsed it away with the hose.

We let our children wash the kitchen floor in their bathing suits, then take them directly to the tub. They each get a sponge but are limited to one bucket of warm, soapy water. To hear there squeals of delight is a joy, but it is even better to know that the floor will be cleaned. I simply have to mop up the water when they are done.

Candles in or around a bath can be fun, if you are there to supervise. If you allow water pistols, challenge your child to snuff out the flame with a water pistol. The bath is the ideal place for bubbles. If they spill, no one cares. When I was a child, we used to soap up a washcloth and then blow through it, forming a cascade of small bubbles. This is really fun, requires no extra equipment, and just rinses away.

Once a month or so we have a spa with our girls. I let them use my fancy bath items, special shampoos and soaps, and often serve them a glass of juice while they are in the tub. When the bath is done, we do their nails, including trimming and nail polish. If we want to stretch it, we'll use hot rollers and do their hair and makeup. Just as it makes a mom feel special to go to a spa, it makes a daughter feel like a princess. When they are experiencing their preadolescent stress, this can calm them tremendously and help to bring mother and daughter back together.

Approach bedtime carefully.

Bedtime is often my favorite part of the day because it signals the end of the workday for Mom. But bedtime must be approached with care because my attitude sets the tone for how my children will go to bed. If I am cranky and short, it's an unsatisfying end to the day. If I can relax and read a story and chat, everyone seems to go to bed a little more peacefully.

Of course this is a great time for prayer, Bible stories, or devotionals. We have four children and have been experimenting with praying together in the living room before they go up to their beds. We found that the individual prayer was stretching out far too long because each child had one-on-one attention. Regrettably, sometimes a practical approach needs to be considered, although individual prayer time is preferred. Sally Leman Chall advises taking advantage of bedtime as a time to make God real to children. She recalls, "I know just how exhausted parents get as night falls. It can be a real temptation to rush through those bedtime rituals, but resist it."[5]

Story tapes or classical music tapes are the ideal thing to listen to before bed. Our library stocks a great selection of books on tape, for the very young as well as for the older child. We also study one composer a month and generally try to listen to some of that composer's music at the end of the day.

Once in a while we play a reversal game and have our older girls tuck us in, if we're all going to bed at the same time. They listen to our prayers, tuck us in, and go off giggling to their own beds. As our kids have gotten older, they have been allowed fifteen minutes to read in their beds before lights out. They also each have a flashlight because we are not so old as to have forgotten the thrill of reading by flashlight.

Make sick days special.

Some of my happiest memories are of sick days. We were a large family of eight children, and getting sick meant that I was the only kid home and was allowed to lie on the couch. My mother would wipe my brow and bring me soup. I felt loved and cared for.

Because we're home with our kids, sick days aren't the inconvenience they were when I was working. I can remember really scrambling and panicking when I was working if I was trying a case and a kid got sick. Now when someone gets sick, we actually enjoy the chance to slow down a bit.

Paper dolls are a mom's secret weapon for sick days, especially for girls. We have purchased commercial ones and have made our own. They last forever if they are covered in plastic. The children can then design clothes and homes for the dolls.

Save paper boxes to make into a city when your child is sick. Use oatmeal boxes and potato chip cans and all sorts of other boxes. When your child tires of playing with the city, take a picture of his creation for a memory book and send it all to the recycling bin.

An old-fashioned flannelboard is good for playing with in bed. We made one by covering a sturdy piece of cardboard with felt from the fabric store. The possibilities for a flannel board are endless. Many commercial suppliers sell flannel cutouts of everything from Bible characters to body parts. Your children can also cut out stuff from magazines, put scotch tape on the back of the items, and arrange them any way they want on the board.

Any kind of a magazine collage can also be fun. Have your children cut out their favorite foods, a paper doll family, pictures of toys and glue them together to create the ideal toy room. What are they interested in? Furnish them with magazines to suit that interest—animal magazines, doll magazines, car magazines, etc. String a rope with clothespins near the child's bed to display her artwork and the get-well cards she may receive from relatives and classmates.

A children's almanac to read can provide hours of entertainment. I once got almanacs for our kids before a car trip,
and they began memorizing state birds, telling me the fastest
animals on earth, and thrilling me with more than I ever
wanted to know, but they loved their almanacs. You might also
try giving your children photo albums to look at.

Give sick kids something to do with their hands. Get a
simple needlework project or some beads to string to make
jewelry. Get a couple pieces of rope and a book from the library on knots, and let your child learn to tie various knots. Or
give them something useful to do, like rolling pennies into
rolls or sorting socks.

Any of these is a nice alternative to letting your children
vegetate all day in front of the television, although a sick day
should include some proper television vegetation as well.

Expanding Ideas for Family Celebration

Have you ever thought about taking a vacation at home?
Authors Kathy Peel and Judie Byrd suggest this as a cheap,
manageable way to spend a family weekend.[6] This is a great
idea for when you need some time to regroup and just relax as
a family. Choose the date in advance, shop for foods and videos, turn off the phone, hang out a sign on the door. Start off
with a fun Friday dinner—like pizza. Decide what bare minimum of chores needs to be done that weekend. Have board
games to play. Make everyone stay in pajamas until at least ten
o'clock the next morning. Do a fun, but close, outing on Saturday. Let the kids have some free time for reading or relaxing.
Serve something easy on Saturday night, like a crockpot meal.
Then after a leisurely evening, go off to church as a family on
Sunday morning. Doesn't that sound wonderful? No errands,
no chores, no soccer practice to attend. Trying this a few times
a year will revolutionize your view of the weekends. It will help
your family view that time as a real time to recharge and reconnect, instead of a time for engaging in a frenzy of activity.

Have a "Praise-Day Party." Nadine Brown says, "Instead

of having your children eat cake and get presents as they would at a birthday party, this will be a time for them to give gifts of encouragement and praise to family members and playmates."[7] For example, a child might appreciate a note from Mom thanking her for her cheerful attitude in doing chores. A sad or stressed out child might enjoy receiving a special bottle of bubble bath from a sibling.

Think about writing out a mission statement. We have a family mission statement detailing our objectives as a family. You may find that putting one of these together can be one of the most significant things you do in celebrating your family. This idea was popularized by Stephen Covey, author of *The Seven Habits of Highly Effective Families*. He tells his family's story:

> We realized that even though most families begin with a sacred marriage ceremony, for the most part, families don't have the kind of mission statement so critical to organizational success. Yet family is the most important, fundamental organization in the world, the literal building block of society. No civilization has ever survived its breakup. No other institution has had its impact for good or ill. Nevertheless, in most families members do not have a deep sense of shared vision around its essential meaning and purpose. They have not paid the price to develop a shared vision and value system, which is the essence of the character and culture of the family. So we became convinced that we needed to develop a "family mission statement." We had to create a vision of what we wanted our family to be like, what we would live by, what we would stand for—even die for.[8]

Here is one example of a family mission statement from Bill Carmichael:

> To love God above all else and be obedient to his Word.
> To love each other, building up rather than diminishing
> each other.

To help each other discover our God-given gifts and
  calling.
To celebrate whenever and wherever we can.
To reach out to others with our time and resources in ways
  that build God's kingdom.
To pray continuously for each other and those around us.
To strive for excellence in whatever we do.[9]

Take time to talk about why you are together. Brainstorm your
vision for your family, then draft your mission statement.

Some families have a family flag. It doesn't have to be
elaborate. We have a simple felt banner hung on a dowel with
our names and felt cut-outs representing what we are about,
things like praying hands, a cross, and a musical note. Make it
together as a family.

Schedule an evening once a month when you sit together
and update your photo albums. Make an appointment and put
it on the calendar. You are not only getting a task done, but by
doing it together you are reliving memories and sharing a special time.

Have your children been exhibiting exceptional character qualities? Have they improved substantially in some area of
their schoolwork? Think about having a family award night.
We awarded ribbons for "excellence in character" to our
daughters after they did a tremendous job to help the family
while I recuperated from a broken arm. Character ribbons
and other awards are available at teacher's stores or through
the Courtship Connection (see appendix, chap. 14). The recognition we have given our own children has always impressed
them as being more significant than the recognition they receive in the world.

Dean and Grace Merrill talk about their family's honor
nights: "One child is selected for special limelight throughout
the evening—which isn't his or her birthday or anything else,
just a selected time each year when the family zeroes in and
says, 'We think you're great!' "[10] The child chooses the menu,
displays her favorite things, and has a homemade star with

glitter pinned on. The family might then choose to interview her, asking her favorite foods, subjects in school, and special hobbies. You might choose to look at a baby book, read some favorite Scripture, make a compliment list as a family, or take turns saying something nice about the person.

We let our older kids take turns having art exhibits. We put up a sign saying "Clare's Art Work" and then display a series of pictures around the living room. It's fun to see the development in the children's drawing, and it is a real boost for them to see the importance we place on their work. This is especially meaningful when the family is having guests over or a party.

Mary Loverde made a unique gift for her mother, which could be incorporated into family celebrations. She reasoned that on Mother's Day, what her mom would really like is to know that "she had made a difference in my life, that all of her hard work and sacrifices had been worth it." She got a cut glass jar with a lid and wrote out a hundred pieces of paper, each with a memory of a treasured moment with her mother. The gift was one her mother treasured.[11] We could do this for a significant birthday for our child, perhaps recording the one hundred most precious moments we have shared. For a friend's fortieth birthday, I wrote out her forty favorite verses of Scripture—ones that had special meaning for her—and put them into a decorated jar. For a child, you could write out the Scriptures that have most influenced your life, or that you would like most to see them remember.

Rituals and Traditions

I pray my children will remember our home as a celebrating place, indeed, that celebration was a family tradition. I pray that memory will keep us connected as they return home to us regularly to the touchstone of their heritage. I pray they will continue to celebrate life with their own spouses and children. It is important to plan intentionally to maintain family ties, or time and the cares of life will loose them.

William Doherty wrote a wonderful book called *The Inten-*

tional Family: How to Build Family Ties in Our Modern World. He says we need to strive to be intentional families: "At heart, the intentional family is a ritualizing family. It creates patterns of connecting through everyday family rituals, seasonal celebrations, special occasions, and community involvement."[12] Family rituals might be what Doherty calls *connecting rituals,* like what we do at meals, in the morning, and at bedtime. They might be *love rituals,* like anniversaries and birthdays. *Community rituals* are things like weddings and christenings. *Daily rituals* are the things that make each day sacred, if they are celebrated in the spirit of gratitude and grace.

Cheri Fuller recommends asking the conversational opening question, "What did you learn today?" She offers these guidelines for making family mealtime count:

> Aim at a generally consistent dinnertime; eliminate as many distractions as possible; avoid unpleasant or negative family business; encourage your children to become involved in the discussion, to participate, and speak up; encourage listening, and not interrupting, respecting each other's ideas and opinions. Think of this hour as a time of encouragement and refreshment for everyone.[13]

We need to hold on to that important ritual of eating together and make the experience one that everyone values.

Many ethnic and cultural groups pass along certain rituals and traditions from person to person, without any formal recording of that tradition. I am an amateur Irish musician. Many of the tunes of Ireland were never written down, so they are passed down aurally from musician to musician, as are many songs and legends. Because I have heard the tunes played by others, I know them and can teach them to others. In many families, the stories of each generation are passed down this way too.

Meg Cox, formerly a staff reporter at the *Wall Street Journal,* now writes and lectures about family rituals. She notes that rituals not only help families feel connected but also "help heal the pain of life's tragedies." Rituals do ten important things for children:

- Impart a sense of identity
- Provide comfort and security (like bedtime rituals)
- Help us navigate change (passages and transformations, like deaths, initiations, giving up a bottle, riding a bike)
- Teach values
- Cultivate knowledge of a cultural or religious heritage,
- Teach practical skills (like baking together, camping skills)
- Help solve problems (like printing an annual calendar with important family days printed)
- Help keep alive a sense of departed family members (when we bake a favorite aunt's pie recipe and serve it on her china)
- Create wonderful memories
- Generate joy in a family[14]

How much time do we spend on special events, such as planning birthday or graduation parties? These events, while significant, are gone in an instant. How much more satisfying life would be if we put the love, the thought, the energy, and the care into everyday life. So much of life is maintenance, the routine tasks we perform each day to simply keep our family functioning, just "showing up." But these maintenance activities require time and thought, or we may be squandering a good bit of our life together as families. Every day we have unlimited opportunities to enjoy each other and share love, kindness, and encouragement—efforts that count now and in the future as children approach their own family life carrying with them all they have learned.

Celebrate the Memories

I like Mary Beth Lagerborg's idea in her book *A Cure for the*

297

Growly Bugs. She suggests, "Stop what you are doing for five minutes at some point in the day and just watch your child, snapping memories from the invisible Polaroid in your heart. Remember that even the most exhausting days have golden moments to treasure; little ones grow up so fast."[15]

What are the Polaroids in your heart? These are some of the memories from my memory book:

- I remember each kid going through an annoying phase of taking all the books off the bookshelf and laughing with delight at the pile of chaos they had created.
- I remember my daughter Clare saying, "I like to love."
- I remember stickers *everywhere*. The girls would even put stickers all over our legs while we stood at the sink washing dishes.
- I remember asking Caitlin, "How did I get such a sweet baby girl?" She said, "From Baby Jesus."
- I remember Caitlin pointing to everyone around the dinner table and saying, "I love you and you and you and you."
- I remember Clare pointed to a tiny sliver of a moon on a brilliant summer night and declaring that it was Jesus smiling at us.

What I will remember from these short, sweet days of childhood is that it really did seem like Jesus was smiling on us because we were all taking the time to rejoice in the day the Lord had made. My hope is that our children will celebrate today with joy, celebrate again often in their memories, and continue their joyous celebration every day of their lives. If they can do that, they will have learned the skill of living well.

Life Skills Checklist

❖ Do we try to find the precious in the every day?

❖ Have we studied some Scriptures about celebration?

❖ Have we counted the seasons of childhood remaining for our family?

❖ Have we written down some fun ideas to share with our family?

❖ Have we shared with our kids some of the fun things we did in childhood?

❖ What are some ways we can smooth the rough spots of mealtime? Of bathtime? Of bedtime? Of sick days?

❖ Do we have a family mission statement? What about a family flag?

❖ What family traditions and rituals do we want to pass on?

❖ Are there awards we could implement that emphasize growth in character?

❖ Are we seizing the potential for joy in our family *today*?

Epilogue

Now What?

If you have read through this book in its entirety, you are probably overwhelmed with ideas. I hope you are also excited about implementing some of them. So, now what do you do?

We are far from a perfect family. In fact, we rather enjoy our faults and foibles. We try to have fun and we definitely seek to live a life characterized by love. We know that life cannot be truly lived by adherence to checklists. Each family is unique and each child is unique, with their own personality and gifting. So, in addition to offering lots of lists, I have sought to provide ideas which you can creatively adapt to your own family, giving due regard to your child's personality, strengths, and weaknesses. Here is one more idea we have used in our family to follow through on our goals for our kids. It is pretty simple and provides a way for you to track your child's progress.

Each year, my husband and I sit down together to talk about each of our children. We discuss their strengths and weaknesses, their progress and the areas which require more intense work. We have a notebook for each child, labeled, for example, *Clare's Life Skills.* For each nonacademic area we are focusing on, there is a sheet of paper, or several, listing notes, thoughts, ideas to follow up on, goals, expectations, and the like. For our youngest child, Daniel, the goals listed are potty training, washing by himself, increased efficiency using a fork and spoon, control of temper, and a few others. The older children have goals like learning a new craft, assuming a new cleaning responsibility, learning to graph their "investments," or implementing a new organizational routine for their rooms. In the past, we have photocopied and used materials from a variety of sources for these notebooks. If a child was working on baking, we would copy a list of desired accomplishments and place it in her notebook.

One of my goals in writing this book was to give my readers ways to think about goals for their own children. How you seek to implement these goals and what goals you choose to add or delete is a matter for your family. You are the expert where your family is concerned. My prayer is that you will take the material in this book and lovingly customize it to meet the needs of your family. It doesn't take a lot of time or investment in resources. It takes intentionality, love, planning, and enthusiasm. God bless you on your journey as you seek to equip your children for the real world. Have fun!

Appendix

A Life Skills Toolbox of Resources

This appendix provides more detailed information, listed by chapter topics, about helpful curriculua, projects, organizations, book reviews, and other tools for teaching life skills to your children.

Introduction: What Will They Need to Know?

A. **Keepers of the Faith** is a unique family ministry, offering teaching tools and encouragement in life skills. There are project booklets available for girls (Keepers at Home) and boys (Contenders for the Faith), although my girls have done projects out of each of these books. The books provide suggestions and milestones for mastering projects such as needlepoint, gardening, cooking, models, pocketknives, and electricity. There is a lot of overlap on projects for boys and girls, including projects on showing appreciation to grandparents and memorizing Scripture. We have used these books to learn many skills, although they do not teach the skills themselves; rather they provide checklists and ideas for mastery.

An accompanying volume is called *A Parents' Guide to Productive Pursuits and Practical Skills for Children,* which gives parents ideas on teaching and encouraging children in these areas. Keepers of the Faith also has a complete catalog of instruction books and kits to accompany the projects, although you could do most of them with library books and some materials from the craft store. They are reasonably priced and the materials are very motivating for the children. This is worth investigating.

Keepers of the Faith
P.O. Box 100
Ironwood, MI 49938-0100
906-663-6881
Email: folks@keepersofthefaith.com
Website: www.keepersofthefaith.com

B. *Training Our Daughters to Be Keepers at Home* is a huge, beautiful volume, comprising a seven-year program with day-by-day lesson plans to teach Christian homemaking skills. Designed for girls ages 10-18, it is a complete (and I mean *complete*) course in godly womanhood, sewing, cooking, caring for the sick, making a house a home, gardening, family finances, knitting and much, much more. A few supplemental volumes are used each year, but the book itself is over 600 pages, making it a great resource for moms and their girls. Available from:

Training Our Daughters to be Keepers at Home
Smiling Heart Press
P.O. Box 208
Fossil, OR 97830

C. **Doorposts** is a company that has traditionally marketed its products to the homeschooling community, but they are so good that I think everyone should know about them. They specialize in creating Bible-based, parent-designed, family-tested products to help us apply Scripture in our homes. Two of their major works are *Plants Grown Up: Projects for Sons on the Road to Manhood* and *Polished Cornerstones: Projects for Daughters on the Path to Womanhood.* These books provide Scripture and practical application of life skills for your children.

Their book, *For Instruction in Righteousness,* is a topical study guide for parents on fifty common areas of misbehavior or bad attitudes. They focus on what the Bible says, give ideas for discipling, and provide object lessons and stories. Doorposts also has some other smaller products, like their *If-Then* chart, which allows you to list disobedient behavior and the consequence for that behavior. *The Blessing Chart* then acknowledges and rewards godly attributes and good behavior. They have many more ideas and products which will be a blessing to your family.

Doorposts
5905 S.W. Looking Glass Dr.
Gaston, OR 97119
503-357-4749
E-mail: orders@doorposts.net
Website: www.doorposts.net

D. Other Recommended Books
Ready for Responsibility by Dr. Bob Barnes (Grand Rapids, MI; Zondervan, 1997.)

Mega Skills by Dorothy Rich (Boston: Houghton Mifflin, 1992). Rich believes parents play a critical role in preparing their children for success and that we need to help children develop: *Confidence:* feeling able to do it; *Motivation:* wanting to do it; *Effort:* being willing to work hard; *Responsibility:* doing what's right; *Initiative:* moving into action; *Perseverance:* completing what you start; *Caring:* Showing concern for others;

Teamwork: working with others; *Common sense:* using good judgment; and *Problem solving:* putting what you know and what you can do into action. This book might be helpful for parents seeking to work on attitudes with their children.

Chapter 1: Responsibility in the Small Things

A. If you are interested in exploring the idea of teaching your child the whole enchilada, or homeschooling them, you might want to check out **KONOS**. Concentrating on character traits, the curriculum uses a theme to integrate several subjects into an exciting educational experience for your child. Each unit contains readings and activities in Bible study, science, language or literature, arts or crafts, music, health, safety and writing, reading and history and character. A full-fledged home school would have to supplement these materials with a math and language arts curriculum, but many families enjoy doing KONOS activities during family time to develop character qualities and family closeness. Some of the character qualities studied are obedience, honor, patience, responsibility, courage, wisdom, cooperation and self-control.

There are three volumes for the elementary grades and two years of study for the high school years are available, with more materials in the development stage. If you are even mildly curious about the family centered learning lifestyle and if one of your major concerns is your child's character development, check out KONOS.

KONOS
PO Box 250
Anna, TX 75409-0250
972-924-2712
Email: info@konos.com
Website: www.konos.com

B. **Family Tools** is a unique company dedicated to helping you raise responsible children. Their specialized products can aid you in improving a child's behavior and attitude, gaining greater cooperation, getting more input on chores, managing money, and much more. These products were designed by parents, for parents, and are uniquely sensitive to the needs of today's parents. Family Tools is a distributor for the *PEGS System* (Practical Encouragements & Guidance System). This is a plastic pegboard with discs depicting chores or attitudes to track for the day. As the task is completed, the disk is turned over, giving a visual, as well as tactile, sense of accomplishment to the child and an easy method of tracking for parents.

Other fascinating products available include *Time Out to G.R.O.W.* which is a creative way to use time-outs. The child is given a worksheet to process what happened, who was hurt and how to resolve the issue so that time-out is used as a time to grow—Get Reproof to Obtain Wisdom. *Choose a Chore* is a job jar system for assigning non-routine chores. *Pick a Privilege* is a jar system for choosing creative rewards to motivate children. All of the products come with extensive instructions and ideas. If you haven't heard of this unique company, check them out!

> Family Tools
> Box 298
> Circle Pines, MN 55014
> 888-384-7347
> Website: www.familytools.com

C. Kym Wright has written a study called *Women: Living Life on Purpose*. The main text consists of several meaty articles on womanhood and child training. An accompanying study guide takes you through Bible passages and developing your own thoughts and action plans. I bring this work up here because Kym has done a marvelous job of creating checklists of practical living skills. Her lists are so complete that they would well equip any child in handling the practicalities of life. Then she shows her readers how to take these lists of life skills and make chore charts for your children. This study is worth its price for this feature alone, but she also has much wisdom to share about husbands, ministry, attitudes, fruitfulness, and more. Kym is the author of several unit studies for homeschooling and is the editor and publisher of the magazine *Open Arms*. You cannot help but be encouraged by this dear lady!

> Kym Wright
> alWright! Publishing/Open Arms Magazine
> PO Box 81124
> Conyers, GA 30094
> Email: editor@openarmsmagazine.com
> Website: www.openarmsmagazine.com

Chapter 2: People Skills

A. Look for these books, or ones like them, in your public library:

The Family Book of Manners by Hermine Hartley (Uhrichsville, OH, Barbour & Co., 1990)

Telephone Time: A First Book of Telephone Do's and Don'ts by Ellen Weiss (New York: Random House, 1986)

What to Do When Your Mom or Dad Says Get the Phone by Joy Wilt Berry (Chicago: Children's Press, 1983)

B. The word "etiquette" conjures up images of white gloves and tea parties for me. But etiquette is more than knowing the proper fork to use with meals. It includes character issues such as obedience, honesty, gratefulness, patience, loyalty, wisdom, and attentiveness. *Etiquette PLUS: Polishing Life's Useful Skills* is both a guidebook and checklist of the social graces. Written by Inge Cannon, this little book guides parents and children through manners and the principles behind them. Available from:

Education PLUS
PO Box 1350
Taylors, SC 29687
864-609-5411
Website: www.edplus.com

C. It might seem rather peculiar to include a handwriting resource under the topic of "people skills," but one of the most important people skills for our children to learn is expressing gratitude. In our family, this has often taken the form of writing thank you notes or notes of encouragement to others. But what if your child doesn't write yet? A picture is always lovely, but what if you could provide your child with a note whose letters your child had to merely trace? **StartWrite Software**™ is a unique program for your computer. With it, you can create pages for your child to simply practice their writing or to express some meaningful message to another. You type in the text, add some precious clip art from the program and print it out for your child to make their own. Your child follows the dots on the sheet to create properly formed letters. It's great for handwriting practice and for special projects. Scripts are available for printing or cursive. I use this to help my kids master cursive and to create special notes to others.

StartWrite Software
Idea Maker, Inc.
80 South Redwood Road, Suite 212
North Salt Lake, UT 84054
801-936-7779
Email: info@startwrite.com
Website: www.startwrite.com

D. The **American Girl Library** offers two volumes relevant to this chapter's life skill. *The Care and Keeping of Friends* (Middleton, Wis.: Pleasant Company Publications, 1996) is an encouraging little book for girls who have questions about friendship. In a gentle way, it tells how to meet other girls and how to nurture friendships.

The other volume of interest is called *Oops: The Manners Guide for Girls* (by Nancy Holyke, Middleton, Wis.: Pleasant Company Publications, 1997). In the warm, inviting American Girl style, children are introduced to social dilemmas and are walked through proper behavior. Covers the usual stuff, like dinners and napkins, but also includes more unusual things, like how to behave at a funeral or have tea with the queen!

Chapter 3: In the Home Skills

A. Sue Gregg's *Eating Better Cookbooks* are the last cookbooks you will ever need. Subtitled *A Comprehensive Wholefoods Cooking System*, this multi-volume series will educate you and your children on nutrition and healthful cooking. Cookbooks available include *Main Dishes, Meals in Minutes, Soups & Muffins, Desserts, Lunches & Snacks,* and *Breakfasts.* Each is packed with delicious recipes and an entire education in healthy eating.

For teaching purposes, *Lunches & Snacks* contains cooking lessons and activities for children age 7 and above. She also has a complete cooking course available with a video and student guide. These surprisingly affordable resources will launch you and your children on a lifetime of healthy eating and cooking.

> Eating Better Cookbooks
> 8830 Glencoe Drive
> Riverside, CA 92503
> 800-998-2783
> Website: www.suegregg.com

B. The **Cooperative Extension Service** is a great source of information on cooking, canning and foods. We purchased a few project books for a few dollars each and virtually got a cooking course for our children. There are titles available on food safety, baking, meats, vegetables, canning, etc. Written for use by children, they are thorough with lots of hands-on activities.

C. Emilie Barnes is the princess of home management. My favorite of her books is *The Creative Home Organizer* (Eugene, OR: Harvest House Publishers, 1995)

Chapter 5: Time Organization

A. Do you need some help in sanctifying your time—slowing down to catch the moments? The next two books may revolutionize your life.

Margin by Richard A. Swenson, M.D. (Colorado Springs, CO: Navpress, 1992)

The Practice of the Presence of God by Brother Lawrence (Springdale, PA: Whitaker House, 1982)

B. A great resource for organizing time together is *Family Times: Growing Together in Fun and Faith* by Jerry & Patti MacGregor (Eugene, OR: Harvest

House, 1999). This is a neat guidebook to creating family fun times. The MacGregors offer practical suggestions for games, traditions, kitchen fun, suggested books to read, and lists of family-friendly movies.

Chapter 7: Around the House Skills

A. For your child to learn home repairs, the best and cheapest resource I could find was from the Boy Scouts of America. They have a series of about 150 booklets in their Merit Badge Series on a variety of topics and life skills. *Home Repairs* is clearly written and perfect for youngsters to use with their parents. Who knows—your child may become the chief handy person in your family. You may order it directly from:

> Boy Scouts of America—Supply Division
> Direct Mail Center
> PO Box 909
> Pineville, NC 28134-0909
> 1-800-323-0732

B. Your local **Cooperative Extension Service** is a great source for information and assistance about gardening, soil quality and canning. You may know of them through an affiliation with 4-H. Through their office, even non 4-H members can have access to 4-H materials to work on projects at home with their children. For example, my local 4-H unit has a two unit gardening study. Each workbook costs about $3.00. The activities in the book take the children through every phase of gardening in an interactive format, written at their level. When they have produced something wonderful in the garden, they can exhibit it at the county fair and compete with other gardeners. This does not require 4-H membership. Other project books available include works on growing flowers, growing in containers and growing vegetables. The Cooperative Extension Service is a gold mine!

C. Other handy resources:
Reader's Digest Complete Do-It-Yourself Manual (New York, The Reader's Digest Association, 1974)
Reader's Digest Fix-It-Yourself Manual (Pleasantville, NY: The Reader's Digest Association, Inc. 1978)

Chapter 8: Money, Money, Money

A. Many institutions have taken on the mission of helping to educate the public in general and our children in particular about finances. You could give your child a superb financial education just accessing the free resources available. One of the best is a Website of the **Jump$tart Coalition**

for Personal Finance Literacy in Washington, D.C. This is a wealth of free information for kids and families: www.jumpstartcoalition.org

B. **The ABA Education Foundation,** a subsidiary of the American Bankers Association, is another source of financial information for teaching your children. Each year, they sponsor the National Teach Children to Save Day to help bring real life money management to young people. A kit of activities is available to address savings and savings skills, as well as credit matters.

>ABA Education Foundation
>A Subsidiary of the American Bankers Association
>1120 Connecticut Avenue, NW
>Washington, DC 20036
>202-663-5425
>Website: www.aba.com

C. The **American Girl Library** has a little volume called *Money Makers: Good Cents for Girls* by Ingrid Roper (Middleton, WI: Pleasant Company Publications, 1998). Girls can get ideas for making extra money which range from the expected, like babysitting, to the unusual, like handmade bookmarks and pencils. This book is unique because it discusses and describes how to organize a business, has interviews with girls who have actually done the various projects and, as a bonus, contains business cards, flyers, price tags, etc. at the back of the book which your girl can copy. Very colorful and fun, this will give your daughter lots of ideas!

D. Linda Hackett had four kids and struggled with teaching them how to manage their allowances and extra earnings. She came up with a system called **CA$H KEEPER**, which consists of a notebook with divider sections and ledger sheets to track income, savings, and spending. What is unique about this clever system is that separate, see-through vinyl pockets are included for each category of cash, making it easier for children to stash the cash, then account for it. This is a neat system!

>Linda Hackett
>Ca$h Keeper
>2879 Bonnie Brae Ave.
>Salt Lake City, UT 84124
>801-272-4182

E. Another fun approach to money management is called **Cash University: Money Management for Kids.** It was developed by a stockbroker who got tired of seeing his kids waste his money. This is a complete program, including an audiotape explaining the program and an instructor's guide for parents. It begins with a story about Cashew the Squirrel who didn't store up enough walnuts for winter. Children then choose a goal, and use a goal reminder sheet, an allowance calculator, erasable board to track chores and cash, as well as their own checkbook which can be used to track funds or exchange money with parents. The program is directed to ages 4 to 9. This looks like a fun, colorful resource to help your kids manage their money and set goals.

> Cash University
> 4881 Kendrick S.E.
> Grand Rapids, MI 49512
> 800-209-4800
> Website: www.cashuniversity.com

F. The first place for the Christian to look for financial advice on money management is **Christian Financial Concepts, Inc.** The ministry, founded by Larry Burkett, has as its purpose that of teaching biblical principles of managing money and they have available a wide range of materials, for adults and children. Several free brochures are available on budgeting, major purchases, tithing and investing. They also carry all of Larry Burkett's books, such as *The Financial Planning Organizer, Larry Burkett's Bill Organizer, Debt-Free Living, Using Your Money Wisely, Your Finances in Changing Times,* and more. Many of these materials are available in Spanish as well. For children, workbooks are available on *Money Matters for Kids* and *Money Matters for Teens.* My children really enjoyed these workbooks, along with their product called *My Giving Bank.* The bank is a 3-compartment bank showing a bank, a store, and a church. It provides a tangible way for children to view how their money is distributed.

> Christian Financial Concepts
> PO Box 2377
> Gainesville, GA 30503-2377
> 800-722-2377
> Website: www.cfcministry.org

G. **Life Pathways** is a division of Christian Financial Concepts that helps individuals to determine their interests and gifting and match them with a career field. Their latest product is *The Career Direct Guidance System,* which is a CD-ROM program used to profile personality, interests, skills and work priorities. The program generates a huge report for study and reflection. The program also comes with audio tapes to aid in this significant process. For older children, ages 13 to 16, the *Career Direct—Youth Exploration Survey* would be quite helpful. These colorful workbooks lead the student into an exploration of interests, abilities and priorities and assist in making key decisions and developing a life purpose statement. I wish I had had these materials when I was younger, and I can't wait to use them with my own children. Our goal in training them at home is to help them to develop a vision for their lives. These materials will bring that vision into focus.

Life Pathways
601 Broad Street, SE
Gainesville, GA 30501-3729
770-534-1000

H. For younger children, check out *Money Matters for Kids* by Lauree Burkett and Christie Bowler (Chicago, IL: Moody Press, 1997). This is a fun book of jokes, puzzles and principles from the Bible written for children to introduce them to money and attitudes towards money.

Money Matters for Teens by Larry Burkett with Todd Temple (Chicago, IL: Moody Press, 1998). This picks up where the kids book leaves off. Handles more sophisticated issues, including how to make money.

I. In my state, the **University of Illinois Cooperative Extension Service** offers a comprehensive program for teaching life and money management called "Welcome to the Real World." The program was designed for school use, but can be adapted to individual family use as well. Children spend some time considering careers and settle on what educational level they will achieve. Then several financial and lifestyle variables are plugged in, and the students are challenged to see if they can live the kind of lifestyle they think they want in the career and income they have chosen. This would be an incredibly valuable exercise for older students, whether or not it is offered in their class at school. The materials may be ordered from the Cooperative Extension Service. Write for information at this address:

University of Illinois Cooperative Extension Service
Countryside Extension Center
6438 Joliet Road
Countryside, IL 60525-4642

Chapter 9: Healthy Habits

A. For information or a referral to an audiologist, contact:

American Speech-Language-Hearing Association
10801 Rockville Pike
Rockville, MD 20852
800-638-8255
Website: www.asha.org

For information about vision screening and optical health, contact:

American Optometric Association
243 N. Lindbergh Blvd.
St. Louis, MO 63141

888-396-3937
Website: www.aoanet.org

For information about immunizations, from both ends of the spectrum, contact:

Centers for Disease Control
1600 Clifton Road NE
Atlanta, GA 30333
800-311-3435
Website: www.cdc.gov

National Vaccine Information Center
512 W. Maple Ave., #206
Vienna, VA 22180
800-909-7468
Website: www.909.shot.com

B. The hardest way to learn to have a healthy, preventative-based lifestyle is through illness, either your own or your child's. The easiest way is through making gradual healthy changes as a family. There is no better source for information about healthy family habits than **Lifestyle for Health,** headed up by Cheryl and Forest Townsley. Cheryl is the author of numerous books and has a bi-monthly newsletter providing encouragement for healthy lifestyle changes. She also has many tapes and supplement products available. Her books include *The Lifestyle for Health Cookbook, Kid Smart, Food Smart, Meals in 30 Minutes* and *Return to Paradise,* which lays the biblical foundation for health. I have learned so much from the Townsleys! I have read and enjoyed several of their books, regularly use their recipes, and have attended a seminar given by them in our area. If you are looking for a Christian, no-nonsense, intelligent, no-hype approach to better health and healthier kids, this is the place to begin.

Lifestyle for Health
8122 SouthPark Lane, Suite 114
Littleton, CO 80120
303-794-4477
Email: Cheryl@health.com
Website: www.lfhealth.com

C. The **American Dietetic Association** offers lots of articles and information on nutrition. They can also find a Registered Dietician in your area.

American Dietetic Association
216 W. Jackson Blvd., Chicago, IL 60606
1-800-366-1655
Website: www.eatright.org

D. Dole Food Company has a fun **5-A-Day Adventure Program** for kids. Printed materials are available as well as a CD-ROM with tons of fun activities.

Dole Nutrition Program
155 Bovet, Suite 476
San Mateo, CA 94402
FAX: 650-570-5250
Email: dole.nutrition@bnt.com
Website: www.dole5aday.com

E. The **American Girl Library** is full of lots of fun titles for growing girls. We particularly enjoyed *The Care and Keeping of You* by Valorie Lee Schaefer (Middleton, WI: Pleasant Company Publications, 1998). My preteen daughters devoured everything in this book and talked to me about the stuff that was confusing or troubling. The book is thorough—covering everything from braces to bras and from periods to pimples. What a neat way to share self-care information with your daughter!

F. Your local county health department can be a great source of health care information for your family. Along with local hospitals, they frequently have printed materials available for children, open houses, and health fairs.

G. For drug education resources, contact:

American Council for Drug Education
164 W. 74th St.
New York, NY 10023
800-488-DRUG
Website: www.acde.org

National PTA Drug and Alcohol Abuse Prevention Project
330 N. Wabash Ave., Suite 2100
Chicago, IL 60611-3690
800-307-4782
Website: www.pta.org

National Crime Prevention Council
PO Box 1, 100 Church St.
Amsterdam, NY 12010
800-627-2911
Website: www.ncpc.org

Partnership for a Drug Free America
405 Lexington Ave., Suite 1601
New York, NY 10174
212-922-1560
Website: www.drugfreeamerica.org

Chapter 10: Your Mind's Life

A. A good book on study skills for the middle years is *How to Be School Smart* by Elizabeth James and Carol Barkin (New York: Lothrop, Lee & Shepard Books, 1988). We found our copy in the public library. It's for the child to read on their own and examine what they can improve.

B. *How to Study and Learn,* Janet Winkler (New York: Franklin Watts, Inc., 1978)

C. *Scholarship: Boy Scouts of America Merit Badge Series* (Boy Scouts of America, 1988). The activities in this project booklet would be the perfect motivator for a boy who is resistant to school and school work. It speaks to boys about the importance of school and how to navigate it successfully. Best of all, you don't have to be a Boy Scout to enjoy any of their materials!

 Boy Scouts
 1325 West Walnut Hill Lane
 PO Box 152079
 Irving, TX 75015-2079

Chapter 11: Spiritual Habits

A. Children's Bibles and devotionals are plentiful. A trip to your local Christian book store will result in finding something appropriate. A monthly publication we have enjoyed is called *Keys for Kids* from:

 Children's Bible Hour
 Box 1
 Grand Rapids, MI 49501

B. **Your Story Hour** produces character-building stories for radio and cassette listening. Its goal is: "Making boys and girls of today better men and women tomorrow." Do you long for some wholesome family entertainment? Then check out this company. It has been around since 1949 and offers cassettes of Bible stories, classic stories, and all-around good stories for children and their families. Send for their extensive brochure. These reasonably priced cassettes will bring your family hours of listening pleasure, and a great deal to talk about to boot.

 Your Story Hour
 Box 15, 464 W. Ferry St.
 Berrien Springs, MI 49103
 1-800-987-7879
 Website: www.yourstoryhour.com

C. **Canon Press** is a small publishing house dedicated to providing "select literature for growing in Christian faithfulness." You won't find the top-10 Christian feel-good books here; you *will* find meaty volumes to sink your spiritual teeth into. Canon Press features writers and commentators on the classical tradition of education. In addition to scholarly works, they also publish a course in logic and a home study course in Latin. One of their goals is to remind us that "a full and good life includes not just doctrinal truth, but truth, beauty and goodness." They also offer a free, bimonthly periodical called the *Credenda/Agenda*. If you are ready to commit to seriously challenging yourself with some readings on the classical Protestant perspective, check out their catalog.

Canon Press & Book Service
PO Box 8741
Moscow, ID 83843
1-800-488-2034
Email: canorder@moscow.com
Website: www.canonpress.org

D. There is no shortage of materials for family Bible study. But if you are looking for a meaty interactive study that the whole family can use to grow together, check out **The Explorer's Bible Study.** From preschool students to senior high schoolers, Explorers Bible Study has resources that are very family friendly. Preschoolers can do a Scripture overview with *And It Was Good* (Old Testament) or *New Testament Lessons for Little Listeners*. These friendly books offer Bible stories, guided prayers, Bible words, and activities and praise hymns. Early elementary students can choose from an Old Testament or New Testament overview as well, although either book could be adapted for use with these children. Older elementary students can choose from the study of Genesis, Luke, and Acts, Exodus to Joshua or Job, Psalms and Proverbs. More books are in the works for further study. Junior and senior high school people can study the same topics at their level.

What's different about these studies? Rather than just filling in a blank, these studies really encourage students to think about the meaning and application of the Scripture. If you want to embark on a meaningful Bible study as a family, or to start an Explorer's Bible Study at your church, they may be contacted at:

Explorer's Bible Study
Box 425
Dickson, TN 37056-0425
800-657-2874
Website: www.explorebiblestudy.org

E. Raising children for the Christian parent is really a matter of discipleship. We are about the business of teaching them biblical values and character.**Whole Heart Ministries** has a wonderful resource, called *Our 24 Family Ways*, to assist in this process. It is a unique table-top resource to use around the table with your family. Principles concerning authority, relationships, possessions, work, attitudes, and choices are presented. Each day presents the character quality, related Scriptures and devotional outlines. This is a 70-page flipbook format with delightful drawings that may be colored. If you are wondering what first step to take to begin to instruct your children in Christian character and values, this is a great resource.

Whole Heart Ministries
P. O. Box 67
Walnut Springs, TX 76690
800-311-2146
Email: whm@wholeheart.org
Website: www.wholeheart.org

F. Write to the local or national offices of various religious denominations to ask for information about their organization and belief systems.

G. **Praise Hymn** is a unique company that specializes in teaching a love for the Lord and a love for music. Their Bible study aids, the *Star Light* or *Star Ways* Bible curriculum, are thorough, hands-on, and very engaging. Materials are available for lower elementary grades through the middle school years. Their music curriculum is in the resources for chapter 13.

Praise Hymn, Inc.
Post Office Box 1325
Taylors, SC 29687
1-800-729-2821
Email: Info@PraiseHymnInc.com
Website: www.PraiseHymnInc.com

H. Memorizing God's Word is easy for children when they see it, say it, sing it, and play it. **Thy Word Creations** offers some lovely materials for children to employ many of their senses to memorize passages of Scripture. There are cassettes to listen to, large type, delightful books to read and songs to sing and play to put God's Word into their hearts. What a great family project! Children as young as 2 or 3 can begin Scripture memory with these aids. Materials for teens and adults are also available.

Thy Word Creations
Rt. 76, Box 28
Glenville, WV 26351
304-462-5589
Email: thywordcreations@iname.com
Website: www.thyword.cjb.net

I. **Scripture Memory Fellowship** is the granddaddy of Scripture memory programs. I had a chance to meet its founder, N.A. Woychuk, and he is the epitome of a mind and heart full of the Word of God. Scripture Memory

Fellowship offers memory books and incentives for whole families to memorize Scripture, all within the context of the family unit. For a very nominal fee, everyone from preschoolers to grandparents can become involved.

Scripture Memory Fellowship
PO Box 411551
St. Louis, MO 63141
314-569-0244
Email: memorize@slnet.com
Website: www.scripturememory.com

Character education as part of spiritual development (Chap. 11 cont.)

Why all the emphasis on character education? As Christians, we must not only ask whether something is right or wrong, but does this action or this thought reflect the character of God? Studying character qualities, what they mean and how they are demonstrated in Scripture is a profitable study to do with our children toward their spiritual development.

A. **Plain Path Publishers** is dedicated to assisting young people in the work of putting God's word into practice by forming habits or behaviors which will lead to character development. Their materials were written and produced by Gary Maldaner, an educator and author. Their most popular work, *Christian Character*, is an examination of the character that should be found in the lives of young people. Using Scripture, real-life examples, personal evaluation, and goal setting, your young people are encouraged to gain an in depth understanding of 28 character qualities. *Christian Manhood* is specifically addressed to training boys to be spiritually strong men. Also available is a series of five little booklets entitled *Polite Moments*. Each volume contains illustrations and encouragement for old-fashioned polite behavior and speech. Materials from other authors are also available from Plain Path. If you are looking for guidance in the area of character education, these materials will provide years of discussion.

Plain Path Publishers
PO Box 830
Columbus, NC 28722
828-863-2736
Email: plain@juno.com

B. **Full Gospel Family Publications** offers a two volume set called *Character Building for Families*. Volume I contains 165 lessons on 12 character qualities. Volume II has 135 lessons on 5 qualities. The text includes Scripture to read and memorize, questions to discuss, and patterns to pray over the day's lesson. What is appealing about these materials is that they are suitable for a wide age range of children and can be used with the whole family—even Mom and Dad will benefit!

Full Gospel Family Publications
419 E. Taft Avenue
Appleton, WI 54915
920-734-6693
Email: pilgrims@juno.com

C. Dale Osborne offers a *Values Program for Character Education in the Family Environment.* Seven levels of booklets are available, each covering several virtues, at a reasonable price. The format defines the quality, gives biblical examples, tells a story in which the quality is demonstrated, asks questions about the story, suggests activities, asks the students to show how they have/ how they can demonstrate the quality, then asks some deeper questions. Finally, at the end of each unit is a unique feature: Parents are asked to sign and date a paragraph attesting to the fact that they have studied the quality and are ready to learn a new thing. For a set of little, inexpensive booklets, your family could gain a great deal of benefit from the exercises and activities provided.

Values Program
c/o Dale Osborne
339 Range Lane
Cahokia, IL 62206
618-337-4580
Website: www.familyvalues.nu

Chapter 13: Creativity

A. Our **County Recycling Center** has a regularly scheduled book rescue. On the designated day, members of the public can go to their site and comb through tons of books discarded from schools and libraries. Check for something similar in your area. I have found an entire set of craft encyclopedias, as well as numerous individual books about sewing. And they were all free!

B. Do you have a serious budding artist in your midst and are you looking for a godly perspective to teaching art? You must check out **How Great Thou Art Publications.** Created by artist Barry Stebbing, a committed Christian, they offer drawing books and lessons for all ages (even adults!) to learn basic and advanced art techniques. And everything is presented in a way that honors God and teaches Christian values and principles. All materials are reasonably priced, can be used for more than one family member and, when diligently studied, will provide your child with solid art instruction from a Christian perspective.

How Great Thou Art Publications
Box 48, Dept. 1000
McFarlan, NC 28102
1-800-982-DRAW (3729)
Email: howgreat@vnet.net
Website: www.howgreatthouart.com

C. A simpler approach to art instruction is take by Jean Soyke, author of *Art Adventures at Home: A Curriculum Guide for Home Schools*. These thorough books, available in two levels, can provide a complete art education for young children through upper elementary aged children. Each book presents 35 lessons per year, with enough provided for three years. Children will work on projects ranging from fingerpainting to tie dye to mosaics. The materials required are not too complicated. Most of them can be obtained from your local discount store. At $19.95 per volume, both of these books can provide you with six or more years of quality art instruction you can enjoy together with your child.

Ms. Soyke has also written *Early Education at Home*. For ages 3-5, it is a 36-week program to provide your child with basic readiness skills and character development. Even working parents can use these fun ideas to enhance "quality time" with their children, while teaching valuable concepts which will help them in school.

M. Jean Soyke
At Home Publications
2826 Roselawn Avenue
Baltimore, MD 21214
410-444-5465
Email: JSoyke@juno.com
Website: www.athomepubs.com

D. So you don't sew, but your young person is pining to learn? There are some really tremendous resources to help you both have fun learning. *I'll Teach Myself* is a series of book written for children to direct them through the learning process. In *Sewing Machine Fun* (Books 1 and 2) children work on projects, do games, solve riddles and read jokes, which all reinforce the skills they are learning. She starts with the basics of using a machine and goes on to introduce some simple projects, such as fabric greeting cards, soft animals, and a carrying pouch pocket. The books are colorful and fun and are designed for the child to read and follow on their own, with minimal skill required of the parent (whew!).

Specifically for children, this company also offers *Step into Patchwork* and *Gifts to Give,* along with many other patterns, tools and accessories. These can be used individually at home or in a group setting, such as 4-H, scouting or a home economics class. These are extremely creative and fun!

Possibilities
I'll Teach Myself Series
8970 Hampden Ave.
Denver, CO 80231
1-800-474-2665
Website: www.possibilitiesquilt.com

E. Do you long for an old-fashioned piano teacher for your children? Madonna Woods of Davidsons Music has some charming materials available for teaching piano at home. Madonna Woods' *Piano Course for Christians* is a book/cassette course in which she talks the student through the most rudimentary lessons in a loving, thorough fashion. The tapes are so personal and encouraging that it is like this lovely lady is sitting beside you at the piano bench. Her course goes far beyond beginners. She offers materials for all levels and styles of music.

Davidsons Music
Piano Course for Christians
6727 Metcalf
Shawnee Mission, KS 66204
913-262-4982

F. **Praise Hymn, Inc.** offers materials for Bible and music study for Christian children. *God Made Music* is a music workbook series for grades K-7. Each book has 34 lessons, each taking about thirty minutes to present. The books contain a variety of music activities and teach children theory and basic music knowledge. At level 3, the flutophone is used to develop some listening and playing skills. At level 4, the soprano recorder is introduced. Other than these little instruments, the series is geared toward general musical knowledge and singing. In other words, even if you don't play the piano, you can give your children a foundation in music. Kids love these fun books! (See page 316 for address.)

G. *Keys for the Kingdom* is a complete, progressive piano course for Christian students. Beginning with the earliest levels, the expression of a worshipful attitude is present in each exercise. The performance pieces are based on sacred music, contemporary hymns, and classical music. The books are bright and encouraging, moving the student incrementally through basic and advanced music concepts. GlorySound, producers of Keys for the Kingdom, as well as other materials, offers the Christian Keyboard Network. For a small yearly fee, members receive a newsletter, discounts on workshops, and free and discounted books. For the committed Christian musician, this is worth checking into.

Keys for the Kingdom
GlorySound-a Division of Shawnee Press, Inc.
49 Waring Drive
P.O. Box 690
Delaware Water Gap, PA 18327-0690
800-962-8584
Email: keys@noln.com

H. The **Carpenter's Son Woodcraft** offers educational and recreational woodcraft kits and accessories. Your young craftsperson might build a doll cradle or a magazine rack with these fun, easy-to-use kits. There are also sets of real tools available for children. We have used several of these projects with our girls and they have really enjoyed them.

The Carpenter's Son Woodcraft
3209 Willowbrook Circle
Waco, TX 76711
254-756-5261

I. Our local **Cooperative Extension Service** has numerous project books on sewing, knitting, and more. The two volumes on sewing which we have, called *Sew and Have Fun* and *Sew Much More* were each just a few dollars, are written to the children and are a complete course in sewing.

We also got two volumes on woodworking from the Cooperative Extension Service. These project books teach about tools and how to use them and take the child through simple projects step-by-step.

J. **Girl Scouts and Boy Scouts.** Anyone can start or join a troop, but you can also register as an independent scout. You can earn badges and work in project books. Many good, worthwhile projects, even if you can't get to a troop. Some of the projects are wonderful for teaching life skills, such as first aid, health and fitness, Ms. Fix-it, money sense, computer fun and a huge selection of arts from which to choose. If your child is motivated by badges and by following prescribed orders of doing things, check into becoming an independent scout or just working on these projects on your own.

Girls Scouts of the USA
420 Fifth Ave.
New York, NY 10018-2798

Boy Scouts of America
1325 West Walnut Hill Lane
PO Box 152079
Irving, TX 75015-2079

Chapter 14: Celebration Skills

A. A home-based business, **The Courtship Connection** is a source for lots of interesting stuff. They sell award ribbons for excellence in character and some resources for character training. They are perhaps best known for their materials on dating and courtship. They offer a free catalog for you to examine all their important offerings.

The Courtship Connection
3731 Cecelia St.
Toledo, OH 43808
419-729-4594

B. If you and your family enjoyed reading and studying John Bunyan's *Pilgrim's Progress,* you will enjoy playing **The Game of Pilgrim's Progress.** This colorful, thoughtful game is both a teaching and a devotional tool as you and your family journey with Pilgrim on the way to the Celestial City.

The Game of Pilgrim's Progress
Family Time, Inc.
Bob Blair
606 Road 540
Bloomfield, MT 59315
888-534-3007
Email: pilgrim@midrivers.commb

Notes

Introduction

1. Robert Barnes, *Ready for Responsibility* (Grand Rapids, MI: Zondervan, 1997), 53.

2. Barnes, 56.

3. S. M. Davis, "What to Expect from a 12-Year-Old," (sermon on videocassette, Park Meadows Baptist Church, Lincoln, IL)

4. Linda and Richard Eyre, *Teaching Your Children Responsibility* (New York: Simon & Schuster, 1984), 4.

5. Patricia Sprinkle, *Children Who Do Too Little* (Grand Rapids, MI: Zondervan, 1996), 163.

6. James Tobin, "Are We Raising Helpless Children?" *Parents Magazine* (April 1998):74.

7. Barnes, 10.

8. Deborah Carroll, *Teaching Your Children Life Skills* (New York: Berkley Books, 1997), 147.

9. LaVerne Ludden, *Job Savvy: How to Be a Success at Work* (Indianapolis, IN: JISTWorks, 1992), 10.

10. Bernard Wysocki, "Americans Decry Moral Decline: Most Turn to Family, More Than State, for Answers," *Wall Street Journal* (24 June 1999): A9.

11. Barnes, 28-29.

12. Sarah and Elizabeth Delany, *The Delany Sisters' Book of Everyday Wisdom* (New York: Kodansha International, 1994), 77.

13. Rick Boyer, "How Do Children Learn Life Skills?" *The Teaching Home* (Dec. 1990-Jan. 1991): 45.

Chapter 1: Responsibility in Small Things

1. Bonnie Runyan McCullough and Susan Walker Monson, *401 Ways to Get Your Kids to Work at Home* (New York: St. Martin's, 1981), vii.

2. Sprinkle, *Children Who Do Too Little*, 10.

3. Tobin, "Are We Raising Helpless Children?" 73.

4. William Damon, *Greater Expectations: Overcoming the Culture of Indulgence in America's Homes and Schools* (New York: The Free Press, 1995), 77.

5. Teresa Mask, "Self-Esteem Taught by School as Important Life Skill," *Daily Herald* (6 May 1999):11.

6. Damon, 79-80.

7. Paula Polk Lillard, *Montessori: A Modern Approach* (New York: Shocken, 1972), 115.

8. McCullough and Monson, 1.

9. Elisa Morgan and Carol Kuykendall, *What Every Child Needs* (Grand Rapids, MI: Zondervan, 1997), 74.

10. Stanley Greenspan, "Mastering Challenges," *Parents Magazine* (February 1996): 86.

11. Sprinkle, 93.

12. "What's New?" *Woman's Day* (20 April 1999): 140.

13. Gary Chapman and Ross Campbell, *The Five Love Languages of Children* (Chicago, IL: Moody, 1997), 17.

14. Barnes, *Ready for Responsibility,* 66.

15. Elizabeth Crary, *Pick Up Your Socks* (Seattle, WA: Parenting Press, 1990), 40.

16. Crary, 40-42.

17. Sprinkle, 121.

18. Morris R. Schechtman, *Working Without a Net* (New York: Pocket Books, 1994), 9.

19. Ibid., 13.

20. Ibid., 18.

21. Lucy Calkins and Lydia Bellino, *Raising Lifelong Learners: A Parent's Guide* (Reading, MA: Addison-Wesley, 1997), 128-129.

22. McCullough and Monson, 18.

23. Crary, 43.

Chapter 2: People Skills

1. Barnes, *Ready for Responsibility,* 100.

2. John Gottman, *Why Marriages Succeed or Fail* (New York: Simon & Schuster, 1994), 28.

3. Barnes, 139.

4. Ludden, *Job Savvy*, 42.

5. Linda Schwartz, *What Do You Think?* (Santa Barbara, CA: The Learning Works, 1993), 176-177.

6. Wes Haystead, *Teaching Your Child about God* (Ventura, CA: Regal Books, 1983), 70.

7. Schwartz, 178.

8. Suzanne Chazin, "Can You Raise a Polite Kid in This Rude World?" *Readers Digest* (February 1997): 135-136.

9. Ibid., 139.

10. Linda and Richard Eyre, *Teaching Your Children Values* (New York: Simon & Schuster, 1993), 207.

11. Oretha Swartz, *Service Etiquette* (Annapolis, MD: United States Naval Institute, 1977), 261-262.

12. Ellen Banks Elwell, *Christian Mom's Idea Book* (Wheaton, IL: Crossway Books, 1997), 161.

13. Chazin, 138.

14. Ibid.

Chapter 3: In the Home Skills

1. McCullough and Monson, *401 Ways to Get Your Kids to Work at Home,* 227.

2. Ibid., 227.

3. Ann R. Martin, "Coming Clean," *The Wheaton Sun* (13-14 Jan. 1999): 35.

4. Nadine M. Brown, *How to Have Kids With Character* (Wheaton, IL; Tyndale, 1990), 18.

5. Eyre, *Teaching Your Children Responsibility*, 36.

6. Sprinkle, *Children Who Do Too Little*, 97.

7. Ibid., 112-113.

8. Emilie Barnes, *Emilie's Creative Home Organizer* (Eugene, OR: Harvest House, 1995), 95-96.

Chapter 4: Life Navigation

1. McCullough and Monson, *401 Ways to Get Your Kids to Work at Home,* 233.

2. Crary, *Pick Up Your Socks*, 74.

3. Michael McManus, *50 Practical Ways to Take Our Kids Back from the World* (Wheaton, IL: Tyndale House, 1993), 77-78.

4. "A Parent's Guide to Internet Safety," as reprinted in the *The Compiler,* The Illinois Criminal Justice Information Authority (Summer 1999):15.

Chapter 5: Time Organization

1. Karen Miles, "The Frenzied Family Syndrome," *Woman's Day* (1 February 1999): 22-24.

2. Karen Levine, "Family Time Bandits," *Parents Magazine* (April 1998): 124.

3. Marnell Jameson, "In Search of the Good Life," *Woman's Day* (1 February 1999): 48.

4. Brother Lawrence, *The Practice of the Presence of God* (Springdale, PA; Whitaker House, 1982), 33.

5. Ludden, *Job Savvy*, 53.

6. Mickey Rathburn, "Balancing Act: How to Help Your Child Juggle Sports, School and Life," *Sports Illustrated Kids* (September 1997): 41.

7. Harvey L. Ruben, *Super Marriage: Overcoming the Predictable Crises of Married Life* (New York: Bantam, 1986), 135.

8. Quoted in Meg Cox, *The Heart of a Family* (New York: Random House, 1998), 11.

Chapter 6: Space Organization

1. Deniece Schofield, *Confessions of a Happily Organized Family* (Cincinnati, OH: Writer's Digest Books, 1984), 68.

2. Eyre, *Teaching Your Children Responsibility*, 38.

3. Ibid., 42.

4. Inge Cannon and Ronald Jay Cannon, *Mentoring Your Teen: Charting the Course to Successful Adulthood* (Taylors, SC: Education PLUS, 1998), 249.

Chapter 8: Money, Money, Money

1. Bob Losyk, "Generation X: What They Think and What They Plan to Do," *Public Management Magazine* (December 1997): 7-8.

2. Barnes, *Ready for Responsibility*, 156.

3. Larry Burkett and Rick Osborne, *Financial Parenting* (Colorado Springs, CO: Victor Books, 1996), 105.

4. Barnes, 161.

5. Ibid., 162.

6. Eyre, *Teaching Your Children Responsibility*, 40.

7. Chris Snyder, *Teaching Your Child about Money* (Reading, MA: Addison-Wesley, 1982), 55.

8. Dean and Grace Merrill, *Together at Home* (Pomona, CA: Focus on the Family, 1985), 125-127.

9. Snyder, 91.

10. ABA Education Foundation, Promotional Materials for National Teach Children to Save Day, Washington, D.C.

11. Carroll, *Teaching Your Children Life Skills*, 64.

12. Neal Godfrey, *Money Doesn't Grow on Trees* (New York: Simon & Schuster, 1994), 60-61.

13. Barnes, 165.

14. Leslie Mann, "The 4th R: Responsible Money Management Is an Important Lesson for Kids," *Chicago Tribune* (8 Aug.1999, sec. 13): 6.

15. Godfrey, 63.

16. Barnes, 166-167.

17. Mann, 6.

18. Burkett and Osborne, 108.

Chapter 9: Healthy Habits

1. The American Dietetic Association, "Position Paper: Dietary guid-

ance for healthy children aged 2 to 11 years," (5 Oct. 1998), in *Journal of American Dietetic Association*, 99 (1999): 93-101.

2. Ann Douglas, "Actions Speak Louder Than Words," *Chicago Tribune* (8 Aug. 1999, sec. 13): 3.

3. ADA, "Position Paper."

4. McManus, *50 Practical Ways to Take Our Kids Back from the World*, 98.

5. Ibid., 1.

6. U. S. Department of Education, Safe and Drug-Free Schools Program, "Growing Up Drug-Free: A Parent's Guide to Prevention," 7. (This brochure available from U.S. Dept. of Educ., 400 Maryland Ave S.W., Washington, DC, 20202-6123.)

7. Ludden, *Job Savvy*, 79.

8. Sondra Forsyth, *Girls Seen and Heard* (New York: Jeremy R. Tarcher/Putnam, 1998), 6.

Chapter 10: Your Mind's Life

1. Jane Winkler, *How to Study and Learn* (New York: Franklin Watts, Inc., 1978), 20.

2. Elaine McEwan, *How to Raise a Reader* (Elgin, IL: LifeJourney Books, 1987), 20.

3. Crary, *Pick Up Your Socks*, 19.

4. Cheri Fuller, *Motivating Your Kids from Crayons to Career* (Tulsa, OK: Honor Books, 1990), 114.

5. Crary, 19.

6. Fuller, 107-108.

7. Crary, 19.

8. Fuller, 111-112.

9. Cheri Fuller, *Unlocking Your Child's Learning Potential* (Colorado Springs, CO: Navpress, 1994), 162.

10. Marialisa Calte, "School Daze: There's a Life Lesson Our Kids Aren't Learning," *Woman's Day* (June 1, 1999): 56.

11. Brown, *How to Have Kids With Character*, 110.

Chapter 11: Spiritual Habits

1. David Heller, *Talking to Your Child about God* (New York: Bantam Books, 1988), 6.

2. Sally Leman Chall, *Making God Real to Your Children* (Tarrytown, NY: Fleming H. Revell, 1991), 16-17.

3. Elise Arndt, *A Mother's Touch* (Wheaton, IL: Victor Books, 1983), 40.

4. Norman Vincent Peale, "Learn to Pray," *Woman's Day* (April 20, 1999): 74.

5. Taken from Kent and Barbara Hughes, *Common Sense Parenting* (Wheaton, IL: Tyndale House, 1995), 62.

6. Ibid., 82.

7. Bill Carmichael, *Seven Habits of a Healthy Home* (Wheaton, IL: Tyndale House, 1997), 238.

8. *USA Today Snapshot* (July 27, 1999), USATODAY.com.

9. Robin Scarlata and Linda Pierce, *A Family Guide to the Biblical Holidays* (Madison, TN: Family Christian Press, 1977), 35.

10. Jane Chastain, *I'd Speak Out On the Issues If I Only Knew What to Say* (Ventura, CA: Regal Books, 1987), 139.

Chapter 12: Decision Making

1. Barnes, *Ready for Responsibility*, 87.

2. Gordon Miller, *Teaching Your Child to Make Decisions* (New York: Harper & Row, 1984), 15.

3. Mark Field, "Some Basics for Sound Thinking: Hastiness," *The Ethics Roll Call* (Spring 1999): p. 5.

4. Miller, 53.

5. Barnes, 212.

6. McManus, *50 Practical Ways to Take Our Kids Back from the World*, 131-132.

7. Andrea Heiman, "How to Make Good Decisions," *Teen* (January 1997): 52.

8. Ludden, *Job Savvy*, 131.

9. Crary, *Pick Up Your Socks*, 22.

10. Ludden, 144-145.

11. Quoted in John R. Jones, *Reputable Conduct: Ethical Issues in Policing and Corrections* (Scarborough, ONT: Prentice Hall Canada Career & Technology, 1998), 102-103.

12. Sandra Lee Smith, *Coping with Decision Making* (New York: Rosen Publishing Group, 1989), 84.

13. Barnes, 192.

14. Ibid., 193.

Chapter 13: Creativity

1. Edith Schaeffer, *Hidden Art* (Wheaton, IL: Tyndale House, 1971), 32.

2. Marlene LeFever, *Growing Creative Children* (Wheaton, IL: Tyndale House, 1988), 11.

3. Ibid., 16.

4. Chall, *Making God Real to Your Children*, 30.

Chapter 14: Celebration Skills

1. Richard J. Foster, *Celebration of Discipline: The Path to Spiritual Growth* (New York: HarperCollins Publishers, 1998), 191.

2. Arndt, *A Mother's Touch*, 92.

3. Jerry and Patti MacGregor, *Family Times: Growing in Fun and Faith* (Eugene, OR: Harvest House, 1999), 17.

4. Foster, 193.

5. Chall, *Making God Real to Your Children*, 160.

6. Kathy Peel and Judie Byrd, *A Mother's Manual for Holiday Survival* (Dallas, TX: Word Books, 1991), 78.

7. Brown, *How to Have Kids With Character*, 185.

8. Stephen Covey, *Seven Habits of Highly Effective Families*, New York, NY: Golden Books, 1997, 76.

9. Carmichael, *Seven Habits of a Healthy Home*, 240.

10. Merrill, *Together at Home*, 40.

11. Mary Loverde, "The Memory Jar," *Woman's Day* (May 11, 1999): 90.

12. William J. Doherty, *The Intentional Family: How to Build Family Ties in Our Modern World* (Reading, MA: Addison-Wesley Publishing, 1997), 8.

13. Fuller, *Motivating Your Kids from Crayons to Career*, 125-126.

14. Cox, *The Heart of a Family*, x.

15. Mary Beth Lagerborg, *A Cure for the Growly Bugs* (Grand Rapids, MI: Zondervan, 1997), 35.

Index

About the Author

Christine M. Field practiced law for eight years before becoming a full-time Mom. She and her husband home school their four children in Wheaton, Illinois, where her husband serves as Chief of Police. She is the author of several books, including *Coming Home to Raise Your Children*, *Should You Adopt?* and *A Field Guide to Home Schooling*. She writes columns for several magazines, including *Home School Digest* and *Open Arms* magazine. Her work appears regularly in *Hearts at Home* magazine and others. Her article on life skills recently appeared in *Focus on the Family* magazine. Christine also maintains a limited law practice, advising and representing couples in international adoptions.

Christine loves to encourage others. She has spoken to many groups, from small fellowships to large conventions. To contact her about speaking to your group, or to share your ideas for teaching life skills, you may e-mail her at MField7842@aol.com, or visit her website at http://www.members.aol.com/MField7842. You may write to her at The Whole Family, P.O. Box 261, Wheaton, IL 60189-0261.